COMING CLEAN

Contents

Introduction

"I let my boyfriend take naked pictures of me. He put them on the Internet and now I'm worried about my husband finding out."

Confession Number One

I launched the Web site DailyConfession.com at the start of 2000 with the intent of creating a place where people could unburden their souls and receive honest and humane responses. I had no greater purpose, no dream of wealth or fame. Enthralled by the World Wide Web, and the access it offered to anyone with an idea, I wanted to see how the world would respond to mine.

Confession Number One, a mere twenty-four words, was, appropriately enough, the tale of a sin that could occur only in the Internet age. But the early responses that came from the visitors to my newborn Web site were filled with a brand of condemnation that was older than the Bible.

"You skank!"

"Hey darlin', can you spell b-r-a-i-n-d-e-a-d?"

"You should not have been a tart in the first place."

"You deserve all you get."

It was enough to make me wonder if my creation was a mistake.

Being Jewish, I had no experience with traditional Christian confession. But I had been raised in a home where you owned up to your transgressions and received some empathy and understanding. DailyConfession.com was supposed to take this experience—of truth-telling and reconciliation—to the world. I even hoped that confessors would get a sense of absolution from the responses of compassionate readers. But if those who bared their souls were to be greeted with nothing but scorn and derision, if the site revealed that people are basically condemning and sanctimonious, then I would have to reconsider the whole idea.

Then up popped Response 55. "First and foremost," wrote the sender, "you all don't need to be complete jerks to her."

Then the writer offered some practical advice. "Tell the boyfriend to get lost. And ask forgiveness from your husband and from God."

Response 55 made me think there was hope out there for my fellow man. Response 56 made me certain about it. "My word," it began, addressing the other sources of feedback. "You are all such perfect human beings. Bound to be Americans. How ye cast judgment on one honest enough to repent of their sins. Photos-schmotos. Give a heck. Who cares?" This response goes on with reassuring words about the minuscule chance that the photos will ever be discovered and includes a "rock on girlfriend!" to boost the confessor's spirits.

Eventually, hundreds of people responded to Confession Number One. Of course, a great many requested the URL—Internet address—for the photos. A similarly large number of them offered derogatory remarks about the confessor. But more than one person wrote that she had made the same mistake. Many more urged the confessor to get right with her husband, or leave him. These kinds of replies, and others that offered sincere advice and perspective, persuaded me that the site would be worth the time and effort I would put into it.

In that first week Confession Number One was followed by a handful of other postings. Then, and ever since, adultery was a major theme. Lying, which is always part of adultery, was also a big one, and a lot of people confessed to compulsions involving rituals of hygiene.

I could relate to that. I'm so concerned about germs that I wash the doorknob after taking out the trash. I was relieved to see I wasn't the only one alive with this kind of worry. And just knowing that I wasn't alone made me feel much better. This reassurance would become a hallmark of the Web site, something that many visitors would enjoy and appreciate.

The site grew slowly at first. In March 2000 we counted a handful of visitors per day, perhaps one hundred in the month. But as spring turned to summer the population at DailyConfession.com began to explode. By January 2001—our one-year anniversary—we were up to ten thousand visitors, or "hits," per week. As I write, in December 2003, we are getting more than 8.5 million hits per week. The number of confessions and responses has grown right along with the size of our cyber community. Soon we will log Confession Number 250,000. At the same time we will break the 2 million mark for responses.

As the site developed, I had to set standards and impose a few rules. I have declined to post dangerous or criminal-type confessions, although they do come in. In two messages, people confessed to wanting to kill the president of the United States. Both were forwarded to agents of the Secret Service, who took them very seriously. Similarly, I won't allow obscene, racist, or sexist rants. And if someone submits a response that is simply a vicious attack on a confessor, or on another responder, it goes in the electronic wastebasket.

For the most part, I use a test of sincerity when deciding whether to accept or reject confessions and responses. Even in short pieces of prose, writers reveal whether what they are saying is heartfelt and true. Fabricators invariably come across as inaccurate and emotionally detached. The same is true for those who write responses. When it's from the heart, I will do almost anything to make sure it gets seen. For this reason, you will read here some rather graphic and disturbing confessions. Some will shock. Others will break your heart. I offer them because I believe that every part of the human experience is worth knowing and understanding.

Our typical confessor is a female between age eighteen and thirty-four. However, the Web site gets plenty of submissions from men, and people of any age seem to be interested in cleansing their consciences. We received a confession from a grade-schooler who stole a teacher's eraser, and one from an extremely senior citizen who began an affair after fifty years of marriage.

Though most confessions deal with everyday events, a trickle of submissions come from victims of abuse as well as from people who are on the brink of suicide. People who cut themselves to ease psychological pain use the confession-and-response format to get help. It often works, as kindness and wisdom flow to the confessor. Many people have sought therapy and begun to recover because of our Web-based community. More than a few battered women, and their children, have found shelter because of our help.

Protected by the anonymity of the Internet, they come seeking catharsis, reassurance, and a certain acceptance. They leave behind tales that speak volumes about the variety of human experience and the true nature of human beings. In the pages of this book you will meet, among many others:

A man so desperate for paid sick leave that he is pretending to be crazy at work.

A woman worried that having sex with her boyfriend on the night of his father's death was wrong.

A man who tried to get his dog high on marijuana.

A woman who steals pink flamingos of suburban lawns.

A boy who slipped his birthday money back into his unemployed father's wallet.

A "virgin" who gave her boyfriend HIV.

A man who believes he was responsible for his girlfriend's death.

A huge number of people who are wrestling with adultery.

An almost equal number of people who suffer over germs, dirt, and public restrooms.

Some of the confessors cop to things they did yesterday, or even fifteen minutes before they sat down at their computers. Others will reveal a secret sin they have harbored all of their lives. I can relate, personally, to that issue. When I was a teenager I accepted a box full of parts for my car, promising the friend who brought them from his dad's store that I would pay him. I never did pay. And my failure has gnawed at my conscience for a long time. But now that I have 'fessed up, I do feel a little bit better.

The Web site categorizes confessions by the original ten commandments. For this book, I have renamed the categories, and my confession would fall into Stop, Thief!

The Kitchen Sink holds all those entries that defy the other categories. Included are a bunch from the very early days of the site. Most are confessions of not sins, but idiosyncrasies that cause worry and shame:

I have started using adult diapers. The thing is, I'm twenty-four.

I am addicted to used panties . . .

I don't have a cat, but I bought a litter box to use myself.

When I sit on the toilet . . . I like to have a conversation with myself.

People who confess to these kinds of problems have not committed grievous acts against others. And though I'm not a clergyman, as far as I can tell they aren't violating any of God's rules. However, they do feel anguish about what they are doing. Their confessions may be considered an attempt to test the human family's level of tolerance, with the hope that even at their most bizarre, the confessors will find acceptance. Remarkably enough, they almost always do. For this reason, DailyConfession.com shows that the astounding variety of human faults and foibles is nearly equaled by the human capacity for understanding and compassion.

O   O   O

Fortunately, it's hardly all pain and suffering in the world of confession. Many peculiar, and even disgusting, habits are revealed, and there is no shortage of humor. Consider the curious confession titled "Body Pillow" that was among the first to be written.

"I have plotted and schemed to make my girlfriend (now my wife) jealous for my own diabolical reasons. However, I am not satisfied to make her jealous of another woman. Oh no! I have conspired to make her jealous of an inanimate object. Namely, Body Pillow!

"I have often cold-shouldered her in favor of hugging my Body Pillow. I have arrived at her house with Body Pillow strapped in the front seat (upright position of course). The personification of Body Pillow is most important in this maniacal scheme. and I have made her sit in the back when Body Pillow was in front. I extol Body Pillow's virtues. Body Pillow never nags me. Body Pillow likes the way I dress. And when we moved into our new home together I carried Body Pillow over the threshold.

"The payoff is when she gets really angry and tosses Body Pillow around the room, baring her teeth and growling like a wild, feral creature. Such lapses in common sense and decorum amuse me no end.

"Long live Body Pillow! BLOO HA HA HA!"

Though it's impossible to resist laughing at the Body Pillow confession, the responses were nearly as silly. Some took the confessor seriously and warned him that he was courting divorce. Others questioned his sanity. But the one that caught the spirit most fully reported simply, "I've got bad news. Body Pillow is cheating with bolster. Oh the humanity!"

The millions who visit DailyConfession.com come looking for entertainment from writers like the Body Pillow man, for inspiration, and for a dose of "reality" that is even more direct, and frank, than what can be seen on television. This book will present the best of all the entries on the site in a way that makes them accessible to all. It will also provide the kind of context—added demographics, social science, and analysis—not available online. Altogether, these elements will provide an entertaining and enlightening view of private life never before seen.

Netspeak!

A Glossary of Internet Abbreviations

You are about to enter the world of instantaneous, global communication. The written word here differs from the traditional published text you are familiar with. For the uninitiated, some of this "Internet shorthand" can look like a foreign language. To help get you up to speed, I have included a glossary of the terms that appear in the confessions.

Actual confession:

Netspeak!

I must confess, every time someone writes in "netspeak" I want to remove their vital organs with a spork.

LOL RFLMAO LMAO TTYL . . .

Why can't you just type out the whole sentence please? Don't tell me it's easier, I'm sure it is, but it takes the life out of the language, (what's left anyway.)

When people talk to me and use netspeak it sounds like they just don't care, like people using LOL when they "laugh?" bah humbug!

This confession speaks volumes with regard to a subculture that exists on the Internet today, and the disdain that many people have for the evolving language of the Internet.

You will find many of these terms used in this book. After

reviewing the first draft with my editor, it was painfully obvious that I either needed to translate the Netspeak or provide a means for the reader to decipher the enigmatic banter of the Talk-Backers from the Web site. I fought for keeping the Talk-Backs as they appear on the site. It gives a very true feeling for the grit and emotion, as well as the style of the language that is becoming increasingly common in Internet conversation. After hours of negotiations and a bribe of a Starbucks mocha latte, it was agreed to leave the Netspeak in the book.

Below is a list of the Netspeak words that appear in this book (but it is not a complete listing of every word in use). Several abbreviations have more than one accepted use or meaning. For the most part, it will help you figure out just what they mean, when they say . . .

2	To, too, two *(context dependent)*
4	For, four, *fore *(context dependent)*
b/c	Because
b4	Before
bf	Boyfriend
brb	Be right back
btw	By the way
convo	Conversation
cus	Because
cya	See you (later)
em	E-mail
gf	Girlfriend
gtg, g2g	Got to go
i	I (me, myself)
ic	I see
jk	Just kidding

lmao	Laughing my ass off
lol	Laughing out loud
ne	Any
ne1	Anyone
no	Know (context dependent)
no1	No one
omg	Oh my God
otoh	On the other hand
peeps, ppl	People
pita	Pain in the ass
r	Are
roflmao	Rolling on the floor laughing my ass off
sum1	Someone
tmi	Too much information
ttfn	Ta ta for now
ttyl	Talk to you later
ttys	Talk to you soon
tx	Thanks
ty	Thank you
u	You
ur	Your, you're (context dependent)
wb	Welcome back
wit	With
wtf	What the f*ck?

Peculiar spellings and typical mistakes—these are words that are not abbreviated but simply spelled in a new way or the correct spelling was substituted for another similar word . . .

cause	Because
kewl	Cool
loose	Lose

skewl, skool	School
than	Then
then	Than
there	Their, they're
to	Too, two
your	You're

"Emoticons" are keystrokes that, when combined, create cute little typographic images, the most common of which is the smiley face.

:)	Smile
:(	Frown
;)	Wink
:P	Sticking tongue out
:-/	Confused or perplexed
:-0	Shocked

And finally, a word on "shouting." When someone has a point to make or has strong emotion on the topic at hand, he or she may "SHOUT." Typing a word or a string of words in all caps is considered shouting. Typing an entire paragraph in all caps is either ranting or simply forgetting the caps lock was on. - :)

CHAPTER I.

That Old-Time Religion

It is often said that more people have been killed in the name of religion than for any other reason. Has a war ever been waged in which both sides were not convinced that God, or the gods, was on *their* side? Civilizations have risen and fallen; nations have been formed and destroyed; entire peoples have been eradicated—all in the name of religion.

But all news on the religious front is not bad: Religion has turned anarchy to order. It has given hope where otherwise there was none. While almost all wars have been waged in the name of religion, so has religion brought peace to warring nations and people.

But you can't talk about religion without also acknowledging the fact that religion can be a very touchy subject. Not only are there countless millions of people who don't belong to any religious group, but there are also millions of others who don't, God forbid, even believe in God—or gods.

So for our first category of confessions we have chosen that which begot the need for confession in the first place—that old-time religion, and the ways in which people keep finding, changing, losing, and questioning it.

I'll Get That!

I ran into my friend picking up our kids at school today.

As we approached, I could see that she had a little dirt smudge on her forehead. As we said hi, I just reached up and started to wipe away the dirt and she stopped me.

I confess that I completely forgot it was Ash Wednesday. It was very funny and very embarrassing.

Sorry!

That is HILARIOUS!!! I can see myself doing that!

Living in LA (Lower Alabama), I don't know all the catholic traditions behind this time of year (I know very few Catholics, and even less that actually play by the rules). I wouldn't have even known what it meant

---

Nothing to be embarrassed over, lighten up!

Yeah my parents forgot about that too. When I came home from school my mom was going . . . 'What's that on your forehead?' So you're not the only one.

Malenkaya

Hey, that's happened to me a few times.

I wash off the ash a soon as i get out of the service. lol . . . I almost did the same thing myself. Oops, sorry, didn't realize your cultist ceremonial ritual meant you had to wear that blackened smudge on your forehead all day.

MollyMayhem

Ha! i almost did the same thing last year to my Catholic co-worker but she stopped me before i could wipe it off . . . i just though she was dirty. LOL. sorry, i'm so clueless about Christianity sometimes.

~Gambitgirl~

I like Ash Wednesday. I especially enjoy the sermon, where the one person is making a big show of devotion, while the other is just striking his breast and asking for mercy. The lesson here is don't be showy about your devotion. Then, they smear ashes on your forehead and send you out into the world.

`Gramps`

I hate that bit of dirt on the forehead thing. Isn't cleanliness next to godliness?

Mastur . . . Bad! (?)

Okay, I confess. I masturbate. To top it off, I'm a girl.

According to my religion, this is bad—very bad!. But to me, it's just a "normal" thing. Other Christian religions accept it and it feels good to me, so whatever . . .

Why do people make such a big deal? I do it too! It doesn't hurt anyone, and would they rather we were pregnant and slutty?

Don't feel bad, feel good instead. I mean that. no one but you yourself knows how and where it makes you feel pleasure. Also if you have a boyfriend, just tell him some "hints" to make you go crazy in bed. Good luck.

LN

---

rock on. Don't ever let anything or anyone make you feel ashamed for doing what is totally natural.

xx

If this is any consolation . . . I'm Christian (Catholic) [[well . . . raised one anyway]] and I masturbate as well. No biggy. And yes I'm a girl too . . . Although I admit that if it is a "sin" I do pray to God to forgive me, lol. (I'm serious) :)

DUDE i'm like the exact same way. I'm Catholic and so anything that's human nature is bad. I do it all the time! in fact i just got off about an our ago! AND i even bring my stuffed animals into it sometimes!!!

---

good for you ;) it always cheers me up when people are able to have religious believes, and at the same time be critical to the dogmas and commandments thrust upon them, and think for themselves!

Kari

Dont worry girl anyone with any sense would do it. Why? Cause at least you get what you want when you do it yourself. U go girl!!

Ouija Works!

I used to be very skeptical of all the spirit stuff and communicating through seances and ouija boards and that sort of thing, but I tried a ouija board with one of my friends, and I confess—that shit works!

We sat there for a while at first, becoming more skeptical with each passing moment, but then, the thing started to move, and neither of us was doing it! I know I wasn't and I know she wouldn't do that. Man, talk about creepy.

So I confess . . . I believe!

I also found out that the ouija warks when i was 16—about ten years ago. Some of the spirits seem very friendly but you open yourself up to all of them. Strange things may start happening around you and you may find it impossible to get rid of. If you throw it away it comes back to you somehow. In different ways. This could get ugly and I don't know why they sell such things. I would pray hard and quickly to God and promise never to mess with the occult again. trust me.

It worked for me and my friend once, too. It was soooo cool, but also kinda creepy. We were actually talking to her deceased cousin for like three hours. I really shouldn't believe, though, because it's really against my religion (supposedly it's a tool of the devil or something), but I saw what I saw, and I know it wasn't fake. We haven't gotten a chance to try it again, though . . . .

I. THAT OLD-TIME RELIGION

Those SO do not work. And they're not a "tool of satan". They're a game, and obviously your friend MUST have been moving it, even if you think she wouldn't. Call me crazy, but I don't believe the Milton-Bradley company would sell something of an occult nature.

Yea, you are opening yourself up to satanic stuff also. That stuff is powered by satan and it could come back to bite you in the ass.
angelface

I'm Roman Catholic but I'm very skeptical, I think the danger with Ouija boards is people take them to be more than just a silly parlour game, start thinking it's real and get obsessed with it. You and your friends moved the planchette unconsciously. You'd be hard pressed to find a clergyman today who believes in demonic possesions, most of them believe that possesed people are just mentally ill.

If it actually worked it wouldn't be sold in Wal-Mart for $12.95.
Tamsin

Honestly, I think you experienced the scientific end of the Ouija board. The board can work in 2 ways, a mystical way and a purely scientifical way. I tell you it was the latter because you and your friend were both hard-core skeptics, so it was more than likely just the natural static in each others bodies moving the felt on the board. If you REALLY want to try it, make your own. Get a piece of card board and wax paper. On the wax paper write all the things a Ouija has, and tape it to the cardboard. Then over turn a wine glass and use that. Just never ever ever EVER ask if anyone is there, ask for certain names, or just questions.
BlondeLies

I keep bloody well away from ouija . . . too many things can happen and go wrong. You've got more guts than me . . .
Senkensha

It's made by "Parker Brothers", it's a game. Get a life.
~Smoke

---

just don't ever use it alone. that's some powerful mojo there & you
should always do it with other people to avoid opening yourself up to
malign influences
~Gambitgirl~

A Birdie For The Priest

I was late for work today, and indulged in a little road-rage as I was
driving there.

So it wasn't the best of times for the red light. And then the light
changed. And the car in front of me didn't move. I was fifteen
minutes late by this time, so I jumped on the horn to tell the idiot
to stop changing CDs and drive. Eventually, they got the message,
and began to move. Then they stalled.

I confess, I passed them as soon as I could, and showed the driver
my finger as well.

It was a priest.

I feel so embarrassed . . .

LOL. He's a priest. He'll forgive you. Or maybe he'll make sure you get
sent to hell. Hehe, just kidding.
BostonGirly

LMAO . . . kind of served you right, though . . .
DontKnow_DontCare

Ha!! You should be. No human being should be treated with that kind of disrespect, clergy or not. Thanks for a great laugh.

ClearSky

What is it that makes you think that you and where you need to be is soooo much more important then everyone else on the road?

SouledOut

Who cares what he is! he could be the Pope . . . some people just should not have licences.

homeboy_g

Oh . . . so if it was a mother with her 3 kids, or a guy having trouble getting his car to move you wouldn't have been embarrassed? Be embarrassed you acted like a total schmuck. Don't be embarrassed that a certain person caught you at it.

FTMhuman

LOL!!!! hahhahaa . . . that's really cheered me up. Oh well, nothing to be ashamed of. Hell you could have torn him out of his car and murdered him and they'd still have no choice but to forgive you.

Mossphenom

You did the right thing. Anyone that can't pay attention to the road, or that just doesn't know how to drive, shouldn't be behind the wheel. That's about 50% of the population, priest or not.

Boainmypants

Hmm, but yet you wouldn't be embarrassed if it weren't a priest. *sigh* Society today.

BAM

Ok, that's worse than mine! On the way home yesterday I flipped off one of those war protesters/supporters (didn't bother to read his sign). These fools stand on the walkways over the freeway and cause accidents. After the idiot in front of me slammed on his brakes to read the sign, I was a little angry.

Anonymous

Why? Because he was a priest or you were an ass. You're lucky he didn't have a gun!

`Gramps`

She Won't Marry An Atheist—But Sex Is OK

I'm in love with a woman, and she's in love with me. We've been going out for two years. We would probably be engaged now and married in a couple years, but for one thing:

She's a Christian and I'm an atheist.

She says she can't marry an atheist. But she will stay with me as long as I "keep trying". We almost broke up last night . . . until I finally gave in and said I would.

I tried to explain to her that's like me saying "only if you keep trying to believe the earth is flat" but to no avail. I asked her what happens when we're 80 and still only boyfriend and girlfriend—and she said fine.

I don't know what to do. I confess I feel horrible and angry and upset and just plain at a loss. I have to try to convince myself of something that isn't real, or force the woman I love (who loves me deeply) to break up with me.

I hate this.

i feel your pain. My boyfriend wants me to get married in a catholic church, I'm also athiest. Its not happening. I don't care who its important to (his mother and grandmother) It goes against everything i Believe in and I'm not going against my beliefs on the most important day of my life to satisfy his mother. Its my day not hers! He also gets very angry with me when we talk about religion. he understands where I'm coming from but he is strong in his beliefs and he wants me to feel the same. I just cant

---

If she can't respect your beliefs than I guess she'll just have to lose you.

---

thats pretty damn unfair. tell her that if she cannot love you unconditionally as you love her, then maybe you should both rethink this relationship. she shouldnt make you change and you shouldnt have to, if you do you will become bitter about it and thats no way to start a marriage knowing that will happen.

Scarlet

I understand both of your plights. But, if your wife is so silly in her attitudes about "trying" to change your beliefs, then why bother? don't you want someone who will love you for you? I personally would not waste a minute with anyone so hell-bent on changing me. You deserve better.

If she truly loved you she would accept you the way you are. Your beliefs and everything. You're not expecting her to change for you so why then must you change for her. It may be hard, but living life with a lie like that will be very hard. What happens when she tries to make you go to church every week? It's sad how some people can't accept ppl for all their "faults" and strong points. Just because you don't believe the same doesn't mean you do not love HER any less.

Kawzmik

Break up with her. Obviously she is too stubborn and so are you. You both need someone else and would be better off!

Even though you love her, her illusions are so ingrained into her head that she will never be able to love you the way she should. This personally is why I try to date only fellow atheists . . . Love should conquer over all: even religion. If the love is there from both parties, then religion doesn't matter. I've seen it done before. The problem w/ your fiancee is too wrapped up in her fantasies to actually realize what she's throwing away.

* *
—

My guess is she is worried about the future, ie. children. Would you be willing to raise children christian even though you don't believe? If so, tell her . . . maybe that will make the difference.

Not to put a damper on things, but there's no solution here. You've been through it, you know what the only answer is. There are other people who would be more suitable for each of you. You might as well stop wasting time and emotional energy and get on with finding them.

MollyMayhem

but i bet y'all are sleeping together. haha some christian. let her go. u shouldnt have to be forced into compromising urself just because she cant hack it. ur better off without her.

tb

Umm, YOU need to break up with HER. Don't get me wrong, I'm am SO not agreeing with your beliefs, cause, yeah, God does exist, and you WILL find out in the end. She got herself into a situation by going out with you. I put myself in the same place once, and got nothing but heartache. If you know that you will never change your ways (well, not really never, cause God has worked greater miracles than convincing athiest that there IS a God) then you need to end it now, cause she will never (I mean this one) grow in her faith as long as she is with a non-believer. "Do not be unequally yoked together with unbelievers" Take this from someone who's been there, you are causing her more pain then pleasure. Let her go, or let God convince you that He exists. Those are your choices, I sincerly hope you choose that later.

LKC

The Worms Crawl In, The Worms Crawl Out . . .

My confession is, I don't believe in God. Not the slightest bit.

The Benefits: Sleep in on Sunday, Do whatever I want without fear of going to hell, Don't waste time praying for help that will never come.

Life is hard enough. I don't need to be worrying if I've committed some sort of sin every two minutes, or worrying if I'll go to hell if I die.

I know where I'm going . . . The ground, to be slowly decomposed with the help of millions of little bugs.

It's liberating to be able to say that isn't it. Life becomes so much more valuable when one realises that there is nothing beyond.

Hell yea! Finally! Another intelligent person sees the light.

Emily

---

thats uh, quite the view you have there, a little sad man, It is wired in our head to believe in a higher power. And you can sleep in on sundays and believe in god. God isn't an alarm clock.

No kidding! Kudos to you! No gods, no masters. :)

* *
_

Yup, and your soul will perish in hell . . . .

Life is hard enough. I don't need to be . . . worrying if I'll go to hell if I die. IF you die? WHEN you die. because you will, and you might feel different then.

All can say is that people who have nothing to believe in are sad. If you dont have faith in something that hasnt been proven you should not have any faith in yourself.

You are totally entitled to your opinion of course, but the end of your confession had a dismissive ring to it. As a believer in God, I found that offensive. Believe in whatever you want to believe in, but please, keep an open mind.

To the girl who talked back and said "another intelligent person sees the light" . . . . I have a phd in marine biology, I didn't get that by praying really hard. I am an extremely intelligent individual. I don't tell you this to reassure myself (as you obviously had that purpose in your blatantly insulting and IGNORANT note) I believe in God. I suppose that makes me a Bible-thumping redneck huh? NO. You make YOURSELF look stupid and ignorant when you make those comments. Being judgmental does not make you look so smart either, honey.

good for you. christianity holds onto too many beliefs that all seem to contradict each other. it's not worth it. live for yourself. that doesn't mean you're a bad person. as long as you still have morality. most of the christians i know are the first to judge people, and put their own matters above everything else. not to mention telling other people they're going to hell. i'm sick of hearing it. jesus hasn't saved us yet, what makes you think he will today?

All you people who say in your reply that you belive in God should start acting like it and stop saying he'll go to hell for not believing. That is neither nice, nor true.

It's about time we heard more atheists speak up. Seriously. Why can't people accept the fact that there is no giant security blanket in the sky named "god"? We evolved from monkeys. They don't have souls. Neither do we. Face the facts: we're all going to die and rot in the ground some day. Nobody's going to heaven. Nobody's going to hell. Just live your life to the fullest while you've got it cause there's no round two. Lates.

S

GOD does love you, even though you don't understand Him right now.
ASHley**

Is Somebody Up There Watching?

I just had a moving religious experience.

I work two jobs. One ends very late at night and the other starts very early. In between I try to catch an hour or two of sleep at my girlfriends place.

Now, my girlfriend doesn't want to have sex before marriage, for religious purposes. Personally, I didn't care either way when I first entered the relationship, but I do love her and plan to marry her, so any sacrifice is worth it.

However . . . as much as we try to stay good and not get carried away sexually, we're only human and sometimes go too far.

Last night during my stay, we both got a little carried away with some petting, and right before she climaxed, an empty glass sitting across the room broke. Nothing was near it. It didn't fall from anywhere. No candles were sitting in it. Nothing. It just broke.

I feel like I should just chalk it up to coincidence, but honestly, that scared the s% out of me.

Either way, she's going to be lucky if I even kiss her before our big day.

Thou shalt not do the nasty in the presence of God, lest the glass breaketh . . . amen.

Tornado

hehe, awwwwwwwwwww . . . I do think it's a sign. So yeah, it's yer lives and live them the way you want to live them.

Malenkaya

You mean she wasn't screaming in ecstasy so loudly that it could have shattered the glass just like in the movies?

DontKnow_DontCare

or someone was in the room, broke it while trying to sneak a peek and disappeared from site after breaking it. ANything could have happened, do NOT assume it was God's way of saying not to do it, if anything maybe yur girl was screaming at such a pitch that the sound hit the glass perfectly and it shattered? The glass could've been an old glass and maybe it was sittin on a coaster wrong, tipped over, and shattered on the table. Everything happens for a reaosn, and that reaosn is NOT cuz God doesnt want u to have pre-marital sex. TONS of people have pre-marital sex and no signs are brought to them but hey, think what you like.

Dethrone_Enslaver

weird, i'd be all scared too

dinkus

LMAO!!!

Prozak

Bizarre. However I think it still qualifies as sex, whether either of you climaxed or not. If the criteria for 'having sex' was to have an orgasm, there'd be a heap of virginal women out there who've been married for years!

moonakey

That is positively freaksome, gotta say. But I wouldn't be too spastic about it . . . Coincidences to happen.

Glasses

HA HA!! the Lord moves in mysterious ways his wonders to perform!!! hahahahha sweepea

sweepea

HA! Normally I'd say that virginity is highly overrated, but someone's watching that girl. I'd be VERY careful if I was you. Even with your thoughts. ooo-OOO-ooo . . . . .

eve_attax

God may care about us as individuals, but He has given us free will and adopted a hands off policy. We should all be so lucky as to have such obvious guideposts in our life. So what broke the glass? Does she have any dead relatives living nearby?

`Gramps`

Drinking Behind Allah's Back

I confess that I love to drink when I go out.

That wouldn't be such a problem if I wasn't Muslim. We are forbidden from drinking. But I love the way a good buzz makes me feel. I'm not a lush, but I love a good "Smirnoff Ice" once in a while.

I confess that I'm not very religious on Friday nights.

---

hey im with you . . . im muslim too, and i feel guilty, but i cant stop now

---

Your kind is not so rare. You're just a Muslim by name and not a practicing Muslim, right?

And you would be different from everyone else who touts their beliefs how? It seems to be an American thing - this practice of affiliating with this religion or that religion and then living outside the boundaries of what it expects from you.

MollyMayhem

Haha, you just made my day! Thanks alot, I really needed a good cheering up.

go girl

Some people just put way too much emphasis on religion!! Give it a break!

I used to have a girl friend who was a virgin for most of the week. Or to put it another way, she was a virgin like you're a muslim. I have no problem with your drinking, just don't tell me you're one thing that you're not.

`Gramps`

I went to school with lots of Muslims who wouldn't smoke or drink, but they would have sex like rabbits—makes no sense! So I'm curious, do you smoke, or have sex too?

What's the difference between a Baptist and a Methodist? The Methodist will talk to you if you run into each other at the liquor store. Welcome to the club. Trust me, you're not the only Muslim who drinks, Friday or not.

How hard is it to live up to your principles? If you believe in all that stuff, then you should abide by the simple rules. If you don't, then chug away.

Just don't drink so much that you wake up with a porkchop in your hand.

Forgive Me Father . . . For J'm Not Really A Whore

To occupy a very boring day this past Sunday, I went to the local Catholic Church and gave my confession.

I confess here, that I confessed there, that I turned from nice young women to prostitute and potential murderer just for something to say.

Omg! That's so damn funny!

Next boring Sunday . . . Go back and confess again. Only this time confess that because you were bored, you made a mockery of the the chruch. I'm sure that will go over very well.

Tha's got to be one of the weirdest confessions I've heard.

Sarah

For a little more fun, you should have dressed up as an altar boy . . . .

Lol I can't believe you did that . . . but it must've been funny!
Cristi

I find the idea of what you did funny; I can only imagine the priest's reaction to your "confession"! However, it is important to remember that what you did also shows a certain amount of disrespect towards an institution that other people hold in high esteem, and therefore makes a mockery of their beliefs, which I do consider to be wrong. Nobody likes to have what they believe in made fun of. I would suggest that you let your little joke lie, and just not do it again.

AngelK

A friend of mine told me he used to make things up for confession as a little kid. Of course, you're an adult . . .

CHAPTER II.

Urges, Obsessions, and Fantasies

We all have them: the little tics others can't see; the quirks we usually keep to ourselves; the "special" things we never admit to; our secret urges; our naughty obsessions; our salacious fantasies.

This is one of my favorite categories, not because it satisfies some lecherous, voyeuristic curiosity in *me*, but rather because we learn here that the things we thought only we did—the things we had come to believe we have title and sole ownership of—are actually not so unique. We find out that there are quite a few other people who share our "personal" obsession or fantasy.

The cool thing that happens here is that in some small way, we come to realize that the thing we thought made us oddballs is honestly not so odd, or at least not so damning.

It is in reading this kind of confession that we learn that we are okay.

From obsessive-compulsive disorders to foot fetishes, these are the things we generally hold very close to the vest as we go through the poker game of life. These are the things that we try desperately to control, when in fact, they control us. These are our urges, obsessions, and fantasies.

II. URGES, OBSESSIONS, AND FANTASIES

A Turn-On

Ok, I admit it. I'm female and watching gay guys make out turns me on. I know, I'm demented, but hey, everyone's allowed to have weird obsessions.

Honey, you have guts. I mean personally I think the whole lesbian thing is a turn on but guys . . . it doesn't float my boat but hey, whatever turns ya on!!

Many men, like myself, enjoy watching lesbian porn. Turn about it fair play, haha.

How is it demented? Lots of guys like to watch chicks make out and that's fairly accepted as normal. I think two guys are hot together too :D
xx

---

hey - guys are turned on by two girls making out. What's the diff?

---

over here thats called a fag hag . . . . nothing wrong with it . . . whatever floats ur boat i suppose.
KaRmA

I agree it sounds wierd, but i am the same way. absolutely love it.
wonder

Really? Me too!
jelly

Clean Freak

I confessed, I am obsessed with cleaning and cleaning products. I work from 7:00 AM to 2:00 PM every day, and when I get home I immediately go for my cleaning box.

It's stocked with 3 kinds of Windex, Comet, Soft Scrub with bleach, lemon scented Soft Scrub, plain bleach, Oxy Clean, sponges, Brillow Pads, toilet cleaner, and other stuff. Then I go to work.

I clean every mirror, window, door, bathtub, toilet, counter top, and floor in the apartment. While doing this, I breathe as deeply as I can to smell the wonderful scent of all these cleaners. I adore the smell of all the cleaners.

When I'm done, I do a once-over with Windex to make sure everything shines.

One time my husband came home while I was cleaning and said I had a maniacal gleam in my eye. But I can't help it. I'm obsessed with cleaning and the wonderful feeling I get from smelling all my cleaning aids.

There's nothing wrong with that and if you every finish cleaning your house and still feel he urge to clean then you can come right over and clean my house. :)

My step-mother was the same way. God, we even had to fold our clothes before putting them in the dirty laundry. As long as your husband can live with you . . . no harm.

Actually I think that's an obsessive compulsive disorder, maybe you should see a doctor about it.

obsessive compulsive disorder is not a disorder unless it poses a problem. obviously, this confess is not an example. :P it must be nice to live so clean.

som

---

you sure those fumes aren't messing with yer brain? :)

---

would you mnd stopping by my house one day? you would probably freak just looking at it . . .

You can't actually believe you're cleaning because you're a clean freak. You're cleaning because that's the only way your brain knows how to get those inhalants . . . You're not a clean freak, you're addicted to fumes.

You sound like my aunt. Once I start cleaning I go crazy and must clean everything till it shines too. Doesn't oxyclean works wonders? I love that stuff.

Ramoneschick

Nothing wrong with that; yeah I admit its a bit obsessive, but it's harming anyone . . well maybe yourself. Try not to inhale those cleaners tooooo much, bleach and ammonia can obviously damage your lungs and breathing passages, destroy mucus membranes in your nose and sinuses leaving you open for more air-borne things such as colds and flu's. You can also get yourself nice and high (which my be why you enjoy it so much *L*) so be careful. Otherwise have fun!

Senkensha

---

if you are doing this every single day after work this does NOT sound normal. plus the fact that you emphasize how much you like to smell them makes me think you are huffing or something

~Gambitgirl~

I Watch Sailor Moon

I think sailor moon is a pretty cool show, but everyone criticizes me for it.

They say sailor moon is for girls (which is somewhat true), and call me gay simply for watching a girl's tv show.

What's a poor boy to do?

---

i used to be obsessed with sailor moon . . . and i still draw sm stuff sometimes –

Sarah Saturn

Well . . . they are kinda hot for cartoons.

---

whats a poor boy to do?" - eat a sandwich

---

pfft! sailor moon is an awesome show "illigitimi non coraborum" its latin for "dont let the b@st@rds gets you down"

kit

Lol . . . I think you are sad not only for watching a 'girls' show, but for watching a 'childrens' show . . . .

SnakeEyes

I know a few guys who watch Sailor Moon who are *not* gay! So keep watching and enjoy it, it's a great toon . . . .

---

hey now. if you watch sailor moon you rock. and its not for girls. its not even for children over in japan, its considered an adult anime. food for thought

BlondeLies

Sailor Moon is such a ditz. Sailor Mars should be the leader.

I am male - 37 - marketing exec. Sailor Moon is most assuredly created by and for adults in the Japanese market. It targets both females and males. You are who the show is designed for, watch it – I certainly do!

Tell them you like watching Anime (which is what Sailor Moon is . . . actually, it's more specifically "shoujo", but don't mention that.) I like Sailor Moon, too, and I'm a guy.

It's The Washroom That's Hairy!!

I confess! Every time I go to a public washroom, I never use my bare hands to touch the taps, the lever for the towel dispenser, the door handles . . . everything! I have this tremendous phobia for those invisible little critters called germs in public washrooms.

The smelly odor of other people's waste products I smell every time I step in makes me want to not touch anything and get the hell out of there ASAP. I hate that smell and it makes me feel that those germs causing those smells are . . . EVERYWHERE! So after I finish with the urinal, I do the following:

1. I go to the sink to wash my hands. Now my hands are clean. But the tap is still running, and I don't want to use my clean hands to touch the faucet or I'll get them dirty again, so . . .

2. While tap is still running, I quickly go to the tower dispenser and dispense a towel, but I do not take it yet. My hands are unclean after touching the lever, so . . .

3. I rush back to the tap still running, and re-clean my hands. Now my hands are clean . . .

4. I grab the towel I dispensed in step #2 and dry my hands with it.

Note that I don't have to touch the germy lever on the towel dispenser again to get a towel since it's already done in step #2. If I want more towels, I simply use the towel I have with my hands to push the lever, therefore, I never touch the lever with my clean hands.

5. Now my hands are dry, I use the towel I currently have on my hand to turn off the tap. My hands never touches the faucet, only the towel does, so it stays clean.

6. To exit the washroom, instead of touching the door handles, I use the towel I have currently holding to open the door and I'm done.

Now here's the part I really feel bad on. If there's no trash can nearby, I just toss the used towel on the floor before leaving the washroom. So what happens is that overtime, the doorway gets a lot of used paper towels on the floor that the poor janitor has to clean up, but my hands remains clean.

I always feel very bad every time the caretaker grunts when cleaning that mess up. I've never been caught yet, or have other people eye me strangely since I almost always try to use the washrooms in the least traffic hours at my university, but I'm sure any janitors reading this really wants to lynch at me right now.

I know this is a really bad habit and I try to stop, but every fiber in my body tells me not to do so every time I step into a public washroom. Is there something wrong with me?

That's okay, you're normal. I do the same things . . . you know, you could make use of your elbows and your feet to turn on taps and such. Depends on the tap, though. Good luck.

Couldn't you just get the paper towel before you start washing your hands?

Well, I think you mayyyy be taking it a little too far, but I'm kind of the same way with money. Will NOT eat anything if I've touched it and not washed my hands. And I'm ALSO the girl who won't share food or drink for the life of her. However . . . in no way am I close to having an OCD. :)

Diasphora

Why not just get disposable latex gloves and make it easier?

I don't like germs myself, either, and I don't like public restrooms because they are so dirty. However, my process is more simple. See, most people that use paper towels do it because they have also washed their hands. So I wash my hands, with my wet hand (so the wetness will be like a shield, lol) close the faucet, THEN I get my paper towel normally. However, I use the paper towel to open the door (but I don't toss it in the floor, I wait till I find a trash can), or sometimes I'll just wait till somebody else opens the door if there are other people in the restroom. So, you're not alone!! :)

First of all, save yourself that extra step of washing your hands twice by dispensing the towel BEFORE you wash your hands the first time, right after you finish going to the bathroom. Second of all, being cautious of germs is a great habit, but only if you do it ALL the time. I have the same kind of thing about bathrooms, maybe not quite so neurotic, but if you think about it, you're not escaping germs . . . . how about those buttons on ATM's? Or counters at stores? Or Money! There's a good one, imagine who touches your money. Doorknobs? What if someone goes to the bathroom, and doesn't wash their hands, and then touches doorknobs that you're touching? Its really all in vain, unless you're a serious hand washer, and that means like after you touch any public surface.

That doesn't sound quite normal to me. I could go on a huge talk back about how toilets are cleaner than kitchens etc, but I won't. All I'm going to say is maybe you should consider some kind of therapy.

The soap in that washroom is probably antibacterial soap which kills all the bacteria on your hands, some bacteria are good, some are bad, the soap is probably doing you a lot more harm that the bacteria on the sink or towel dispenser, make sure you rinse well. Hope that doesn't creep you out!

Everything you come in contact with (money, elevator buttons, desks and chairs, doorknobs, other people) is *covered* in germs. By all means be clean, but I think you're carrying this a little far. Though I do hate it when someone goes to the bathroom and doesn't wash their hands, then I have to touch the door handle after them. Yuck!

ElStreak

If 17 Hairs Fell Out Today . . .

I counted hairs that dropped this morning when I brushed.

17 hairs.

And when I brushed my teeth One hair dropped. I dunno, maybe more? I am getting crazy over this recently. Whenever my scalp itches, more hair will drop. And there'll be a weird smell. Like my shampoo smell only stronger and a little weird. And I don't wash my hair everyday, one like maybe once in two to three days.

I've always wondered if a person drops about 60-100 hairs a day, and it takes so long for a hair to grow back, soon won't you go bald?

I am afraid of my hair thinning, is it normal? And not only that, I use anti-dandruff shampoo and I still have dandruff.

Now I don't wear black . . .

---

my hair falls out all the time . . I'm in the same situation as you. I'm scared I'll go bald someday! I don't think my hair has gotten any thinner but it has to have cause it's been falling out every day for as long as i can remember . . lol . . we should start a club or something :)

Stop using the dandruff stuff, it's probably too harsh for your hair. 2) Use baby strength shampoo and see if that doesn't help somewhat. 3) Talk to a hair stylist. Good luck

Eagle Girl

Well, I have always had thick hair . . . I'm only 13 and I shed A LOT. In the shower after I shampoo, about 17 hairs come out right there. So I lose some hair, but my hair is still really thick.

Don't worry about becoming bald (at least not yet) because its a fact that we shed from 70 to 100 hairs a day.

How long is your hair? I had the same problem when my hair was app. shoulder length. Turns out it was old hair that had fallen out and gotten caught in the rest of it. I cut my hair (to 4 inches) and now there's no problem.

---

your teeth have hair??? go to the doctor matey

I heard Head and Shoulders (anti-dandruff shampoo) make you lose hair if you use it too frequently. I don't know if it's true though. Maybe.

AHHHH!!!! Dooooo something!! No, seriously . . I have no suggestions . . . Go to a dermatologist??

I'm in the same boat! I'm only 20 years old and just sitting here a ton of hair gets dropped and i can see it on my white desk. I started using Rogaine and it totally helped, except that it's like acid and my 'lover' likes to kiss my head and one day her lips and mouth started burning and she couldn't figure out what it was. I said it was a lotion for dry scalp . . Eek. I think I'm going to try Propecia.. expensive, but it's just a pill. Damn, we should talk man!

You have dandruff and are losing a lot of hair because you don't wash your hair enough. YUCK how can you go 2 to 3 days without washing it. Get some head & shoulders and wash it daily or at least every other and go easy on the conditioner keep it off of your scalp.

My Weirdest Quirks

Here are my 2 weirdest quirks:

1. Once I saw a movie in which a man who answered his door and looked through the peephole, was shot in the head through the peephole. Ever since, whenever I have to open the door I put a finger up to the peephole and see if anyone shoots it. Better to get shot in the finger than in the head.

(No one has actually shot me yet, but you never know . . .)

2. Whenever I put something in the microwave and set the time I run away as far from the microwave as possible. I do this because I think that one time it might explode, and I have to be far from it so I don't get hurt.

Hey man don't feel too bad about the microwave thing, Being a little hick from the sticks I didn't even see a microwave till I was like 9 and to this day I am really weird about them.

---

well that's not THAT weird. maybe you'll get over it one day! lol . . .
i used to do the same thing about the microwave

I do the same thing! But its only when i'm making popcorn. i think that the bag will explode or something.

Chica

---

you aren't supposed to stand in front of the microwave anyway, it emits waves that are carcinogenic.

---

gah! know the movie you're talking about. whenever i look out my peephole i always half-seriously think "gosh, i hope there's not a big gun barrel on the other side" LOL. you are not alone

~Gambitgirl~

Hehehehehee that's kinda cute. The finger thing is a good idea . . . but I doubt your microwave is going to blow up . . . . run from the radiation or something :)

Highashley

HAHAHA!!!! When I heat up water in the microwave in a coffee mug for whatever I take it out with a very long pair of BBQ tongs. I heard that a guy took out a hot cup of water from the microwave and it exploded and made him blind!! So I keep it as far away from my body as I can. Now you have more to worry about . . .

I do that peephole thing 2.

That's very interesting . . . you know, it's not that weird if you think about it.

If Only . . .

For some odd reason, I feel that by doing the smallest thing, I can change my destiny.

I read time and again how. "If only he had taken his usual route home . . . he would have avoided the accident and still be alive today . . ." or "If she would have looked up a split second earlier, she would sill be alive . . ."

So, while doing whatever I am doing; for instance, driving home, I will slow down and even stop – in the middle of the road [traffic permitting] just to change the timing and location from where I would be if I had simply driven home. I honestly feel like I have just forever erased the future that destiny had planned for me, and now have a new path to take.

I think I think too much.

So what if it all backfires and these "precautions" actually end up getting you killed. Then maybe that was part of your so called "destiny". Think about it.

Leigh

You and my friend Joe need to hang out . . . he thinks he was put on Earth to change everything that destiny and fate has already set before us. I hope you're not reading the books and I hope you're not convinced that the alluminaty (sp??) is real . . . talk to someone before you go crazy.

elegantly_wasted

I'm exactly like that! Oh wow! I think like that all the time, constantly! It's not like it rules my life, and it's only really noticeable when I do it on the little things—like departing times or how slow I walk to my car before leaving for somewhere.—

Diasphora

Umm, Final Destination is a "good" movie to calm your nerves!!!

CandyMan

Well, have you ever thought that it WAS your destiny to stop in the middle of the street (traffic permitting), or to leave a split second before you were supposed to? Maybe THAT was your destiny, rather than doing the latter . .

IndianPrincess

Did you ever think maybe it was your destiny to slow down and stop in the middle of the road? LOL

Kim

What if by stopping in the road, you change your destiny for the worst? Or by doing something else like that things are shifted to the worst? But then again, what if you can't change anything, only delay it?

KAIN

I think destiny is pre-planned, If you get into a car accident they will say "I don't know why she would do this, but she just stopped in the middle of the road" rather than "if only she had been a split second later"

But what if you didn't slow down that one time and had gone that little bit faster, maybe that person will miss you? You cannot change what is going to happen to you, it's going to happen and you cant hide from it.

Legally Sane

I had recently been diagnosed as bipolar. I was taking my medication but I wasn't doing well. I told my doctor that I wasn't doing well but he just blew me off (turned out he was pretty lazy)

Anyway, I starting getting paranoid and stopped taking my medication because I began thinking that my doctor was an agent of Satan and he was trying to poison me.

I decided that the world would be better off without him being in it as an agent of Satan so I decided to kill him. I started to leave my apartment and show up at his office to shoot him. (I was so psychotic that I didn't stop to think that I don't own a gun.)

On the way out an Angel of the Lord spoke to me and told me that only God could take a life and not to shot my doctor.

Terrified, I overdosed on lithium. It must have been the right thing to do because I snapped out of it.

I have a different doctor now and I started off by telling him this story. Now if I tell him I'm not doing well his ears perk up.

Thank God you made the right choice and now have a doctor that is much more understanding . . I wish you all the best with handling this disorder.
DarkGirl

LMAO - true or not, that's one of the best stories I've heard in a while. Thanks for the chuckles :o)

I am so thankful that you had a sane moment and found another Dr. A dear friend of mine quit taking his medicine, lied to the Dr. and his wife and ended up killing himself. The world has suffered a great loss, he was a dynamic, loving, giving person. Heal your mind, body and soul, and have a wonderful life.

Evie

PS Did you tell the other Dr. you were going to kill him?

These are not symptoms of bipolar you describe, but more likely paranoid scizophrenia. If so, you need to stay in therapy and on your medication. If you dont, you could seriously hurt someone.

Damn . . . that is one scary story. doctor better listen up . . . sometime the patient DOES know more about what's wrong with them than the doctor. doctor's who think they know better just b/c they have a fancy degree & don't REALLY listen to their patients need to take this as a big warning . . . more than one life could be at stake. to the confessor, I'm really glad you're doing better now & found a more responsible cargiver

~Gambitgirl~

Actions speak louder than words.

Aristotle

I'm glad things worked out ok for you. Keep at it.

Phatboy

Yikes.

Safegirl

I'm so sorry you had a bad experience and I'm glad you didn't end up doing anything dangerous. Doctors should always keep close tabs on how their patients are doing and show the utmost concern. Hope things get better for you. :)

My BF is bi polar. I'm so sorry that you had an experience like that. He had an episode recently where he threatened to kill his boss and his family while they were sleeping. It was scary. His doctors are taking him off his meds to see if he's okay without them.

I'm glad your new doctor listens better. I probably would too.
~brainie

I Love White Women

There I said it: I love blonde white women.

I am a 29-year-old black male living in the United States, Manassas, VA. In the town where I live, there are many inter-racial marriages and I want so bad to be in one.

Whenever I see an inter-racial couple or kids, I check them out and hope that one day, my turn will be soon. I love sexy blonde white women. However, I am too afraid of being rejected by some racist ones, so, I don't approach them.

I can't help it, I love blonde white women.

Arrrggghhhh! What the heck is wrong with brunettes and redheads? Is a bottle blonde better than a natural brunette? We need to get over this thing that the only type of beauty is barbie-doll blonde, blue eyed, and busty.

Racism is a terrible thing. I'm white and I think it's awful when people say derogatory things about other ethnicities. I know rejection is difficult to face, but instead of letting it make you a bitter person, let it make you a better person. Date around and you might just find a blonde that loves you—and if not, then learn from your mistakes and keep looking. God bless you, and rock on!

Xanne

Woo! I live in Woodbridge right outside Manassas. Although I am not blonde I do have a blonde friend who needs a man in her life.

Come to Canada . . . more races that mingle

I'm a Blond White Women and I think Black men are god damn SEXY and I think little Mixed race babies are so cute . . . pitty the majority grow up and have 2 deal with identity crisis's!

CheekyGyal xxx

I'm a white male, and I like redheaded white women. Blondes are too standard.

Smoke

hey confessor I can help you out with that i am white with blonde hair i'm 21 and love black men give me a call we could hook up sometime!!

acidtrip

Ain't nothing wrong with that at all. What I DO have a problem with is the fact that I have to drive from Woodbridge to Manassas to get to a half-way decent mall. What a piece of caca that Potomac Mills mall is!! But so long as you aren't trying to steal the girls from me, have fun with the white women.

Yes bottle blondes are sexier. Blonde says, "I care to be as sexy as I can be". It may not be fair but that is the way it is in our society and us guys all know it.

Nice to see you're searching for the inner person. Why don't you just buy an inflatable doll and take it with you instead? It'll have all the intelligence you're looking for.

`Gramps`

dude i hear you! i love guys outside of my race too! my last bf's were (in order) japanese, Thai, El Salvadoran & Afro-Native-American. hey, we like what we like, doesn't mean we'll necessarily write off a great person just b/c they don't fit out fantasy picture, i mean i've date plenty of white guys, but we just like what we like. i hope you find yourself a good white girl & be happy & have lots of kids LOL . . . biracial babies are just the cutest!

~Gambitgirl~

I'm Gonna Own A Shoe Store

I have to get this out to someone.

I have an extreme shoe fetish. If I see a girl who is even remotely attractive, but is working a nice pair of shoes, I immediately want to jump her bones.

I'm not just talking about the high heel stripper "CFM" shoes and boots either. If a girl wears the right kind of tennis shoes with the right outfit or pants then she has my complete undivided attention.

Also bare feet, I don't care how well taken care of, are my biggest turn off . . . and flip flops are the worst trend since hammer pants.

It's great because most guys get in trouble for looking at a chicks boobs instead of her face. Most girls I talk to just think I'm shy because I look at the floor a lot, but I'm really just checking them out.

Lots of men in shoe stores think the paycheck is just a fringe benefit. Ladies, if there is a man selling you shoes he almost certainly has a shoe or foot fetish. Trust me, I have experience in this arena . .

mmm kinky . . .

I thought Al Bundy was dead . . .

`Gramps`

I know how you feel. I think a woman's best assets are from the waist down -butt, legs & feet. When I see a woman in a nice business suit with dark hose and a pair of pumps, OMG it's better than a bikini! Pearls and pumps, baby. Although, I do like the eyes, too.

Women shoe fetish . . . nothing really new, but still odd to me. Whatever makes you happy!

VICE

Just wondering . . . . if you got into a relationship with someone, would you deman that she never takes her shoes off?

Wow I thought it was just me who absolutely loathes bare feet! They're just creepy - have fun with ur fetish!=D

Leanne

Let Me Count The Ways . . .

The ways I am obsessive / compulsive / crazy:

1. In my backgammon set, there is an extra piece for each color. I must alternate this piece with another every time I play, so that no one piece is left out of the game for too long.

2. The toilet paper must go on the roll a certain way, facing towards me, not the wall.

3. My job is to put books in jiffy bags and seal them with tape. If the tape becomes crinkled when I put it on, I must get new tape. The tape cannot be crinkled.

4. When I am sitting around, I constantly trace the shape of objects in my mind. Constantly.

5. When I drive, there is either an imaginary runner keeping up with me the whole time, or he is leaping from one point (say, a stop sign) to another (a telephone pole.) He's always there.

6. Everything has a place, and if I find that it is not in its place, it seriously irritates me.

7. I alphabetize everything possible.

8. I make to-do lists and I cannot do anything that isn't on that list.

Not to be mean, but there is medication for this

I used to do the thing with watching the pretend running man while driving, only it was while I was riding in the car, and I imagined myself rollerblading and jumping over obstacles like electrical boxes & curbs, things like that. I understand.

OMG IM LIKE EXACTLY LIKE YOU! I do every single one of those things except #3 but i do that when i tape anything else. That's so crazy its like your reading my mind

---

The man prances on light posts for me to. I named him Spiderman, and I can't blink while he is on a pole I drive past.

I got that runner/jumper guy too

I hope that you don't get a lot of talk backs saying that you need to get help, etc, etc, etc from people who don't know what they're talking about. Granted, I don't know what I'm talking about either, but I think your quirks are adorable! Be proud of them!

You need to see a shrink, some of the things you are saying aren't that bad cause everyone likes to be a perfectionist but seeing imaginary runners is just a little crazy if u ask me

---

Hahahaha! that imaginary man is the best! i always have something jumping over signs and trees and what not! mostly when i'm NOT driving though and just sitting in the backseat or on a bus.

I actually do the imaginary runner thing! But a variation. When I am a passenger, I imagine compulsively that I am running next to the car, and for some reason, one leg always twists behind the other . . . weird.

I Don't Feel . . .

I confess, I feel so sick, that I am so . . . emotionless.

I was looking through a site, and there were all these disturbing pictures people had sent in, like of a guy's head blown to pieces from a motorcycle accident, and another of this guy who got hit by a train, and his head was almost flat.

I feel so horrible, because I hardly *felt* anything. I didn't throw up, I didn't feel sick, I wasn't shocked or disgusted or anything.

What I DID feel was . . . fascination.

I liked looking at these photos and wanted to keep looking at more. It's that fact that makes me feel sick and horrified at myself.

Ahhhh good ol' rotten DOT com, so disgusting yet it really is just like a car wreck- you don't want to look but you cant tear yourself away . . . .

I know exactly what site you're talking about. i too have felt what you feel . . . nothing.

So does everyone else who looks at that site. Do you think the web site would still be running if you were the only one that felt like that? It's basic human nature or something . . .

You younger folks do not recall when the National Enquirer specialized in gore; that's how it got such a huge reader base. They switched to the current format in the early 70's. People are drawn to this stuff. If you are concerned over your reaction see a professional. They may help you understand your fascination.

Did you go to gruesome DOT com??? I went there once but after one picture I got freaked out and I've never been back. Just stop going . . . you don't need those images in your mind.

There is nothing unnatural about that; maybe not average but you're hardly a freak. Those sites exist because many people have a fascination with that kind of thing.

xx

Rotten DOT com is a great site.

i think i know what site you are talking about . . . YUCK that site is horrible!!!

~*bijin*~

I admit I was directed to rotten myself and saw a number of those pictures. Quite a number. Eventually, they did make me queasy. But for about the first 30 or so, I, like you, felt nothing. Odd, I know. I guess we just had to be there.

MollyMayhem

Let me guess . . . . rotten DOT com? We've all been there and done that. Its the thought that it could be real that is so fascinating I think.

kawzmik

Bizarre Compulsion

After reading others' confessions on here, I've decided to come clean.

The truth is, I've been in therapy for a year for compulsive behavior. This started after I got married to my wife. Here goes: Every Sunday I go to Wal-Mart (because they've got the best sales) and I buy 21 toothbrushes.

I use a new one to brush after every meal, every day . . . 21 toothbrushes a week average me around $50. My wife is supportive but she tries to make deals with me, like, use two brushes a day.

I've sincerely tried but if I change my normal routine I sit and pull my hair out, literally. I'm developing a little bald spot.

I'm hoping therapy will help and one of these days, I can be normal like everyone else.

You will be fine, you are lucky to have such a supportive wife and therapy is the answer. You could have a worse problem like drugs or alcohol, which ruins your life. Plus you must have the best teeth, I'm jealous.
~DarkGirl~

You can order huge amounts of toothbrushes from supply companies for a lot cheaper. I worked at a shelter and we would get like 5000 at a time. Find out about it from companies that sell paper towels and toilet paper for commercial restrooms. They also supply hotel chains with soaps and shampoos. That is a bizarre and wasteful obsession. But for the meantime, check out other options than Wal-Mart.

And I thought I had issues . . . No disrespect intended, good luck bro.

Your compulsion is treatable, meanwhile, find the nearest dental school or attend the nearest dental convention, they sell toothbrushes in bulk, it'll be a lot cheaper, believe me.

Would it be cheaper to buy a Water-Pik, with replacement tips? Just wondering. Otherwise, become good friends with your dentist. Dentists often have free samples or promotional toothbrushes.

Dude, I wish I was as unique as you are.

Aww that must suck hehe but it would be quiet amusing to see a guy stand in line with 21 toothbrushes don't the cashiers recognize you and think what the hell? What do you say to them?

(Ramoneschick)

Have you read A Man Named Dave? It's the last book in David Pelzer's trilogy. In it he overcomes all his self-doubt and continually just tries his hardest at whatever he puts his mind to. You can do it. Have faith in yourself.

---

good lord. I usually despise the over-diagnosis of ocd on this site by armchair shrinks & undergrad psych majors . . . but this sounds pretty darn serious. wow, that must be very hard to live with

~Gambitgirl~

Of all the compulsions you could have, stringent dental hygiene is DEFINITELY not one of the worst, count yourself lucky :)

One day you will. The therapy will help. And I'm proud of your wife for being so supportive. It just takes a lot of patience sometimes.

~Karebear~

Not only do I brush with the same toothbrush all the time, I've even grabbed the wrong one occasionally. Or someone else will use mine. You have this compulsion, you recognize it, and you are trying to get help. I wonder what traumatic event pushed you to this weird thing. Get a bad tasting toothbrush once?

`Gramps`

How Was Work Today?

I have been married for three years. I confess that I have become a little obsessed with my husband's work.

He is in real estate, or so he says. I have never been to his office. I have never met anyone else that he works with. He does have a company car and cell phone.

It's been bothering me for the past few months and I just figured on why. He has direct deposit, and I'm happy that he makes good money, really good money. But it's always the same amount deposited every two weeks.

If he sells commercial office space, I would think that his pay would vary with the commission on his sales. But they don't seem to.

Maybe I've seen too many spy movies.

---

maybe you should say something to him about this . . . umm . . "concern" of yours . . watch his body language . . and the way he looks at you . . if anything's off . . he's definetly lying . .
~§µgå® ßëRr¥~

It's far more likely that your husband is telling the truth. Or selling drugs.

My mom is in real estate you dont get money that often but when you do its usually a good ammount. your husband is up to something. i think its time to investigate. another thing no company car or phone. it doesnt work that way

---

Three years and you've never been in the office or met any one he works with? There are too many strange things here — I'd check it out, but be ready to deal with him being angry or to find out something you may have preferred not to know or both. Good luck.

Might be working for the CIA? They say that people that work for the CIA sit at lunch with people that they don't even know their real name.

no i dont think ur being delusional or paranoid . . . maybe u should have a PI investigate whats going on because something doesnt sound right. kudo's on being so perceptive!

And maybe you don't really want to know exactly why your reasoning adds up to what you think.
MollyMayhem

Hire a private detective. Please post what you find out in another confession, I confess I am VERY intrigued . . .

Maby you should just follow him, a little spying and distrust never hurt any marrage! He's probably working for the C. I. A. or something and thats just his cover story haven't you ever seen meet the parents.

No. I'd be questioning his job too. Maybe he works for the fbi.

Fortune Favors The Brave . . . And The Kinky

I'm 25, female and everyone sees me as the goody two shoes girl next door. Well it's not far from the truth. Good student, good daughter.

The thing I've never told anyone is that for as long as I can remember I've had fantasies about being spanked. No idea why. My parents never did and neither did any of the schools I went to. Until recently I haven't felt comfortable enough with a boyfriend to bring it up.

Well I've been with my current guy for a year and a half and last night I got my courage up and told him. Yes, I finally got that spanking. No little love pat either. He really had me squirming.

He said I deserved it for keeping secrets from him. It stung a lot more than I imagined it would but OH MY GOD was it exciting.

I'm so proud now that I finally have my own kinky sex story to confess.

Mmmmmm . . . . . I love spanking too :) well done for getting up the courage to ask for it, but before you do it again make sure you've decided on a 'stop word' something completely unrelated, like 'rosemary', something you'd never normally say during intimate moments, then if things hurt you can use your stop word and he'll know you're serious, so many people get hurt during this sort of play because their partner thought that 'no' actually meant yes, have fun but be careful :)

~kitty~

Good for you! Whatever floats your boat I guess. Enjoy!!

~iylya~

Lucky you, your boyfriend took to it so easily. Kinky? No, there's so many other things in that classification.

MollyMayhem

Good for you!! Sobi

Ummm, hate to tell you what your story did to ME! ;). Sounds like you have a good relationship. Trust is good.

I like to be spanked also. The harder the better, and I have no idea why I like it so much! Well, I'm glad that you had the ability to say what you wanted, and it looks like your boyfriend couldn't have been more happy than to oblige!

^_^ [— meow

Oh, that's awesome that he did it for you!!

Humm . . . I just don't get it. My wife likes me to spank her during sex. It obviously really gets her going . . . WOO HOO! But I still can't comprehend the turn on. She'd freak at the slightest discomfort any other way, even if I lick her nips just a little to wet. I know spanking does nothing for me. Oh well, spank away!

Something to tell the grandkids . . .

`Gramps`

YEAH! lol

~50centmami~

Congratulations. That is very cool that your boyfriend is kinky enough to play along and contribute to the fantasy! I hope you indulge him when he tells you about his own fantasies. ;)

The Momma Cat In Me

A few months ago I gave birth to the most beautiful baby boy ever.

My confession is that sometimes when I'm holding him and he's all sweet smelling and soft and adorable, I have the urge to lick his head . . . like how momma cats lick their kittens.

He's so beautiful - I am so weird.

That's adorable! As long as you don't give him a bald spot from obsessively licking his head you can tell him the story when he's older, and I'll bet you it'll be great for a laugh. Do it!

That's sweet.
áéíóú

That's not weird at all. You just don't see it on TV, that's all. And yes, he is just as wonderful and beautiful as you think he is - it's NOT just because you're his mommy! Enjoy your wonderful gift!
Don

Lick his head? I wonder what my mom thought or did to me . . . . .

Aw how sweet ^_^ can you say primordial instincts? i don't think you're weird, but others might, so try and refrain from licking his head- end rant

---

You are not "weird" at all. You are a mother who loves her child.

Well, congrats on your new baby!!!
~Sarah~

HA HA HA HA that is too funny . . . . and cute. Go ahead and lick his cute little head!

Your tongue will get all furry. You should just rub your forehead against the cat.

lol just cover him in kisses, Catwoman.

Hose And Pumps!

I confess that I am really, really turned on when a guy dresses up as woman. I am a 20 year old female and totally straight. Seriously, not an ounce of lesbian in me, but I just love it when guys dress up like women.

It's so sexy especially when they were nylons and high heels! I like it I love it I want some more of it.

I've been to one drag show in my life and it was just too intense for me - my lusting - I just wanted most of those guys so bad.

Why is this?

I have no interest in other girls. I just love guys! It makes me laugh so hard when they dress up as women but it's just so good too.

You like it when men are feminine. I love the Red Hot Chili Peppers Video of "My Friends."

Hehehe!!! I love the same thing! I try to get my boyfriend all the time to do it!

I am 19 and i completely agree with you. I love it when guys wear women's clothes, and it is a very big turn on for me. Did you know that plenty of heterosexual men cross dress?

Me too! YAY!

I really wish there were more women like you!

That's not too bad. I mean, Orlando Bloom does look a little bit girlish with that blonde wig and all. I wouldn't worry about it.

elmo44449999

I don't think guys who dress as women are doing it so they can hit on women. You've got a tough way to go if you're going to nail one of them.

`Gramps`

I'll bet a couple Monty Python skits would drive you over the edge . . . Whatever turns you on, I guess. But you do know that an overwhelming majority of the men in those drag shows are gay, right? Lust away anyway. It's nice and safe.

Eviltwin

Nylons and heels - both invented by men wanting to keep women in discomfort and pain. Hmm, maybe that's what you enjoy it - the grand payback. You should choose a career in planning the big Mardi-Gras parades, plenty of men in nylons and heels.

MollyMayhem

This is like "projected transvestitism" or something . . .

I can not relate to that. the notion of a man in a dress or hose is a total turn-off to me

~Gambitgirl~

Maybe the fact that they're wearing female clothes, actually makes their bodies seem MORE masculine in comparison.

CHAPTER III.

Stop, Thief!

Theft, stealing—we all used to know what those words meant. We had only to hear them to envision Oliver Twist slipping stealthily past some unsuspecting mark, gently grazing the man as he picked his pocket. Twist was a thief: If caught, he got forty lashes; if successful, forty pounds might be his. All was black and white, with no shades of gray.

Now we think of theft as having far more forms and faces. Consider, for instance, the theft of time: taking unauthorized breaks at work or sleeping on the job. Or consider using the company's resources for personal gain. For instance, who hasn't called a friend from work or sent a long-distance fax on the company's dime? Or used the company's computer to create a résumé, using the company's paper and printer to print a hundred copies and binding the résumé with the company's materials and machines—all to get a job at another company! Yep. That's theft, too.

Times and technologies have changed, and so has thievery. You can now be "pickpocketed" from halfway around the world thanks to the Internet, credit card fraud, and something relatively new called "identity theft."

Or have you ever borrowed something and forgotten to return it? Have you ever received too much change back from the cashier and not mentioned it? Have you ever stolen someone's heart . . .

No matter what form it takes, we know that Twist is in our midst when we hear the cry "Stop, thief!"

Family Visits

I am a 22 year old struggling to pay my tuition fees for college.

I confess that every time I visit my parents I steal little odds and end, such as toothpaste, toilet paper, tampons, postage stamps, any canned food, bar soap and shampoo. I don't mean too, but I can't afford to buy my own.

Sorry mom and dad!

They really do know. I wouldn't be surprised if they don't put fresh supplies out for you to take. It's OK; when you have kids, it will be your turn.

TigersGuy

I'm sure your parents probably know you do this, And if you asked they might even give you a little more than what you are stealing

---

Don't you think your parents would have just let you have those NECESSITIES if you had just asked? It is one thing to ask for cash, another for a tube of toothpaste.

They're probably aware of your stealing; where else would it be going . . . why not just ask for a hand? I'm in college too . . . I often have to beat my mom off with a stick to keep her from giving me mounds of supplies if I mention that I'm low.

Well, considering these are your parents and they love you, I don't see why that should be a problem. I am sure if you asked for these things they'd give them to you. Plus . . . I can't imagine they haven't noticed . . . just let it go as not to make you feel bad.

That's not considered stealing. My dad pays my tuition and I still take things from my parents. Usually I ask and I don't go overboard. It's a parent's job to make sure their child, (a hard working adult student one counts too) is able to survive.

College students do stuff like that. I'm pretty sure that everyone has done something like that. Something you might wanna try, have your parents take you shopping when you go home. They notice that their stuff's missing, they just don't say anything. And I'm sure they'd be willing to help you.

. . . and you think they have not realized this? Another college education gone to waste . . .

~SweetSunny~

This is not stealing, think of it as them paying you for taking care of them in 30 years when they need to go into a nursing home! (Besides, all college students do this, and I'm sure your parents notice)

WTF? Can't you just ask them? Do you have that poor of a relationship with your parents, that you cannot just ask them if they would buy you some toothpaste? Gees, I'd just ask my Mom and Dad, I know they would take me out that day to get whatever I needed. They would rather I go to them for help then resort to stealing or doing without! You can go about this the honest way and ask your parents, or you can continue stealing . . . either way it is going to cost them money!

Atheist Addiction

Well, first off, I am an atheist. I hate religion, believe there is no higher force, and all that happens to you when you die is you decompose.

But for some reason, every single time I stay in a hotel or resort, I have to steal the bible from the bureau! I just can't help myself! I have a nice collection of bibles on my bookshelf, all of which I've never even really opened.

What an odd addiction for a person like myself. So far I have 12 and counting.

I'm going on a vacation at the end of this February . . .

Do you realize those cost money? They cost 5 bucks a bible (the Gideon's that put them there just spoke at our church). You are not using them, and you did not pay for them. They may help someone, but thanks to you they can't. Good to know my money (yes, I donate to Gideon) is helping fuel your "addiction" (I think spitefulness is a better term myself)

Well you really are not stealing them because they are put there by people so that people do take them this is what they want. But they really want you to read them but if that is what you choose ok. but i thought i should tell you that your not stealing them when they are there because they want you to take them. There is a special club that i forgot the name of that goes around and puts them in hotels.

Well, you need to stop it. Just because you do not recognize God does not give you the right to steal it from those that might come to know Him by reading those Bibles. The Gideons, the ones that fought to get those out in every hotel in the US, I'm sure appreciate your efforts to steal the Word of God from hotels. I hope you have fun in hell.

Although it saddens my heart greatly whenever I hear that someone does not believe in Jesus, you are entitled to your own opinion. But it is not fair of you to deny that option to someone else who might use that motel room. I encourage you to open one of those Gideons and try to disprove it . . . you wont be able too.

You should open one, then you wont need to steal anymore

Maybe you're just trying to pawn off your beliefs on others - taking God away from them like you've taken it away from yourself. Now I'm all about whatever suits you, but don't be making other peoples' decisions for them.

Talk about sacrilege

I'm an atheist who collects rosary beads. Cheers!
Twistedsplinter

You have some serious problems. First, you're a thief. Second, if I can allow you to have your non-beliefs, then allow me to have my beliefs. In other words, live and let live. Maybe you'll grow up one day.

God'll get you for that . . .
`Gramps`

Maybe you're not such a devout atheist after all. Sometimes, our subconscious knows better than our conscious does.
"Blueper"

It's one thing to not believe in god . . . it's another to HATE religion. what's up with that? what point does it serve? why are you so mad?
~Gambitgirl~

Missing Something?

Two days ago I found a "porn" DVD in my 15-year-old son's computer.

I took it out, put it on my dresser and was planning what I was going to tell my husband and then our son. I went back about my business, but curiosity got the better of me and I dropped it into the DVD player in my bedroom.

Oh My God!

I have decided to wait a while to see if my darling little boy asks about his missing DVD. I doubt he will. I'll never bring it up.

I confess that this is my very first porn DVD, and I think I'll keep it.

I know, bad mom.

So you've discovered he's a chip off the ole block then? What the hell were you thinking? Go buy your own porn and leave the kid alone . . . now what is he supposed to masturbate to?

MollyMayhem

"Bad mom?" No kidding.

Raven

Damn when i was 15 we didn't have no dang fangled porn DVDs . . . we had to get it off the internet. These kids today . . .

the_captain

Not at all a bad mom, just curious. I say equal rights opportunities for all porn enthusiasts out there!

So what if your son is curious? As long as it isn't anything weird like child porn i don't see that ist anything other than harmless.

/twisted

HAHAHA wow . . . well i guess u now know the appeal of porn huh? a little erotic, isn't it? well all boys are curious at that age. let it go. although it doesn't creep u out a little to know ur getting aroused by the same thing as ur own son? hahaha just hadda throw that in there lol tb

Hey get your own porn you little thief. I just hope for your sake son never finds that dvd. Because if he does you will never hear the end of it.

Share with your husband! He will love it!

No you aren't a bad mother. Your son needed that porn - and apparently so did you

Give him the porn back . . . eventually he'll probably figure out you took it and that will just be a bad experience all round.

You are guilty of being just as curious as your kid and you invaded his privacy. I would put the dvd back where you got it and never say a word if I were you. Imagine the anxiety your son might feel worrying about what you think of him, worrying where the dvd might have gone, feeling embarrassed at the thought that you might have discovered something so personal of his, etc. To keep the video is a form of sexual and emotional abuse. Put the darned DVD back already.

You are a sick and perverted person that is just plain wrong, If my mother ever did something like that i would run the hell away and never consider her my mother anymore. I don't think that that is setting a very good example for your children.

LOL, jeez, mom, are you telling us that was your first viewing of pornography? I think you should talk to your kid about it, but still keep it (and benefit from it every once in a while—you are, after all, an adult and HE isn't.)

Messed Up In My Favor . . .

My bank accidentally deposited an extra $400 in my account and I don't know what to do.

I really need the money because I am a college student and I am totally broke. I know it happened last week because they're computers went haywire.

I know I should return it, but if I spend the money, will I get in trouble? Do they have end of the month reports and will they find the missing money?

My mom says she raised me better and I should give it back.

I confess that I'm honestly not sure what I will do.

Spend the money. Believe me, banks can afford to lose $400, you on the other hand can really use it.

If you keep it you will only cause a lot of trouble for yourself in the future. Keep it, and eventually you will say, "Oh sooo should not have kept that money." You might be giving up food and other groceries but you're also giving up possible jail time and additional fees from the bank and fines from the state. Those will make your financial situation alot alot worse than it is now.

Yeah you will get in trouble, even though the bank messed up. Unfair, I know, but so are banks in general. You get 1% interest but their loans have 15%!!! You pay fees for using ATMs etc. oh well, give the money back or you'll owe them!

K Man

More than likely your bank WILL catch you and you will have to pay it back. And if you don't report it, the bank wont trust you because surely someone with such a small income as your would notice an extra 400 bucks. Report it and make the bank love you

---

Sooner or later they will find out. Tell them and give it back, you may end up in jail if you decided to take it.

They will figure it out fairly soon. Don't spend it!!

GIVE IT BACK! They will find it out and automatically take it out . . .

Something similar happened with ATM machines giving away money in the UK and the people who took advantage are now in prison . . . its a biatch I know but honesty really is the best policy!

They will track down the money and they will ask for it back. Trust me, I have to deal with it daily. I am one of those people that have to track down moneys placed in incorrect accounts. and you WILL be asked to pay it back immediately if you do spend it.

Give it back! They're bound to find it eventually! Plus it's just the right thing to do.

god_chic

I'm not entirely sure on the exact technicalities, but if it's their fault, then you get to keep it. It's their little way of making sure they don't screw up too much. I think they have to contact you within a certain period (about a month), and if they dont - the go spend it! Your mum is right in a way, but then no-one else's balance is generally affected, so enjoy it!

Big Tipper

The "new guy" at work asked me out on a date.

I guess to impress me, he took me out to a very expensive restaurant. The meal with two bottles of wine was almost $200. He paid in cash and left a $50 tip.

While waiting for the valet to bring up his car, I told him I left my clutch at the table (I really did). I went back to get it and the money was still on the table.

I confess, I took a $20 bill and stuffed it in my bag.

Sorry, but a $50 tip was just too much.

A guy spent $200 on a person like you? What a waste of money, you don't seem worth it.

I hope he dumps you

You stole from the waitress. I guess you've never worked for less than minimum wage. If he wanted to leave a $500 tip, that was his decision, not yours! I hope he finds someone better than you, and I bet that he does . . .

You are greedy. It was HIS money to spend. I predict he finds out your true nature soon enough and dumps you on your selfish, thieving butt!

His tip was about right, 10% is the lowest level you should leave and certainly too low for a fancy place. Do you realize that the waiters/ waitresses make their money from the tips? It's part of their pay, their actual pay is very low. You not only have no class, but you are theft to boot. What you did is no different than if you had grabbed the waiter's wallet and taken $30.00 out of it! And I noticed you felt no need to give your date half of what he paid to take you out, after all he paid way too much for you, obviously. :-(

Leaving only $30 dollars was not enough. Don't you realize that it is customary now to leave 20% not 10?

I hope you were worth the twenty.
Arkie

As a waitress - 20 bucks is 10 percent of 200. You suck! Not only did you steal from your date . . . but you just ripped off some poor guy trying to do his job. ::mumbles about the indecent people of the world::

Somebody makes their money waiting those tables. who the hell are you to steal from some poor waiter or waitress!!!

Who are you to judge it was too much? . . . You're just a thief, don't try and justify it!

You'd better hope he's not a regular there. If he is, they'll tell him you came back and took the money. Bet you didn't give it back to him . . .
`Gramps`

Not Just Anything Shiny

I confess that I'm a kleptomaniac.

I steal anything. Anything at all. Whether it's worth anything or not. If I can take it without being caught, I do. Most of the time, I end up throwing what I've stolen out because I feel bad.

I have even stolen a ring off a corpse in a funeral home.

Sometimes I just need to steal.

III. STOP, THIEF!

Ok . . . that's just really sick

What you really need to do is get help. Seriously!! You have a problem and you need to talk to a professional. Do it now.

That poor dead guy. What if that was a very special ring to that person?

You should feel bad. For stealing period.

It'll be fun until you get caught then you're screwed for life with a criminal record get some help.

People like you stole my Pokemon cards

So what are you waiting for? The problem won't just disappear on its own. Go find a therapist who can help you. You'll feel a lot better about yourself once you've broken this habit.

Ok you need help. It sounds as tho u are a compulsive stealer. There's therapy for that!

~Sarah~

Woa. Was this at a wake for a funeral that you stole this ring? Please tell me you don't go visiting morgues just to get some jewelry . . .

Gross, man. You need to get help NOW.

`Cramps

Ok, I was gonna be sympathetic but the corpse thing was terrible. You can get help for this, it's a mental illness.

messageinabottle

I'll Do What I Have To Do

We are deeply in debt. Mostly because of medical bills. The creditors call every day. My husband's check is being garnished already and just today another creditor called to say that if we can't pay they are going to garnish his wages.

We don't have the money to pay for the necessities like food and utilities. My medical bills each month are really high. We can't even come up with the money to file bankruptcy.

I confess that I can't take it anymore. I am sick of creditors who don't understand that we don't have the money. I am thinking of either holding up a convenience store or breaking into someone's home to get money.

I don't think I have any other choice.

Been there. Got caught. Not good.

Umm, okay. A convenience store only gives you, on average about 25-50 bucks. That's not worth the time you'll spend in jail if busted. As in breaking into someone's house, that's just wrong. A business is one thing, but taking someone's stuff that they had to go out and buy with hard earned money, I find that unjustifiable. I know life is hard, and I'm not sure what to say, but I'm sure somebody will have a helpful talk back with a better idea than robbery.

Well at least you'll have a roof over your head . . . I'm referring to JAIL.
Joss

Do that, and in addition to being broke, you'll be in jail with a criminal record. There's worse problems than being broke. What are you doing, if anything, to improve your situation?

Well were in the same boat dear, but i would never think of robbing someone. Why not cut way back on expenses, sell the car if you have to, if you have kids that are old enough make them get a job, as for food etc, try eating just once a day, that's what we do. Eventually you'll have your bills paid off.

Crime will get you free lodging, but it won't pay your bills. I don't mean to sound harsh, but if you've got high medical bills, what else are you doing that would bring creditors out of the walls? You need to find a debt counselor who can help you. There should be free services available in your city.

`Gramps`

 Oh, and I suppose having your ass thrown in jail will do wonders for your debt? Think again. Try a debt consolidator . . .

If they were just medical bills I could understand, but it sounds like a lot more than that. My aunt is a truck driver and was out of work for more than a year having knee surgery then was diagnosed with breast cancer. SHE can pay her bills even though it is a struggle because she did not use credit cards for simple, daily expenses. You got yourself into this mess, don't hurt other people just because you do not know how to run your finances!

If you can't pay your creditors I guarantee that you wont be able to pay attorney fees or bail.

You don't want to take the chance of spending MORE money for bail. Don't run the risk, maybe you can try to find a job, too.

Declare bankruptcy before starting to thieve. Better than jail-time, no?

I Have A Hunger For Religion

Lunch at the university cafeteria is expensive and our campus is located nowhere near restaurants within walking distance so I have to find a way to conserve money.

The Student Baptist Ministries offer a half hour bible talk along with a half-hour luncheon.

I admit, I attend those strictly for the free lunch, even though I am an atheist and have no business there.

I admit, I am a cheapskate.

Hey, Free food is Free Food.

I bet you're not the only one. Ever think of bringing lunch from home though?

BostonGirly

Somehow i don't think they mind . . . isn't that the point of the free food?

Jeroo

Hey there is nothing wrong with that, it is about time somebody actually got something positive from religion . . power to you . .

Maimu

There is a saying 'The way to a person's heart is through their stomach'. Besides, the ministry is not just for the soul, but for the body too. I hope you find peace and success so that you can feed yourself. God Bless you; God IS Blessing you.

TigersGuy

That's pretty well my motivation for participating in any on-campus things. Who wants to spend their own money? Nothing draws a crowd quite like free food.

Dontpointhatfigeratme

LMAO . . . you should have a talk with the poor guy who wrote in yesterday about being too poor to eat and has been surviving on Purina . . . .

DontKnow_DontCare

I'm an atheist too. How can you stand hanging all those bible-thumping Jesus freaks? Go buy some ramen and spare yourself an hour of agony.

lil_wench

They're not naive, they know that free food will lure you there.

dinkus

Ok hopefully i'm not going to hell but . . . HAHAHAHAHA!!!!! that's awesome . . .

Jailbait

hmmm u go 2 church 4 the food. Isn't it ironic that you have little money but somehow you can go to a church and they will provide food? Hmmm seems like its God's way of helping you

XxXpLiCiT

Pavlov proved it a long time ago. You're just further proof. Now you won't be able to go to church without getting hungry. Look at the bright side: some of it may actually sink in!

`Gramps`

Dine In - To Go

I confess a few years ago me and my friends decided to eat at this restaurant.

It was a nice view and all but the food was really bad. Once we were finished eating, we called a passing waiter asked for the bill.

15 minutes later, still no bill. So we called the same waiter and asked for the bill. 10 minutes passed, still no bill.

So this time we called a different waiter. Yup, we waited again for 15 minutes and no bill.

So we decided to walk out of the restaurant.

It was funny though, no one stopped us. Serves them right. The food was lousy and yet we still were willing to pay them. Then they wouldn't give us the bill so screw them!

i would have done the same thing

~Gambitgirl~

Way to go, I hate shoddy service. Hope ya didnt leave a tip.

~J

You waited 40 minutes for the bill? That is like the restaurant holding you hostage! I would have walked out too, especially if the food was bad. Actually I'd be torn between complaining or leaving without paying. Wow the only time I've ever come across service (and food) that bad . . . I complained and got the meal free anyways.

I have done this exact same thing- we were even waved out and asked to come again- ha ha.

No excuse you come up with can change the fact that you stole that money. No one forced you to go to that restaurant, or to eat that horrible food, but you did both. So you needed to pay. It does serve them right, but you don't deserve the extra money.

In this particular situation . . . . . I don't blame you a bit!

Perhaps the waiters are consorting to put an end to the bad food.

MollyMayhem

You're only required to make a certain effort. Sounds like you did your best. By the way, I've also noticed that sometimes, the view gets in the way of the food the restaurant prepares.

`Gramps`

I would have probably left what I thought I owed on the table, but only for fear of getting busted for stiffing them. I certainly wouldnt have waited for 40 minutes, maybe 10.

wisconsin

No, I Haven't Seen It...

Sorry sweetie. You didn't lose your razor yesterday.

I couldn't find mine so I stole yours. My legs are nice and smooth, and you had to go to work all scruffy.

I would have put it back after I used it, but you can somehow always tell when I do that. And I didn't tell you because I know you hate it when I use your razor.

I'm going to the store right now to buy you a brand new one.

And maybe one for myself too.

LMAO . . . my sister used to steal my dad's razor . . . that is, until he caught on and bought her one just like his!

DontKnow_DontCare

He can tell because the damn razor is dull after you've done both your legs. Compare the surface area here, honey. It's not magic! Now, what are you going to DO with those silky smooth legs to make it up to him?

Unluckyatlove

---

dude, SERIOUSLY, i dont get why guys get all huffy when their g/f's or wives use their razors..I mean damn, if you can have sex with her, whats the big deal about sharing a razor?!

meow54

#3 Its not the act of sharing that is the problem. Its the act of shaving with a dull a$$ razor once she is done with it.

bigcheze

You bet we can tell . . . it"s like you trying to use a pair of scissors after I cut the excess of my guitar strings with them. The aftermath of leg shaving is clearly visible! I hate it when my wife does that too!

TheSmokingHypocrite

My Dad and my brother used to get so pissed when I used their razors; they just dont make women's razors that do quite as nice a job!! (and if any of you ladies know of any brands that do, please . . . POST!!)

Erin07

Just get a mans razor. i like the venus brand though. works good for me!

~CARLA~

unluckyatlove is telling it like it is. Face small. Legs huge! Like shaving many faces. Many shaves, dull blade! Dull blade, nicks on face! Get yourself one of the new Gillette triple blade shavers. Smoothest thing I've ever used . . .

`Gramps`

Are you my wife?!?! She does that all the time! If she likes mine better than hers why won't she get one! Ah well . . . At least her legs are great! ;-)

Seriouslywondering

Mach 3's work wonders . . . i still wonder why they made those crappy pink cheapo ones for women! men only shave their face and women have to shave practically their whole body . . . . .

JayMing

To ERIN07 . . . I use the venus razor . . which works really well for me. I also use hair conditioner instead of shaving cream, and my legs are smoother than ever!

darlindiva

I'm so with you girl! i used to gank my dad's Mach 3 all the time . . . until he bought me one for myself

~Gambitgirl~

CHAPTER IV.

Family Matters

Blood is thicker than water; it's also a lot harder to get out of the carpet.

The family unit is an amazing, dynamic social group. On any given day the individual members could be at one another's throat about who is going to drive the new car home: the father, because he paid for the damn thing; the son, because he is the only one who can appreciate and handle the car's brute horsepower; or the mother, because she is in charge of the family unit and the father knows the power she wields over him.

Should someone come along and want the parking space the family is trying to vacate and tap the horn to hurry the process, the family unit immediately ceases all internal aggressions and unites to focus on the interloper. This family that was about to terminate the bloodline over a set of car keys is now joined solidly at the hip, ready to repel, with extreme prejudice, he who would oppose any individual member of the family.

It's hard to figure out how they do it—live together under one roof for years at a time, sharing everything from soap, to soda, to secrets, to beds, to bathrooms, and all other real estate in between (and most of the time, it's very little real estate). They are forced to live an otherwise unnatural communal existence.

It's no wonder that every once in a while, things are said, feelings are hurt, and trusts are compromised. This is our dirty laundry. So butt out—these are our family matters.

Circumcision

My wife and I recently had a baby boy. We had to decide which religion to bring our child up in, since I am Jewish and she is catholic. She agreed that Judaism would be fine, but drew the line at circumcision.

While she has been gone these last two weeks, I had our baby circumcised. She doesn't know, but I guess she'll find out in a week . . .

Might I add as a wife who's husband did the same thing to our son after discussing and agreeing against circumcision, he is now a SINGLE man who sees the son he butchered on WEEKENDS only! I hope your wife also boots your ass to the curb after disregarding her choice and doubts about it! You are certainly not a man I would choose to spend the rest of my life with . . . . I made the choice after such an act and am happier now, knowing I do not have to worry about what else he will/has done behind my back!

You so broke her trust. You should really be ashamed of yourself.

You are definitely waiting for an argument. I wish you best of luck.
~DarkGirl~

Ooh, your wife is going to be SO pissed. I hope you know babies are only Jewish If their mothers are. So, that leaves you with a non-Jewish, circumcised baby. Whoa, you're in some trouble.

Someone's facing divorce . . . . Or no sex for months . . . your game, glad I'm not you :)
^DaZ^

Congratulations on your child's mutilation! I bet you're proud, lying to your wife and slicing apart your son's genitals.

Dear me, how complicated, those things . . . For your wife: if Judaism would be fine, why draw that line??? For you: is this the way to deal with conflicts?? I wish you all the best, but i am not jealous

While I do prefer circumcision (I had my son circumcised) it is a joint decision between you and your wife. How dare you go behind her back and do something she did not wish for! You could have at least talked to her about your feelings towards it before doing something as stupid as you have just done. Don't be surprised if she sues your ass and leaves you. I would.

Uh, yeah, I think she will notice the missing foreskin! That was a little wrong to do that without talking to your wife first!

Dude you are in SO much trouble. Where do you get off making a decision like that without even consulting your wife? i hope this isn't an indication of how bossy you are in other parts of your relationship

~Gambitgirl~

Wow. She gives up rearing the boy in her religion, lets you raise him Jewish but just doesn't want you to . . . the little boy, and you won't do it? So you do it behind her back! Selfish bastard, anyone?

So you're not man enough to stand up to your wife? And by the way, it's Catholic! That's a capital C, sonny! Where are you going to be hiding when she notices?

`Gramps`

Keep It Down!

I know I'm supposed to be a dutiful daughter and honor and obey you, Mom and Dad. And just because you're married with kids doesn't mean that you have a totally celibate life.

But is there any way that you could wait to have sex until AFTER we're all asleep or at least in our rooms?

I know that's how we came into this world but I confess that I really don't enjoy hearing you two through the thin walls and doors.

I resolve this year to get and use earplugs if it doesn't stop.

Sorry, but it sounds like your parents have little or no respect for you. I suggest you bring it up, as awkward as it may be, think of all the much more restful nights you'll enjoy.

Why should it stop? Get the earplugs and stop whining.
MollyMayhem

The next time they do this- wait until the next morning then ask for ear plugs . . . if they ask why then tell them there was too much noise last night for you to go to sleep. OR when they start to go at it- turn your radio on just loud enough for them to hear, then turn it up 10 minutes later, and again 10 minutes later. Eventually they should get the message.

If you tell them you can hear them they will be embarassed enough to take care of the problem . . . so your only problem is how to let them know you can hear them . . .

Ewww. That has to be gross hearing them. I know this is going to be embarassing, but sit down with your mom or dad (preferably the parent the same gender you are) and have a talk with them. They probably don't know they are being so loud. They will probably be as embarassed as you are.

If you don't actually say anything to them or indicate anything about it, just turn your radio up really loud every time they make love, and turn it down just after they stop. They'll figure it out.

---

omfg you poor thing! i also had the misfortune of listening to someone have sex, someone i REALLY didn't want to hear! it's the most nasty, yucky feeling ever, makes you want to rip your own ears off doesn't it. my sympathies.

You could try talking directly to them about the problem. Tell them you find it awkward and embarrassing, and ask them to have some consideration for other people. Sure, they pay the bills and all, but you still have to live there. It's cool that they're still that much in love with each other, and still frisky, but a little consideration goes a long way. Or you could just turn your radio or TV up really loud to the point where it becomes distracting to them.

LOL yeah I've had that problem. *shudders* I know when I have kids I dont wanna go without sex, so I keep my mouth shut for their sake. But still, I HATE hearing it . . .

Hey — be glad your parents are happy together! You're very lucky.

I could have written this myself. It's quite horrible isn't it? I always keep my discman by my bed just in case . . .
~Crow~

Do I understand what your saying . . . yes . . . but hey at least your parents can still get some . . . it takes the tention out of the family . . . thats a good thing . . .

In And Out

Oh my god! Last night I confessed to my parents I was gay. (because, heck, I am!)

But I didn't do the normal letter or email or phone call or visit, I did it in a rather unique way. I got them to visit me.

When they arrived I said I had something to tell them, and for them to come to my bedroom, they did. I got into my closet, closed the door, opened it again, stepped out and shouted "Mummy, Daddy, I'm gay!" - They laughed their ass's off!

I confess that it went much better than I thought it would.

Oh! That is just so cute. You adorable thing you - wish I'd done something like that when I came out for the whole experience would have been far more enjoyable. Kudos to you, my love
~Serpentis~

Whoa . . . did they take you seriously? That is funny as hell. Ill be your fag hag if you need one . . .

LOL. Very creative.
~ReD~

That was a very unique way to tell your parents . . . I'm so glad everything went well for you =0)

That was really funny and clever! I wish you luck and happiness!!

LOL, that's cute. you give new meaning to the phrase coming out of the closet. i love stating the obvious.
Skittlehead

Consider yourself lucky. There was one young fellow who had to break his dad's jaw because even though his dad already knew he was gay he attacked his son's boyfriend when he saw them kissing.

They laughed because of the way you said it. They were probly glad you said it right to them and they didnt have to find out elsewhere plus you literally came out of the closet and I think anyone would've laughed at that.

good for you *thumbs up*
~Waddles~

That's hilarious! I'm glad it went so well. You have really cool parents.

Good for you! I'm glad you have open-minded parents that saw the humor in it.

Probably because they didn't believe you. Try taking a bf home with you . . .
`Gramps`

I Had So Much Fun

My wife and I went out last night for a few drinks. I had a few more.

I swear that I don't remember anything past about 10:00pm last night. I woke up this morning sleeping on the couch. My wife had already left for work and I am so late that I just called sick at my work.

I confess that I'm truly unaware as to what the hell I did last night, but in the four years we have been married, this is the first time I've slept on the couch.

I wonder how much trouble I'm in.

I'm really sorry for whatever I did.

Gee maybe you should stop drinking. Could this be fates way of telling you to get your ass on the wagon?

Awwww someone's in the doghouse!!! LOL, no, maybe you just decided to sleep on the couch, or you smelled bad and she couldn't breathe. Good luck talking to her!!!

~Sarah~

Wow, your in deep

Ahhh your probably not in trouble you probably just passed out there and she couldnt wake you up.

'fresh'

Busted

You were supposed to confessed AFTER you found out what you did! I wanna know!

Have you ever heard of flowers? If I were you, I would show up to her work on her lunch hour & take her out to lunch so that you can talk. When she gets back to work, I would make sure that the flowers are on her desk!!!! I know that unless you did something REALLY stupid that this would work with me!

Maybe you passed out and she just dumped you on the couch rather than trying to carry you upstairs to the bed.

That happened to me once. Turned out I ruined the whole 5 yr. relationship in one evening and was left alone for what I had said. And to this day, I still don't know what I said . . . nor do I drink.

Oh nooo!! Will you let us know what DID happen as soon as you find out? Xxx

This is why some people just should not drink period. Maybe it's time to slow down a bit?

Haha thats kinda funny. Hope it wasn't too bad:)

Going To Be A Mom

I am a 19-year old lesbian. For that, Mom and Dad, I am sorry.
To my Sister: I had sex with your boyfriend. I'm sorry, I had to.
My girlfriend and I wanted a baby and now this dream can come true.
I confess that I am pregnant.

I feel sorry for your child. You sound desperate for long-term therapy.

Now this is a soap opera!
~*bijin*~

Hope you have a beautiful baby. But who's the dad?
Jelly

It had to be your sister's boyfriend, it couldn't be any other of the millions of men in the world? I feel very sorry for your sister and your baby. Both have a relative who is a sleaze.

You HAD to have sex with her boyfriend? What, did he rape you?

Why are you apologizing to your parents for who you are??? If anything, they should be apologizing to you for not being tolerant. God loves you regardless, trust me on that one. But I think it's just low that you had to choose your sister's boyfriend in order to become pregnant. Wasn't there anyone else available? Either way, it's clear that there's more going on here than meets the eye. Why do you resent your sister so much?

This has to be one of the strangest white trash confessions I have ever read.

Enjoy your single mother status when your girlfriend leaves you and your family disowns you. Not so smart now are you.

Nothing against lesbianism but YOU, you are a horrible person.

There is a reason homosexuals can't reproduce.
Arkie

You go gir

A 19 year old single anything doesn't need the demands of motherhood. To top it off, gay and lesbian relationships, especially at that age, are unstable. When you are left alone, you will have to shoulder the entire responsibility. But then you could always nail your sister's stupid bf for child support.
`Gramps`

Won't Give In

I have not spoken to my wife in three days.

We are having a bit of a fight right now, and neither has relented on this "Cease Talking" condition.

I confess that whatever we were fight about three days ago must have been pretty serious, because I can't remember the last time we went for this long without making up.

I also confess that for the life of me, I can't remember what we were fighting about.

Hahaha, serves you right! Sounds like my sister and I when we were 10.

Well isn't that just precious, why don't you kids head back to the clubhouse now and let us adults enjoy the peace and quiet.

MollyMayhem

It's been 4 months and I still haven't talked to my "girl", 3 days is nothing. I guess my "ex-girl" now, lol . . .

---

maybe you forgot something important and she's mad at you for it.

Dinkus

I dont know what to tell you about that except to sit down with your wife and talk about everything thats bothering you. dont nitpick but dont just NOT TALK when both of you must want to talk to the other.

You'll get over it once one of you gets horny . . .

---

not remembering what the fight was about is a good sign that its time to kiss and make up.

(Dr. Goldfish)

Haha, nice. =) ASK HER!!

Time to break the cease talk, then!
Loo

Lol . . . that's very funny but DO NOT under any circumstances let your wife know that!
Joey

silent treatment for 3 days . . . and you can't remember why. maybe your wife is pissed that you keep forgetting stuff lol
~Gambitgirl~

Did I Just Say That?

I was honest with my wife today.

It's the middle of winter, we're all eating more and exercising less and I mentioned that she was getting a little "girthy".

Wrong thing to say.

I knew that as soon as the words were leaving my lips. We have been married 11 years, tell each other everything . . .

I confess that I made a bad mistake. It's below freezing tonight and the couch in the den smells, is squeaky and I don't have a quilt or blanket.

I am very sorry for my lapse in judgment.

You should feel terrible . . . you think she can't see the extra pounds?

I can't say that she overreacted . . it WAS kinda mean, honest or not (even though you weren't trying to be mean). Lay low til you're on speaking terms, and in a few days just kinda give her elevator eyes, look impressed and like you're enjoying the view..give her a compliment like "Oh baby that dress looks reaaaaal NICE on you!" ;) Good luck.

Raven

---

ah the golden rule . . . always say "no" when your wife of g/f says "do I look fat?" it should be a reflex.

the_captain

LOL . . . That's hilarious! You'd be on the couch awhile if you were my husband.

~countrygirl~

I don't think it's right that you make an honest observation and you have to sleep on the couch.

If you guys are honest with each other and tell each other everything, why is she so mad? I have the same relationship with my boyfriend, and if he had said that to me, I would've simply gone on a diet and started exercising. In fact, I would've been glad that he said something, because what's the alternative? Him thinking it and it affecting our sex life? Sounds like your wife is in denial.

Hell no dude don't be sorry, the truth should be out, you have a right to ask her to keep herself fit for you, cuz i assume you do that for her already and that's why you would say it. My g/f even told me that if she starts to get fat she wants me to tell her and she'll exercise to get better as I would for her. Relationships are about making the other person happy and keeping them sexually interested as well as emotionally and mentally, and if she refuses to stay fit, then she's not doing her job to "honor and obey" which are in the wedding vows.

Chances are that you had no intention of hurting your wife, but you did and now must apologize for it. And I just had to mention that I'll bet that you yourself are not a "spring chicken" in the winter months.

Oooooooh . . . Not good, man, not good. I thought the "thou shalt not tell your wife the truth about her weight" rule was practically programmed into men when they got married . . .

If its the truth then your wife should be able to deal with that, how else is she going to do something about it?

-Kieyza

ROTFLMAO! Any man who has been married more than 10 yrs (22 myself) has committed a "heinous" act like this! Bad part is- she'll never let you forget it (parties, family get togethers, etc.) Dogs make great companions for those "on the couch" nights and they won't make fun when you stick your foot in your mouth!

Big Daug

Prom Bomb

Many, many years ago - my senior prom. I was with my girlfriend, having a typically boring time.

My little brother (a junior - the junior class sponsors our prom and are invited to attend) was there with his date. She was (is still) very beautiful, exotic and willing as hell.

I drove to the dance that night, my brother came with a buddy of his that was nowhere to be found when little bro's girlfriend "became ill".

I volunteered to take her home and told my date I would be right back.

Little brother, after all of these years I never had the heart to tell you that your date, the girl you eventually married, had sex with me in my car that night.

Truly Sorry. Still won't tell.

You didn't know . . . it's not THAT big a deal. And it's SO good of you to keep it quiet and not injure their marriage. =)

Oh, so because a woman is "willing as hell" that gives you the right to abandon your morals and just do it? How pathetic that is. And I'll bet that to this day you still see the whole thing as being her fault right? Because she was so willing? You make me sick.

good for you! FREE LOVE! im proud of the generation that is doing this shit and keeping it to themselves, then like losers they pour their feelings on 2 sarcastic teenagers ready and willing to critisize them. we thank you for making us laugh.

wait a second . . . he married her??? oh boy . . . it was ur responsibility to tell him. i mean, now she could be cheating on him left and right, and u pretty much know about it. shame on u!
tb

Aha! There's no denying it now. the cat's out of the bag.

Hehehehehehehehehehehehehehehehehe

You never wanted to tell your brother that his wife is a skank?

So not only did you have sex with your brother's date, but you also slept with a junior? All the fault is on you, because you should have known better. people like you make me sick to my stomach, literally.

So you're saying that your sister-in-law was the town punchboard? Or was she just willing with you? The only smart thing you've done is not tell your brother. Stay smart.
`Gramps`

Any Thing You Say

I have been divorced for seven years now. I have been seeing someone for the past three years, we live together and are very happily committed to each other without the bonds of matrimony.

We just visited my folks who liven in Colorado. I was quite surprised by the fact that when we arrived, my father pulled me aside and informed me that due to the fact we were not married, Sharon and I could not sleep in the same room together.

I hugged my dad and told him that it was not a problem and we would respect his wishes.

I confess that probably for the first time in my life, I disregarded my father's wishes. Five times.

I'm don't feel too terribly bad. I have always been a good son, but this was one thing that I couldn't do for dad.

Sorry.

His house, his rules. Next time stay in a hotel.

You could have gotten a motel room instead of going against your father's wishes in his home. Marry the woman. There are benefits she will have should anything happen to you.

MollyMayhem

Sounds like your inner teen ager is still sneaking around trying to get a little. Not man enough to stand up to your father? You could have stayed at a motel, couldn't you?

`Gramps`

Yes, you should respect your father's wishes. However, you shouldn't lie to him then sneak around behind his back. Next time you go to visit, make reservations at a local motel. Then you can be a man about it and say "I respect your wishes, dad, that's why I've rented a room at Motel 6." Then, you'll find out what's more important to him, enforcing his moral code or spending some extra time with you. Either way, you win because you get to visit your dad and sleep with your gf. Also, you get to keep your dignity.

The kids these days have no respect! ;) By the way, don't try to impress us with the "five times" thing. The more astute among us will know you're lying.

It's Colorado . . . what do you expect?

When your young and in love 5 times is nothing. Secondly don't condemn these kids it irrates me even though I'm 42. I do however agree with all the others who said that you should have stood up to your father and told him your going to a motel.

Well, y'all weren't sleeping, were you? Check Miss Manners on the subject—she agrees with you!

I'm a bit surprised at the talk backs so far. Mostly they are just giving you beef for not going to a motel instead. I think that was manly of you to accept it (even if you disregarded the complete rules . . . ;)). I know I would have pissed if my parents had done that to me. Like you don't know what sex is? Geez, you've been married, you live with this girl, etc, etc. Kudos for you to not getting pissed.
Leigh

---

ease up he could have stayed for more than one night! and therefore had sex five times. ie 2.5 times each night. The father said no sleeping in the same room, he said nothing about the sex? but yeah, do it in marriage

---

he's still your dad & it's still his house. either stay somewhere else or respect his rules . . . or just stay home if you can't control yourself. i know you're "all grown up now" and all that but still, have some respect for your parents
~Gambitgirl~

I understand how you feel. my mother didn't wnat me to sleep in the same room with my significant other when we went spend a weekend with them but we broke the rules too . . . . . . It actually made it more exciting at the thought we could get caught . . . . . hehe

podnah

How Could You?!

My seventeen-year-old son just got back from visiting my dad for the weekend. Seems my father told my son about what he did for me on my seventeenth birthday. - He took me to a brothel and bought me a date with two women.

I confess that I am trying to come up with a appropriate punishment for dear old dad . . .

Ouch. Nothing hurts like the truth. Sounds like quite a birthday, though!
Loo

wow really? my parents would never do that for my little bros. I feel like I should be grossed out or something but I don't. Way to go grampa.

Wasn't your son embarrassed to know that? I'd be embarrassed if I found out my dad had to pay for it.

Hopefully your son doesn't take after you or your father.

i guess you gotta do the same thing!

And while you're at it, come up with an appropriate punishment for you for allowing your son to spend time with your dear old dad. Way back when, you had the option of NOT going through with the 'date' dad set up for you. Did you go through with it? Of course you did. Don't be too quick to think less of Dad when you were such a willing participant. Just because he now has the bad taste to talk about it to your son doesn't give you the right to punish him. Use it as a good example to set for your son and take dear old dad with a grain of salt

MollyMayhem

A date? You mean good old sex with a prostitute, right? Why not say things as they are, eh?

Leave dad alone. As long as your son knows he is not getting the same gift . . .

At first i thought this was a woman confessing . . . so i read the confession again . . . lol

---

Punishment? You should thank him every day of your life.

Why would you punish a dad that cool?

Dad tried to be your buddy by getting down to your level, and he's trying to do the same with his grandson. I wouldn't trust granddad with the grandson any more. And if grandma complains, tell her why. See if he still thinks that was such a great thing.

`Gramps`

CHAPTER V.

Working Late... Again

It has been said that man is not monogamous by nature; the very thought of monogamy can be very stifling to some, especially when you consider that the word means being married to just one person for the rest of your life.

Just one shot to get it right.

Religion plays a huge part in marriage. Of course, almost every religion celebrates the joining of a couple in wedlock. Religious sects mandate that the union must be of two people of the same faith. Some decree that, once consummated, the marriage can never, ever be dissolved. And just to stir things up a bit, the Mormon prophet Joseph Smith Jr. told his followers that although a woman could have only one husband, a man could take many wives.

Given all the "rules" regarding marriages, it's hardly surprising that millions of men and women, terrified by the thought of a lifetime commitment to one person, decide to avoid the subject entirely. But despite all the rules, mandates, social pressures, fears, and frustrations, there were more than 2,344,000 marriages in the United States last year. (There were also 1,135,000 divorces.)

Interestingly, adultery, the ultimate marital "crime," is rarely the reason for divorce. Most cases of adultery end before being discovered. And truth be told, it is estimated that as many wives cheat on their husbands, as husbands cheat on their wives.

Adultery seems to be a spontaneous act, one that the guilty party swears that he or she never gave any forethought to. Usually when describing it, we often hear the words: ". . . and then one thing led to another." Of course time, location, opportunity, and copious amount of alcohol also come into play.

Bottom line—adultery happens in all walks of life, all religions, and all countries. So if you're trying to keep score, don't be surprised if it gets a little confusing figuring out just who's Working Late . . . Again!

Right Choice

I have been engaged for almost a year. I am to be married next month.

My fiancée's mother is great. She is putting the entire wedding together and invited me to her place to go over the invitation list because it had grown a bit beyond what we had expected it to be.

When I got to her place we reviewed the list and trimmed it down to just under a hundred. Then she floored me.

She said that in a month I would be a married man and that before that happened, she wanted to have sex with me. Then she just stood up and walked to her bedroom and on her way said that I knew where the door was if I wanted to leave.

I stood there for about five minutes and finally decided that I knew how to deal with this situation. I headed out the front door.

There, leaning against my car was her husband. He was smiling. He explained that they just wanted to be sure I was a good kid and would be true to their little girl. I shook his hand and he congratulated me on passing their little test.

I kept it to myself that I thought their "little test" was asinine bullshit, but I'm marrying their daughter, not them.

I also kept to myself that the reason that I was walking out to my car was to get a condom.

I'm still getting married in about a month.

I was about to give you lots of praise and tell you to tell her parents to go screw themselves. Then I read your last line and that all went out the window.

You were going to get a condom so that you could have sex with your fiancee's MOTHER? And you are still going to marry this girl, when, if the oppurtunity presented itself, you would cheat on her? That is not fair to her . . . not fair at all, and disgusting. Tell her you are not ready for the wedding, or a bet that in two months, you'll be back here confessing your one night stand.

You are disgusting! How could you even consider doing such a thing with your fiance's mother. Especially when you are going to be married in a month! I think that you had better take a good look at the reasons you have for getting married. If you are willing to cheat a month before the marriage, a time when you should be thinking of no one in that way but your future wife, then your marriage is pretty much doomed. Save yourself and your fiance a lot of grief and call it off now! You are definately not ready for that kind of commitment

NINA

At first I thought you were a decent human being and then I read the second to last sentence and only one thing comes to mind: PIG. I hope your fiance/wife sees through you.

omg! that is funny! but bad of you at the same time!

That's some funny shi . . . I can imagine the sigh of relief when you got in your car to go home. Man that would have been a scene if you went striaght upstairs . . .

hahaha thats great. what weird parents. :::note to self::: keep condoms in car, not purse lol.

~SprklingDiamond

Laughing my a— off you sick puppy lol hey you should be real proud you made straight a's but got no a—

LMFAO!!!!!!!!!!!!! lucky escape!! u mite not be so lucky next time =P

Wow—nice way to trick the reader, there. In all, that would have been a crappy thing to do. I know this is all such an extreme understatement, but I'll leave it up to everyone else to kick your ass for it, because I know that's what they'll do. Ah . . . how DC has opened my eyes . . .
diasphora

I have no idea what to say about this except that you are all sick.

I liked you, liked you a lot, until the condom part, you're a rotten person. Do not marry her, she deserves better than you!

Art Teacher

OK, last night while I was preparing for dinner, my husband surprised me with a gift. I was totally surprised when I opened it to find two tickets to Bermuda.

The problem is he booked it for the same weekend as my son's school carnival. I am in charge of Baked goods, so I told him to try and reschedule. He was not happy about my request, and threatened to go without me.

My confession is that I hope he does, because I am planning on seducing my son's art teacher at the carnival.

:O Thats so horrible! That art teacher better be hott! :O
Yaquel

---

thats harsh, forget the art teacher, you married your husband so you should stick with him, dont do it.
~J.J.~

COMING CLEAN

Go girl!

Wow.. you're husband gets tickets to go to Bermuda and you'd rather hang around and go to a carnival? It would be nice and good if it was because, oh, you were going to dod it because you love your son. But noooo . . . you're doing because you suck. Man, he doesn't deserve you, he deserves better. So does your son. I feel sorry for them.

---

shame on you!!!! hey maybe hubby will get a little when hes in bermuda . . . . meanwhile your sons art teacher will turn you down . . . . then youll be stuck all ALONE!!!!!!! HAHAHHAHAHA

Whoah, rewind. You're husband has bought tickets to Bermuda for you and you're hoping to seduce another man. Well' I hope he does go on his own also and fall in love with someone who deserves his generosity which you obviously don't.
Phatboy.

Ah, the ideal American marriage. Good luck to you.
`Gramps`

Let me get this straight . . . Your husband loves you enough to get you tickets to Bermuda and you chose a bake sale over your husband. I can see why you are/or wanting to cheat on him. You are despicable. I sincerely hope he dumps you and you die miserable and lonely. You are a selfish person, underservinf of the love of another person. Your Joss will catch you. It always does and you can't avoid it.

What? Are you retarded? Your husband does something so sweet & you can't go so you can seduce someone. You need to wake up & realize before it's too late & someone who can appericate him steals him away.

---

that confession started out awesome & ended really horribly. woman you are an ever-lovin' fool! if my hubby came home with surprise tix to Bermuda i would drop everything!that is a romantic & thoughtful gift and all you can think about is how you want to schlep your son's teacher. gawd, your husband certainly does not deserve a woman like you. tell him i'll go to bermuda with him! you are a freak

~Gambitgirl~

I don't understand how people can actually plan to do something so horrible to someone they are supposed to love! Do your husband a favor and divorce him. It would be much nicer than staying married and pretending to be happy . . . all the while planning on sleeping with other men. You are terrible . . . and need to grow up!

I can't believe that your husband would be upset at you for being there for your son. I don't know about the art teacher thing though . . .

Three Of A Kind

We are Three of a kind. A wife, husband and a girlfriend. We all live together and raise two children so someone is always here for them, and we share the husband. We are all professional well paid adults. The children love the girlfriend totally.

The husband is fantastic looking and we are both tall, thin and very sexy and good looking. Life is too short and love not need be confined to just one person.

This is not something we hide either. The families know and expect all of us as one family now. We two women have a lot of fun as we are now great friends. We share our hopes and dreams together with my husband.

Well if it works for you then its cool though I am interested in some of the talkback you are going to get as a result of this post especially from the moralistic people.

~DarkGirl~

Who sleeps with him?

---

thats really cool, few people have that kind of lifestyle, i could almost pity and envy you at the same time

---

The Boogie Man, he still watches, though speaks little=)

I dunno, I do believe people should be able to live as they want. (Homosexuals, interracial relationships, etc.) But this just seems wrong. I don't know what else to say.

---

thats not gonna last long . . . .

I can't stand it.

Good for you! I wish more of the world were as comfortable with flexability and as free as you all are. Who's house do you go to for thanksgiving, though?
~Lolita

That's really cool. And I'm female . . just so everyone knows.

If what you wrote is true . . . . I'm jealous, really. I wish I could muster the self-esteem to share my BF with someone else since he likes new experiences so much. You guys rock . . . =)

That doesn't sound like a very healthy environment for kids to grow up in, but, whatever, you'll have to deal with their screwed up asses when they get older, not me.

You'll probably hear a lotta crap about morality, ethics, the poor children, yada yada yada. I say to each their own. Love is love, especially in this unloving, uncaring world we live in.It's better to love and live within healthy relationships no matter how you define the relationship between adults. America. Land of the FREE!

i found all of your confession interesting until you go to the point about bragging about your wonderful physical attractiveness . . . that just soundslike only hot people can have open relationships, which sounds bitchy. whatever works for you guys . . . although i'm not sure how mentally healthy that is for your kids, they're probably a litte confused as to why their family is soo different from other children's

~Gambitgirl~

Emptied The Dugout

I'm a bit older now, but not too old to have forgotten.

I was 22. It was with one of the pennant winners (not saying which). The day before the first game of the 1972 World Series, I bedded every starting player of that team, and two of the coaches.

I loved that team.

Well heck, You've got to support your team. Right

Don't listen to those talkbackers who will berate you and call you a "slut". What they should be doing, is insulting the society that made you feel as a young woman that all you had to offer was what was between your legs!

Please, move on now. It was a different time and you are not a lesser person just because you have done some crazy things.

Oakland Athletics over Cincinnati Reds. I was just wording if you helped the "A's win or contributed to the Reds losing . . . Went a full 7 games . . . The 70's Free Love! Those were the days!

Grand Slam! Truth be told - this is my fantasy. Not as easy to do now (STDs, camersa, the media, etc) but still . . .

. . . And they loved you. For twenty minutes. Then they had a good laugh at your expense.

if it was the reds, you MUST let us know how pete rose was!

Wasn't there a movie like that? Didn't you get sore? Where did you dump the excess?
`Gramps`

Hmm . . . obviously, it was either Oakland or Cincinnatti. And that was the beginning of an era for The Big Red Machine. Now, were you into Rollie Fingers, Bert Campaneris and Vida Blue OR Dave Concepción, Pete Rose (maybe) and Johnny Bench? My guess is that you're an avid baseball fan like myself.
áéíóú

Sounds like Susan Sarandon from BULL DURHAM . . . but she picked out only ONE guy per season, and "[she doesn't] date a guy hitting under .250 . . . unless he's a good glove man up the middle or has a lot of RBIs . . ."
The Smoking Hypocrite

Sure brings new meaning to "getting loose in the bullpen", doesn't it?

I'm just curious . . . was it one by one or all together? Did they line up for their turn? The practicalities of it intrigue me.
SugarSpun

ewwwww cooties!
~Gambitgirl~

No, He's Not

My husband was not too keen on the single guy who moved in next door to us last August . . . until he realized that he talks with a lisp, walks with a hand on his hip and wears eye liner.

Now hubby doesn't mind that I go everywhere with my "fag friend" as he calls him. We go shopping, to the movies, even the occasional "girl's night out".

I confess, I know for a fact Tim isn't gay. He may well be bi, but he is most definitely not gay.

Just use protection, since you seem intent on ruining your marriage.

LOL, oh sorry, bad girl, eh what do I care? I just love this, brilliant, magnifico.

Well now, aren't you and Tim the sneaky ones.
MollyMayhem

It's alright as long as you are just being friends with him and not cheating on your husband with him.
~Sarah~

Lisp+eyeliner+likes shopping=gay! Your friend is either gay or in the closet.

Oh lovely. Two things here: Clearly, your husband is a raging homophobe and I don't know why you would want to be spending time with someone who is so anti-gay anyways. Secondly, if by "for a fact" this means that you have been intimate with your friend, then you are not a very nice person. Please do each other a favor and get a divorce . . . now!!!

I wear eyeliner - male - 23 - definitely not gay. You alude to doing the neighbor. That is wrong, wrong, wrong.

So are you saying your husband trusts you with this neighbor and you re-pay him by cheating? Woopee! You found out he's not gay, now what?

So why are you hanging out with a heterosexual man who is not your husband then?

Thats so nice that you found out hes not gay bu tis it worth you marriage?

---

just because you wouldn't hang out with a homophobe doesn't mean that everyone else shouldn't either. Her husband may be a loving husband, regardless of his personal views.

---

no doubt hun. i had a male friend who wore MAKEUP and he most certianly was not gay. in fact, he got more action that most other guys i knew
~Gambitgirl~

You Are? Me Too!

I have been married for five years, I am 27.

My neighbor moved in about three years ago and we have been having an affair. Mostly just for sex but still I feel horrible.

I told my wife and she told me that she was having an affair with the neighbor's husband!

Oh, this marriage was a mistake.

---

wow . . . this is really sad

diamond_in_the_rough

Sooooo . . . maybe the four of you should get together and go bowling, one night . . . ?

Tornado

Do the neighbors know about each other's affairs also? Dang, real life IS stranger than fiction . . .

DontKnow_DontCare

Hey, maybe not . . . just call yourselves swingers and it's all worked out. lol

Brainie

---

wow, now that its all in the open you guys should double date and stuff. this could be turned into something positive.

Dinkus

Ha! Ha! What goes around comes around! Nice to know you moved into the right neighborhood. Everyone else is cheap and easy too!

DC_Junkie

That sounds like an easy one to fix. Just switch!
BostonGirly

Classic irony. Now you either have to work it out or start sharing. Either have their points.
~Blondie~

i'm sorry, but this confession just made me laugh . . .
god_chic

I don't see how it was a mistake, you two were made for each other. Maybe all four of you can get together now and cut through ALL of the BS.
Unluckyatlove

Are you bragging or complaining? I agree that this is kind of hilarious, but it's also very sad. Sounds like none of you have any emotion involved. It's just sex. Including the marriage. Get counseling or get out.
`Gramps`

We Seem To Be Naked

I confess that a few months ago I went out with my best friend and his wife, and another couple. We had a few too many drinks and all went back to his house.

He was tired and went to bed, but the rest of us stayed up and played strip-drinking games. We ALL ended up naked on the floor.

When I went out on his deck to smoke a cigarette (still naked), my best friends wife was out there (naked and drunk as well). We were both talking and we suddenly embraced and started kissing each other.

After a few moments, we realized what we were doing and stopped.

They have since divorced (for other reasons). I have never told my fiancée, and she never told her husband. We are still best of friends and see my friend weekly.

I never told him either.

---

sigh and people think I'm strange when I tell them that I don't drink
CoolChickie

Sounds like a wild party!! If you feel nothing for her now, then I suggest forgetting it ever happened. Nothing really happened, and telling anyone would just cause upset feelings, and it seems there is nothing to be gained or solved, if you did tell.

red24

---

being drunk is no excuse for cheating, but at least you stopped. and you're right, NEVER tell your fiancee.
Dinkus

She doesn't need to know. It was just a kiss and it hasn't happened again.
Jello_Biafra

Three cheers for willpower! At least some confessors have some sort of Moral Values

Mossphenom

She sounds like poor wife material to me.

SirFartsAlot

Well, it should remain a secret. You kissed- so what. Everyone experiments sometimes, and if you don't have any feelings towards her that is more than friendship (or to any other females) there is no point ruining your relationship with your fiance. Good luck.

sarah_Filan

Man, oh, man . . . keep the lid on that one. Confessing only burdens the Betrayed although it might make the Betrayal's conscious feel better. Nothing good would come of going there.

Whatever

If I was naked with another naked woman and we began to kiss . . . . . well that is all she wrote!! Isn't he concerned about everyone being naked!

Lemon

Traffic Cop

I had sex with a policeman to get out of a speeding ticket.

The worst part is that during the act, I found out that he knows my husband.

I can't believe how some people degrade themselves. You should have said you'd have sex to get out of the ticket and when the officer said yes, used that against him rather than committing to the act. Or you can stop speeding.

Dontpointthatfigeratme

Your marriage must be worthless anyways, no self-respecting woman would prositute themselves over a speeding ticket.

Shera

Personally i would have taken the £60 fine and the 3 points on my licence and walked away. I'm sure your hubby would have preferred that you did the same.

lylya

You better hope he don't tell your husband. I can't believe that you had sex to get out of a ticket and then you are cheating on your husband. You are doing much wrong. When your world comes crashing down don't cry.

Daniel

During the act you found out he knows your husband?? LOL . . you were carrying on a conversation while having sex? Listen, don't degrade yourself just to get out of a ticket. The ticket couldn't have been so bad, that you felt the only way to get out of it is to have sex with the officer. Just think about how many of his cop buddies he's told and how many more times you have to look forward to getting pulled over.

MagicallyDelicious

Sucks to be you . . . . but hey at least you didn't have the ticket . . . *Nita*

DarkAngel

I'm not going to comment on your morals. But you can bet that the cop doesn't dare say a word to anybody. He'd be out on his ear in nothing flat if anyone ever found out . . .

`Gramps`

Typical cop - take advantage of the uniform to do or get whatever you want.

Eyespy

Welcome to prostitution . . .

Zarcynic

That is so tacky. And what do you mean, 'during' the act? You were talking about your husband while having sex with a police officer? And to think, sometimes I question whether we evolved from monkeys.

Cocobean

The Cable Repair Man!

My Husband ordered cable TV for our new home and the man came today to install it.

He was a very sexy black man. I've never cheated on my husband till today, and now I wonder if hubby will know why were getting the premium channels for free.

Well you know what the say about Preaches' Wives and Children how wild they can be I guess it's true because I sure was today.

Please Forgive Me. It just happened.

VERY cliche . . .

~Kerri

Getting something in return for sexual favors is . . . . uh . . . . PROSTITUTION! You're admitting you're a pastor's wife or kid, too? Yikes, Honey. Get down on your knees before God and beg for forgiveness. And you should confess to your husband, too. Secrets kept from one another lead to more secrets . . . more sex? Affairs? It all starts in the mind. You need to be accountable to your husband and to God for your actions. It's one way to ENSURE that it won't happen again.

LMAO . . . where do you live? All the cable guys here could pass for plumbers . . . fat, hairy, homely, butt crack that ate Cleveland . . . .

---

omg I didn't think things like that actually happened in real life . . . congratulations you're living in a port flick.

god_chic

---

what does his being black have to do with anything? oh and things like that dont just happen, toots.

tb

I'm not sure which is more insulting, the fact that women are obsessed with cheating, or the cheesy excuses they come up with for cheating. "Oops! I just accidentally banged the TV repair man!"

Hahahahaha . . . well, you got something out of it. Bad but good. =P

GRRR!!! You make me sick, YOU have a husband then you cheated on him witht he Cable guy, haven't you ever heard that saying 'you can look but don't touch', and they say men cheat more than women, HAH WRONG!

~Peach~

How very nice! While your husband is out working his butt off to support you, you're screwing the first stranger that knocks on your door. What a wonderful wife!

If this is true . . . NOTHING "JUST HAPPENS!" I hate it when people say that. You have a brain and a husband. Put two and two together you you should have realized that you shouldn't have done that!

:::VICE:::

You probably aren't just getting free premium channels, but maybe some STD's for your faithful husband!

Never, Ever!

About the adultery section...

I'm 22, Female and I just finished reading every single confession in this section.

I confess that I am absolutely certain that I will never, ever get married.

Many people will talkback and assure you that there are "nice guys" out there. Either these people are lying for the sheer thrill of misleading you, or they are in denial and live very sheltered lives. I don't blame you at all for feeling this way.

Forgive my negative attitude, but as far as I can tell, there are only two good guys in the world—my Dad and my boyfriend. Both are taken. Sorry.

I'm twenty years old, female as well, I hear you! DailyConfession.com has really opened up my eyes, not that I wasn't doubtful of marriage or men before . . . but reading the adultery section sealed it. The minute they get bored and something better comes along they act like rutting pigs. Actually it is not just men, it is both sexes, nobody has any amount of self restraint anymore. Thank you DailyConfession.com!

[Webmaster's Note:

Hold the bus! DC has been around almost three years. We have a little over a million confessions, both live on the site and archived. Of those, about 187,000 are confessions of adultery.

Now, these are the people that did something wrong and confessed it here on DC, the documented largest online confessional. Many more have committed the sin of adultery and have not confessed.

I'm no statistician or math whiz, but near as I can figure, using an abacus and all ten of my fingers and all twelve of my toes, this represents about 0.00000002% of the world's total population. There are a lot more people out there that we haven't heard from.

So, yeah, a lot of folks are playing outside of their sandbox, but this is a very small sampling of all of the sandboxes in the world!

We might get a different prospective if we had hundreds of thousands of confessions from the peeps that remain ever-faithful to their spouse. But then, where is the fun in reading about someone who has been married 18 years and never cheated . . .]

I'm a guy, married 27 years, never, ever cheated on my wife. The only porn I view, I view with my wife. I love her more than anything, and would never do anything to hurt her.

Good, then we will not hear about how you cheated because of your getting married for the wrong reasons

Don't let a few people with no morality put you off marriage. When you meet the right guy you will know he's the one. None of us can ever be certain in life about anything. If we avoided everything that was likely to go wrong or hurt us, life would be very very dull! Please enjoy life, and don't let the fear of being hurt hold you back.

~iylya~

Can't blame you there . . . .

Oh, don't give up just yet, I'm sure the right guy will come along, oh, wait you mean . . . oh okay, well don't let them give you the wrong idea, these are just

---

When you find the one I am sure you will change your mind.

~50centmami~

Don't worry, not all men are cheaters like a lot of the guys on this site. :-) There is still hope! *ZeLdA*

---

hence why i NEVER read that section. if i my future spouse ever cheated on me i probably wind up having to make a confession in the "thou shalt not kill" section

~Gambitgirl~

CHAPTER VI.

Revenge, Bitter and Sweet

F ace it: No one likes to be crossed. So when someone slides into the parking space we saw as ours, we don't get mad—we get even.

Revenge comes in all shapes, sizes, and levels of humiliation. We may let it be known that we are exacting revenge, or we may let our victim think he or she has simply had some "bad luck," unaware that payback has occurred and revenge has been sweet.

Some people actually turn the normally simple act of revenge into an art form, involving elaborate plots that may require a support team and cast of several to pull off over a period of days or even weeks.

More often than not, revenge is warranted, although sometimes a poor sport may seek revenge because he or she is miffed with someone who bested him or her. But whatever the reason, revenge is used to get satisfaction and to get even, and as the saying goes, "revenge is a dish best served cold."

So when a coworker mentions to the boss that you were late (again), or when the umpire makes a bad call at your son's Little League game, or when you walk into a room to find your lover in the arms of another—you may find yourself wanting to seek revenge.

If you are one to subscribe to the ideal of "an eye for an eye," you may want to take a few notes, because here you will find some truly classic designs for extremely effective acts of Revenge, Bitter and Sweet.

Life's Little Hazards...

This was a first.

My boyfriend and I have lived together for six years. He wasn't feeling well yesterday and stayed home from work. I love him, and really like his '01 Pontiac TransAm with Ram Air. It sounds so choice with the engine just idling.

Since he was staying home, I took his car to work. I decided to surprise him with lunch. He decided to surprise me with another girl in bed with him.

Amazing recovery, I thought, as I stormed out of the house.

I got back into his car, drove to the country golf course. A really nice place actually. I hopped the curb at the seventh hole and parked the car in the middle of the water hazard, water half way up the door. I caused quite a scene, with about a dozen golfers running up a assist me. I got a ride with one of them.

What I did was a little childish, but truly felt wonderful! He hasn't pressed charges yet, and I haven't kicked him in the balls – yet.

LOL! That is so funny. You rule!

~SnakeEyes~

---

ouch. I hope you kick him nice and hard. I would love to have seen your scene though. Would have been very funny indeed

---

Nice job. I don't blame you for it, I would have done the same . . . . only with the other girl in the trunk.

~Smoke.

Ouch!! Thats cold!!

But very very funny :) congrats. cheaters deserve what they get, and you done him good! and if he DOES press charges?

yeah. kick him in the balls.

Lady Corbi

Better to trash his car than to commit violence on him or the other woman.

And kind of a fitting action, since the car was an expression of his male ego, you were expressing your contempt for him and his actions.

---

you should've smashed his damn car!!

---

sweet! i love your work girl!

You go girl! That loser deserves what you gave him. What was immiture was him not being man enough to end the relationship before he cheated on you. P.S. Kick him in the balls too! he, he

---

It's obvious that you were emotionally overwrought, and lost control of the car on that curve/straight away before you got to the water hazard. I'm glad you made it out alive. In the meantime, get some steel toed boots.

`Gramps`

---

oh my goodness girl . . . if i would have been you, i would have done a lot more than that to him. he wouldnt need a car when i got finished with him

---

Haha Kick him to the curb but kick him in the balls first . . . . . then hand him his car keys and imagin the face on him when he sees his pretty car not looking as pretty as it did before!

HAHAHA! LOL! Now kick him in the balls!

Good job! Although I don't normally approve of revenge, he certainly deserved what was coming to him. I hope you dumped his lunch on his head, too. :-)

Car "Accident"

The other day, my boyfriend and I were on a long car trip. I had had a lot of coffee at breakfast and had to pee really badly.

We passed three service stations and at each one, I asked him to stop for me. He wouldn't, since HE didn't have to go, he didn't want to "waste time" stopping. He always does this.

Finally I got so mad at him that I just uncrossed my legs and let myself pee my pants. I had to go really bad, so I soaked myself and the seat. When my boyfriend saw the dark wet patch on his beloved new car's front seat, he was sorry for not stopping for me.

I pretended that it was an accident, but, I confess that I did it on purpose and enjoyed it because I was so mad at him.

Good for you!!! Next time he WILL stop. But why do you want a boyfriend like that anyway? It seems like he only thinks of himself.

I have to say he kind of deserved that. Its unhealthy to hold your pee for a long time anyway and he shouldn't have been so stubborn.

~The Fallen~

That is so funny! I totally wouldn't blame you for having to pee on your boyfriend's car seat. It serves him right!

---

ew. why sacrifice your self-respect to prove a point? sounds like you only embarrassed yourself . . .

-me-

---

what else were u supposed to do? i mean he's a selfish bastard and u need to dump him, not just for this but for his lack of consideration and his controlling behavior. u could get sick if u hold urself too long neways. what was this jerk thinking?

tb

Hon, next time you get mad, let him know you're *pissed off*. There's no pride in being passive aggressive.

~ADA~

What you did was discusting, unsanitary, and YOU'RE the one having to ride the rest of the way on the soiled seat . . . I think your worse off then he is –

KimberlyGirl

LOL you were pissed off alright. I did that once, but it was in school the kindergarten teacher wouldn't let go to the washroom . . . because it was 15 minutes to the bell. But I really had to go and couldn't wait any longer so I pee'd, right in the middle of story time on the carpet. lmao He turned red and appologized, should have let me pee in the bathroom damn it!

I love sensitive guys like this. I hope you're young and playing the field a bit and are not in an exclusive relationship with this jerk, hoping that one day you'll get married and start a family. He is a selfish moron and he's not gonna change. Me judgemental? Never! ha ha ha ha

Good for you!!! He TOTALLY deserved it for not stopping. The only bad part is, you had to sit there is wet pants!!!

Second Bloody Nose This Week!

My wife constantly kicks and hits in her sleep all night long. Usually she connects with a pillow or the night air. But on occasion, she nails me.

I confess that in these rare instances that she whacks me in the face, I gently, ever so carefully place my feet into her side (or back, or whatever is facing me at that moment) And slowing push her completely off the bed.

Half the time she continues to sleep right there on the floor.

I confess, I get even.

HA! your poor wife. At least put a blanket under her so she doesnt fall on the hard floor, and over her so she's not cold. Or, hey, you could do the Dick van Dyke/I love Lucy thing and sleep in two twin beds.

::grin::

---

that's so mean, why don't u just sleep on the couch!!or if not, just wake her up and let her know what she's doing. if u were in her place i don't think that u would enjoy waking up with a back pain on the floor!!

---

hahah thats good stuff. why dont u two try going to a sleep therapist. there may be some underlying cause for this action. lol and u could be a little nicer and gently place her on the floor or the couch, since ur already awake. unless u think she'd deck u for it when she woke up lol

tb

HA HA HA HAH A HA!!!! AAAAA HA HA HA HA!!!

GreenQueen

Maybe she has a sleeping disorder that you should check with your doctor about. Unless she is doing something life threatening don't wake her up, but watch for signs of sleepwalking ect. Also, shoving your wife off the bed for something she doesn't know shes doing. How rude!
Debbi

That's kind of mean! Your wife could be doing this because she is suffering from some type of trauma-related anxiety, and all you can do is kick her out of bed? Maybe you should try talking to her and see if something is wrong, and try to help her first!

I hope I never marry anyone like you. Why can't you just wake her up? Or go sleep somewhere else!

That is hilarious!!! I think I would probably do the same.
BJ

HAHAHAHAHAHA!!! OMG ok that is too funny. How mean! But darn, how great. As long as you don't hurt her it's ok, ya know? MAybe you should let her know of her actions at night, though.
~Sarah~

i don't blame you . . . even if she's not doing it intentionally i'd probably dump her on the floor too if she bloodied my nose or pummeled me in my sleep
~Gambitgirl~

Oh my goodness . . . I hope my husband doesn't lash back like that . . . I hope he realizes that I just have dreams where I have to fight off the evils of the world and save the world itself. I hope every jab, every kick, and every uppercut avoids the love of my life, but if it doesn't, I hope he can refrain from pushing me off the bed.

She's asleep, you're not. And you're trying to get even? Sounds like you're behind already.
`Gramps`

Look Familiar . . .

I just stamped "DECLINED" on the request for employment of the gentleman I just interviewed.

He is very qualified, has more than enough experience and has a great attitude (and is extremely handsome, too!). But in two weeks he will get a letter explaining that we will be unable to employ him at this time.

If he would have remembered my name, or the fact that we went out on a date just six years ago in high school, I might have given him a second interview.

But he didn't.

So I won't.

Foot Note: After he slept with me in high school, he never called again. Guess I am still taking it a little personally.

Revenge can be so sweet . . . . . .

Although it might not have been eithically businessly, youd did the right thing! When guys do stuff liek that they can really mess with your self esteem, and it's your right to do the same thing!

---

good for you! stick it to him!

Six years ago? You really must not have much to think about. Get over it and move on.

---

i don't think prejudice against players is illegal, go for it.

---

haha! in my book that's called sweet sweet revenge, enjoy it. and hey why not? i mean just consider it a bonus to your job . . .
~girly girl

That's not fair, and it certainly isn't professional. Don't let your personal matters interfere with business. You aren't in any position to be hiring people, especially with that poor attitude of yours. Don't take your bitterness and hostility out on him through the job. That should be dealt with at another time and place, and it shouldn't have any bearing on his chance at the job. You are abusing your power of hiring people. You don't deserve to be in that position. Do you have any idea how hard it is now to get a job? You robbed him of an honest opportunity just because you can't be mature and you're just downright petty. I hope I never meet you in life. Your actions disgust me. Try acting professional, get over the past, and grow up.

Me . . .

Gotta love karma! Way to go :)

How very professional of you! Did it occur to you that maybe as you were in an interview situation he didn't want to bring it up and risk looking unprofessional. Or be risk being seen as trying to unfairly influence his chance at a job. Hope for your sake he doesn't work out why he hasn't got the job or you might find yourself facing some sort of lawsuit - and quite frankly it would serve you right.

I bet you're the sort of person who keeps a list of all the people who ever upset you just so you can get back at them. You will notice that I have not signed this talk back so you cant add me to your pathetic list.

He probably did remember you and hoped that you didn't.

Frankly, I approve of what you did. Justified or not, your attitude would have been an anchor around his neck if he worked there. You did him a favor.
`Gramps`

---

unprofessional . . . but AWESOME. note to eveyrone: careful how you treat others b/c you never know when it will come back to bite you on the ass
~Gambitgirl~

The Unwanted Co-Worker

Dear "Bob",

We work for a small company, and as such our performance reflects in our paycheck, when the company does not do well neither do we.

That being said, Bob, we know you read this site all day long and spend most of your day "surfing" and that is when you manage to come to work.

You are late everyday and lazy when you arrive. Customers are not receiving the attention they need to maintain a relationship.

So I confess, we have been spiking your coffee with a laxative. This is the reason you have experienced the stomach cramps and the runs. This is why you have used all of your sick time and are now having to use your vacation time.

All eight of us take turns finding ways to irritate you, we meet at lunch and discuss our plans. We really hate the way you kiss up with the bosses to keep your job.

Quit kissing and go to work.

Or just quit.

You could just tell him you have a problem with him. Or discuss it with the bosses. You are adults. Grow up.

Ooow!! Very funny. Hope "Bob" sees this. Funny thing is, I am at work now and . . . . hey?

Ultimate Revenge . . .
~Malenkaya

OOOOOOHHHHHHH I hate Bob!!

Excellent! Don't get caught!

---

they are on to you "bob" you should know all offices have magical eyes and ears ! nothing goes unnoticed !!!!- suffer like your jocks !
::big grin::

That's so mean! I mean, I understand your annoyances and why you did it but I think you should have talked to "Bob" about it first, and then if he didn't change you could do allthat stuff to get back at him.
~Sarah~

I used to be an HR generalist, so here's what I have to say: I hope you realize that if Bob (or management) finds out, not only can you be fired, he can sue you and you all can be arrested. Just thought I'd pass that on.

---

um hello ppl!! havent you ever heard of directness. frickin a this is just pathetic behavior .. why dont you grow up and just talk to him like adults.. you are being very immature and you seem to be very afraid of confrontation.. get over yourselves and just talk to him. place yourself in his shoes.. and if you are worrying about offending hiom by a direct approach then bla you are dumb..you all need to get a life

---

What surprises me with this . . . is not so much that someONE would do something so stupid, mean and vindictive. I mean, there are hateful people all over the world, right? What is amazing . . . is that a GROUP of people would come together against a co-worker. You would think, out of this group of "adults" one would have the balls to tell all of you that you are jerks. I, personally, would tell Bob what you were doing. He has a right to know who is causing him physical harm.
"Blueper"

Getting Cold Out Tonight

My roomie kicked me out this past weekend to make room for her boyfriend of 3 weeks.

I am fine with that, except for the fact that she gave me two days notice. Not nice.

She waited until I was completely out of the place Friday evening to lock me out and take my key. She was leaving to go get her man and wouldn't be back until Sunday.

As she left she didn't notice that I turned the heat completely off. The temperature went down into the low teens Saturday night. Heard she had a few busted pipes . . .

Damn.

Hehe . . . She deserved it.
Debbi

People will be calling you immature and petty for doing this . . . but you are totally in the right. Anyone with half a brain would have taken sweet revenge (and nobody was hurt, so what is the big deal?) You go grrrl!

---

haha . . that's right, don't get mad . . get even!! ;)
§µgå® ßëRr¥

Oh well, sucks for her!!! That's why you never pick guys over friends.
~Sarah~

---

she deserves it. wtf is that crazy girl doing booting roomates for some dork she's only dated 3 weeks. i would've trashed all her crap before i left!
~Gambitgirl~

Any woman who will ditch you for a new guy who'll just use her then loose her is not worth your time anyway.

Oh, your poor friend (laughing hysterically to myself)

---

haa thats great . . i mean bad . . haa ah well . . i really wouldnt have thought of that myself or wouldve had the nerve to do that . . you know you really had the worst happen to you . . so whats a lil back in her face . . sevres her right . . even though revenge is nothing that we should do . . bc she prolly has bad karma from that and what goes around comes around so she porlly wouldve eventually gotten hers . . but ah . . you just sped that up a lil . . haa

---

Bra-vo! (applause)
áéíóú

On the angle of sweet revenge, I understand, but since she lives in an apartment, you probably just cost the owners of the property a couple grand in the money it is going to take to refurbish the apartment. Along with the insurance company she is undoubtedly going to have to contact to curb her losses. So I say hey, way to go. Feels good to be immature doesn't it?
~A~

As they say, 'Payback is hell!'
Saxman

---

this brings a whole new meaning to the saying "revenge is a dish best served cold"

Enough Is Enough

I left my drunk, philandering, ass of a boyfriend last night.

He came home very drunk. He had a hotel room key in his pocket (I undressed him to get him in bed). He never wears cologne but he reeked from some girl's perfume.

I confess that I almost wish I could be there tomorrow when he wakes up to find me gone – along with every shred of clothing he owned.

Yeah, I'm bad, so sue me.

You go girl! I would've done the exact same thing!
Jelly

i'd do the same in your position, the moron deserved

high five!

You go girl!

Way to go! Dont turn back honey, he'll keep doing it. Just move on, there are better men out there.

No honey, he is the bad one.

I do hope, after you've had time to let your anger settle, that you'll take the high road here and give back his clothes. To keep them means you still want him in your life, you want that connection, that relationship that you know is worthless. I'm like you, when its over, I'm gone, not a trace, except I leave to tell-tale signs or reasons for there to be more contact. Get on with your life.
MollyMayhem

Good for you, you should have taken his car keys too!!

I hope you also took towels, sheets, etc. and all the phones so he couldn't call. Ohh, also the keys to his car so he would have to walk, butt-naked somewhere to get some clothes. LOL

Justice Served

My senior year, my math teacher told me he, ". . . didn't like jocks, he didn't like smart-asses and he definitely didn't like me."

He made my senior year hell and I almost didn't graduate because of this ongoing issue between us. That was eleven years ago, and I have put it all behind me.

Until today.

I confess that I have never taken so much pleasure in writing a traffic citation as I did today. After he signed the ticket, I couldn't help myself - I took off my sunglasses and asked if he still didn't like jocks.

He recognized me.

LOL . . . too funny! Revenge is sweeeeeeeeet

::i::

Revenge is sweet. That is a beautiful story. I only hope that I can have such wonderful opportunities in the future.

Brilliant. Should've asked him to step out of the vehicle and clocked him.

I hate it when teachers play favorites. Most of the time the favorites and non favorites get marks they don't deserve. oh well. I guess it's that way for everything.

~Malenkaya

---

wait, did u give this man an un-earned ticket? if so that wasnt right. otherwise, talk about poetic justice. right on man! and u didnt even have to do anything illegal . . . lol

Ah, so there IS hope!
Ohseedee

Talk about Karma! I bet you loved every minute of it!

. . . .The best revenge is living well. Good job dude!

BEAUTIFUL!!!! Karma at it's best.
~Kerri

That is soooo cool! I would give my left nut to be able to do that to a couple of people I can think of.

Heh, heh, heh!! Nice on mate, wish I could have seen the look on his face!

Lung For A Lung

About 3 years ago, one of my close friends found out that I started smoking.

She was mad at me, so she took the new pack that I had, and went into her bathroom, and flushed them down the toilet, with me finding out about it later.

I confess that the next time I was over at her place, I found her stash of weed, and flushed that down the toilet. I told her that at least what I was smoking was legal.

She's never mentioned my habit again.

LOL . . . fair enough.

xx

That should teach her to throw away your things down the toilet, that should teacher her. I'm Glad u did it!

~Silver~

Ha ha! Smokers revenge!!! Look, I realize that she was just trying to help you, but talk about being a hypocrite! She had no business getting rid of something that you chose to pay your own money for. Good on you for getting your revenge.

---

well good for you for standing up for yourself . . but think about it . . neither of you should be smoking . . period . . no matter what it is . .

§µgå® ßëRr¥

Yeah, but what she's smoking is SAFER!

---

how hypercrytical was she! i would have done the same thing!

COMING CLEAN

Why people take up smoking is beyond me. It's gross, expensive, dirty and very unhealthy. Quit today. Good call flushing the weed, however.

haha, good for you.

Awesome! Hate those damn hypocrites..

oh man! u took her stash and flushed it down the toilet? thats so wrong. thats worse than any other confession here!

I have recnelty given up smoking, but would never condone flushing away a pack of cigarettes unless they were your own to do it with. I might have given up cigarettes but I still smoke weed (in pipes) and that part makes me cry!!!

yeh! frickin' hypocrites . . . i know weed has medicinal purposes but it also contains a lot of carcinogens also so that whole, "tobacco is bad for you & weed isn't" is bull
~Gambitgirl~

Legal or not, smoking is smoking. Loved the story.
`Gramps`

Urine, Engine Oil, Green Ink And Perfume . . .

My student neighbor stole my clearly labeled laundry detergent bottle three times from the laundry room.

I confess that the fourth time I replaced the detergent in a new bottle with a mixture of engine oil (for viscosity), green marker ink (to stain), one cup of my urine (for spite) and one bottle of cheap perfume (to make everything smell nice).

He stole the new bottle, used it and yelled loud enough for everyone to hear when he saw his clothes. He later told me that he lost $600 worth of clothes because they acquired green streaks.

I told my landlord about his stealing and my landlord is going to kick him out at the end of the lease without his $500 security deposit. Also I told everyone else in the apartment. So now 50 people know.

My neighbor wears the ruined clothes to wash his car, jog etc, etc. He has no idea that everyone else know why as he walks past in his green stained badge of thievery.

You go! That is a sure way to find a thief!

angleface

You Rock . . .

DarkGirl

That's a little harsh . . . I'm sure you could've told him to quit before going to that level. In fact, I think that's kind of childish . . . Ahhh well . . . it's your life obviously

~fragelistic~

Absolutely classic. You are a GOD in my book! I bow down before thee . . .
~Briguy~

HAHAHA! That's pretty harsh,but really funny.
[Tamsin]

Good Move.
~Smoke.

Great idea! He have such nerve . . . . I would be so ashamed to be caught nonetheless telling you his loss.

I think you have a firm grip on the term "Justice". Way to go!!!
TigersGuy

EXCELLENT!! I'm a student myself but I totally sympathize with you. If he can't afford detergent for god's sake, maybe he should move back with his parents. That's just low. I mean come on he has to have a job of some kind right? You did the right (and hilarious) thing! :)~
Qwerty

Thats hilarious! Kind of evil,but he deserved it anyways,i guess.
~yum plum bubble gum

I've always wanted to do something like that, but sadly no one attempted to steal from me once I knew better.
frown

This is great! You nailed him.

Not quite the ultimate revenge, but way up there.
`Gramps`

Wedded Bliss Miss

My boyfriend and I used to work together. He cheated on me. Worse - he cheated on me with a co-worker. Even worse he cheated on me with a co-worker who proceeded to paint me as the one trying to come between them and I felt pressured to leave my job.

I have moved to a new state, away from my friends and family.

Now he wants to marry me. I will marry him and after about half a year I intend to cheat on him every chance I get. He wants kids and I intend to get on birth control.

Why do you want to screw up your life to make him unhappy? It's not like he can't divorce you without you consent anywhere in the world pretty much. You are just immature. Find a new guy and then maybe you will be happy.

THAT is messed up.

---

he'll just leave you at some point, with or without the divorce.

Sorry to say this, but this is the silliest, and stupidest confession I've ever read on this site (no offense). What's the point of marrying him if you don't love him? Besides, two wrongs don't make a right. Go find yourself a real man who will take care of you and will respect you. Just my two cents.

---

you're Satan aren't you? Just say no and dont marry him, that will hurt him enough. Marrying him then being a bitch is not the plan, he may end up having you killed if you get too bad. And if he finds out about birth control, he might do something to make them not work then get u pregnant and you're screwed cuz if you abort a baby, and he doesnt want it, he can sue you because you did kill his child, and have yur marriage anulled. So think before you try to ruin his likfe like that, cuz yours will get ruined too

Why bother? Don't spend so much of your life trying to get back at him. Find someone else, and get a life. ^.~*

FabledAngel

---

why are you getting married to him if you hate him? For revenge? He's going to treat you like garbage. And if you DO get pregnant, you're stuffed. You're making a very stupid decision here. Grow up a bit and think about what you're doing. Move on.

You are so in denial. You still love and want him. I bet you're poking holes in his condoms right now so he knocks you up and you've an excuse to stay with him. You're a joke. I know it's harsh, but if you go through with it, it's true!

Please don't waste your life to get revenge on him. If you feel the need to, put some deep heat jell in his drawers, but don't sacrafice your life to make his miserable. Move on, find someone who loves you, that will be punishment enough for him.

Ay

Don't be so stupid you're just gonna ruin your own life. My friend was in a similar situation, and she still hasn't got over the guy in question. think about how stupid it is to marry someone just because you feel bitter towards them. My poor friend . . . !

WOW! You're really going to stick it to him! I'll bet that really makes you feel good! If you hadn't mentioned job, I would have guessed about 12 years old. But that could still be true mentally.

`Gramps`

---

omfg . . . that is a messed up plan! i you really want to hurt him then don't marry him & if he asks why tell him it's b/c he's an untrustworthy sack of crap . . . for the love of god DON'T MARRY FOR REVENGE! all you're going to do it make your life all about pain & bitterness & getting even . . . is that REALLY how you want to spend your life? is that really how you imagined yourself getting married? c'mon, think woman!

~Gambitgirl~

Umbrella Boy

My Ex and I had been together for 5 1/2 years, we had a house together and were happily engaged.

That is until we had this huge fight, he told me that he was moving out and went to walk out the door with an umbrella (it was raining).

I got so angry that I kicked his leg and he tripped down the stairs, the umbrella pierced his left testicle. He was screaming with pain so I called an ambulance.

Once the doctor had checked him out he told my (ex) boy that it would need to be removed. I still can't believe that he had to get his testicle cut off because of me.

Well needless to say we are no longer together.

I'm so sorry.

Clearly an accident. Just send him a card and a gift basket - bottle of champagne, cheeses, crackers, nuts . . . :)

I would imagine he can sue the socks off you now. Maybe an anger management course would be a good idea for you to take. That's absolutely horrible, what you did!

He got what he deserved. Well, actually I don't know, I'm a guy and just reading that confession brought tears to my eyes.

OMG that is great. I'm dying just to key my exs car I envy you. cake or death? right testical please. here ya go!!! YUM! that is the best.

LOL. If it were me , I wouldnt be sorry, and i bet you're really not either.
* J *

OH . . . MY . . . GOD! owwwwwwwwwwwwwwwwwwwwwwwwwww
~Gambitgirl~

If it were me I'd bankrupt you. Why is it that women cry foul if a man even thinks of laying a hand on them, but think the reverse is ok? Grow up.

OMFG if any body, WOMAN or MAN did that to me then I honestly dont think they would be living . . .
BlessedxName

Every man who just read your confession has his legs crossed right now. That said, what happened should not have been enough to cause a break up. It was an accident. A stupid accident. But it should not be enough to break up a commited couple. You two had other problems.
`Gramps`

please explain this to me, why are people praising this behavior? a guy wants to leave, so he deserves to lose a testicle? i think everyone's crazy. quit with the violence, i'm tired of it.

wow! castrated before marriage—not after.

CHAPTER VII.

Love, Unbidden

Sniff
sniff
sigh

I'll never forget "Mary," my eighth-grade English teacher. She was the first teacher I had who was female and under forty years old (as I recall she was maybe twenty-three), and she knew what we were talking about when we used words like "cool" or "groovy" and accepted the fact that the term "hey, man" was not gender specific.

She was my first crush.

I would help her during class, I would volunteer to help after class. I would do anything that would allow me to be close to her—because after all, I was in love. She was married. I could deal with that. As long as she would call me by my first name and smile at me, I was content. This lasted for all of nine months. Then came summer and Andrea. I was a lustful, fickle fourteen-year-old.

Love can be a powerful thing. Love, when the object of desire is unaware, can be a painful thing. And when the object of desire is not interested, love can be a dangerous thing—remember what happened when John Hinckley Jr. set out to win the heart of actress Jodie Foster.

Unrequited love is a part of growing up. Sometimes it lasts a few days. Other times, it can last years. And when we finally give up and try to move on, the pain and suffering can be so intense that we are sure we are going to die from a broken heart. And then along comes another Andrea . . .

Eventually you finally grow up and one day it happens: The person with whom you fall in love actually loves you back! You date, get married, have children and grow old together. But beware—you can suffer a relapse. After being married for eighteen years to the love of your life, you can be in the mall one sunny afternoon and run into an old high school flame whom you haven't seen since graduation day and, well, here comes that pain again.

For the most part, we manage to get through all of this with mostly fond memories, a few small bruises, and maybe a scar or two. And be assured that it happens to everyone. Rich or poor, good looking or plain, from royalty to the rank and file, at one time or another we are the victim of a Love, Unbidden.

My Hunky Housemate

I'm in love with my housemate. he's tall, 6'6". VERY muscular. (I bought him a pair of size 34 501s, but he couldn't get them over his thighs because they were too large!) He's gorgeous. Especially when I "accidentally" catch him sneaking into the kitchen/to the bathroom late at night in just his boxers! (ooh . . . his boxers. Also too "tight" for him in some areas:) heehee!) And his SMILE . . . Oh God.

Sadly, I think he must be gay. I never see him with any girls. He spends all his time working out, or reading (yes, he reads Dostoevsky and other people with unpronounceable names). He's so hunky and well-dressed and well-mannered (so BRITISH, his manners!) he must be gay.

He rarely goes out late. Finally, the ONLY posters he has are Dog ones! What hetero guy doesn't have swimsuit calendars!

What to do . . . .

First of all . . . oh dear god . . . Where do I start with this? . . . oh dear god . . . First of all . . . let me catch my breath. I'm afraid I'm about to pass out. Forgive me if I'm breaking out into hives. Okay. Reading those 'unpronounceable authors' does not mean you are attracted solely to members of the same sex. I don't know who told you that. It DOES mean that he might actually take an interest in something other than the superficial. He MAY NOT be completely witless. Will you be upset if this big walking body actually DOES have a brain? I do hope not. He might be upset that YOU don't, though. :)—I prefer to remain anonymous this time, thank you very much.

That is the most disgusting picture I have ever seen! When I saw the legs I thought I was going to throw up!

do him! But if he doesn't want to do you he's probably gay or has morals or something . . .

---

im a heterosexual and i have no swimsuit calendars. I got video game and metal band posters. So thats what guy doesnt have swimsuit calendar posters, a video game and heavy metal lover who doesnt need them cuz he loves his g/f and she's the only girl i need to see.

He has to be Gay, I'm sorry but if hes straight hes . . . , no he is Gay

---

He might not be gay, he may be waiting for ms right.

Phatboy

---

or he could be too obsessed with his physique to bother with woman. muscle-heads can be that way. or maybe steroids have made him impotent . . . it's possible

~Gambitgirl~

So come on to him and see if he responds. I don't know any muscleheads who are gay.

Safegirl

Drop a hint or something . . . . and that picture is freaky! Some muscles are OK but he crossed that line!

~SnakeEyes~

My husband also has impeccible manners and dresses very well, and he's heterosexul. He never dated alot of girls like other guys simply because he did not want to be a male whore. Maybe your guy also realizes that a guy who sleeps with dozens of girls is not a stud, he's just a male whore. Ask him. If you are really close, he should be comfortable telling you.

not all hetero guys plaster their walls in swimsuit calendars. That's a stupid stereotype. And maybe he just has other interests in his life right now rather than looking for a relationship. Geez. Don't make such assumptions. If he is, cool, if not, cool. whatever. just don't assume! Jeepers.

~Tonee

J Do! Do You?

I have been with my boyfriend for five years and we have lived together for the past two. I am 27 and he is 26. We are very much in love, and I'd love to marry him.

Recently I have thought about asking him to marry me.

But I confess I'm really scared. What if he says no? Although he does talk about the future WHEN we get married, and WHEN we have children...

I really want to ask him, but now I know how guys feel!

Respect to any guys who've asked, because I can tell you, I'm officially scared to death!

I say go for it! Everyone talks about women being more independant but only 1% of women ask men to marry them. If you are both in love then ask him what your heart is telling you.

~J

maybe he's feeling just as scared to ask you, that's why he hasn't yet. obviously he wants to marry you, otherwise he wouldn't be making all these plans and talking to you about the future, so let him ask you when he's ready.

dinkus

I'd wait for it . . . but that's just me. =)

From my own experience - You guys should probably go ahead and break up now.

It sounds like he wants to marry you also. Be patient . . . HE will eventually ask.

:::VICE:::

These talks about the future can't have been too in-depth if you haven't planned a timeframe for the actual event. Unless you're willing TO talk about it together, I wouldn't count on it happening anytime soon, even if you ask.

MollyMayhem

Under Sex Contract

As a 20 year old female. I find myself in the position of being the only one of my friends that is a virgin. And, I for one am sick of it.

Thus I have made a decision . . . if I find myself a virgin in six months I am going to ask one of my friends, Scott, if he will have sex with me. This will be easy because I know that he would be willing to, and I am attracted to him as well.

I would suggest this today, except he has a girlfriend. But, I have signed a contract with my best friend, thus I am required to uphold this . . . so regardless of ANY possible situation I confess here and now that I will no longer be a virgin as of August 4, 2003 at 7:00pm.

I can't wait to see his face when I toss a condom at him and say "lets go" . . . .

Its so much harder to stay a virgin then it is to have sex before your married. I think that is something to be proud of, not throw away for cheap meaningless sex.

are you sure you wanna waste your first time? Why are you so eager to begin a sexual relationship? What's so bad about waiting?

if you insist . . . you really don't have to waist this, right? I would just wait for the right one to come if I were you. Now ppl are prob. gonna portray you as a slut or something.
Britt

That is way sad. Those friends are not your friends. They are manipulative asses. Save it for someone you care about . . . it will be worth it.

What a fun way to lose your virginity . . . NOT! I was a virgin until I got married at age 27. Friends thought I was different because I was a virgin throughout high school, college, etc., but I was PROUD, not ashamed. Sheez.

So it makes you less of a person to be the only one of your friends who is a virgin? It makes you a better person in my eyes but that's just my opinion. Sex is something that you should share with someone you love, not just some guy you've picked just to "do it" with. Get some morals!

Sheesh, you've got it twisted somehow. I'm guessing your girlfriends give you a hard time and tell you how great it is. Well, it can be, but why force it!! Honestly find someone you love and then have sex. Why have sex for the sake of having sex. It's like eating for the sake of eating. Hopefully you can savor the experience a little.

WOW!!! You have some great friends. I am 24 and lost my virginity years ago, however, my friends would respect whether or not I was a virgin now . . . .not make bets on it. Hopefully, either you will smarten up by August, or regret that day for the rest of your life.

Hey, that's my birthday! But anyway, exactly why are you doing this? If it's because you want to have sex, well, I guess that's one way of going about it, but if you're only doing it because you feel "inadequate" being a virgin, then maybe you should reevaluate your opinion on self-worth. Also, if your friend still has a girlfriend by your contracted date, it seems a little selfish to demand he cheat on her just so you can have sex. Go find a drunken frat boy instead, if sex is all you're after.

clonedkitty

LOL, that's great! I mean, I understand how you feel. I am not a virgin at almost 17, but I think that as long as you are sure you won't regret it in the long run, there is nothing wrong w/ it. But that's just me talking . . . Don't forget that I'm not even 17 untill April . . .

~Sarah~

Bad idea — if you're friend is still attached in 6 months, you will either intrude on his relationship, or you may end up having sex with whoever is around at the time. This may put you at risk for STD's (condoms are not perfect) and may also cause you to have a less than enjoyable first experience, which may then follow you. Wait until you find the right person — you've waited this long, a little more time won't hurt.

Fire! Fire!

For over three years now I have a mild . . . ok huge obsession with firefighters.

Whenever I see them on the road, I will stare, wave, smile, do just about anything to get their attention.

I once drove past a grocery store, saw the truck in the parking lot, did a U-turn and went in the store to buy bread. I didn't need the bread, but I bought it anyway just to see them.

I have stopped by a station and had a tour. That was great! I even have a "guy friend" who is a fire fighter, and when I learned what he did, I was even more attracted to him then before I found out.

I have three - count 'em - three fire fighter calendars. Every time I hear the sirens I will stop working and run to the window to watch them drive by. They are the greatest!

I have so much respect for them, and gosh they so darn sexy . . . .

I love FireFighters too. My Father & Brother are FireFighters, and so is my Boyfriend :) I Love Em'

~Silver~

I'm a volunteer fire fighter, but I am a female . . . .

kittie

---

they are pretty hot stuff, arent they?

Gosh, you sound infatuated.

MollyMayhem

That's funny. Just remember . . some of them are tubby and a few are jerks . . theyre not all perfect.

come to london and support them on their strike for a decent wage.
BlueMonkey

A-MEN!!!!
sly

seeeeeehhhhhhckssssssiiiiie! mmmmmmm, boy!

Mmm ... Fruity

I'm a 19 year old closeted gay guy living in the dorms at college.

My confession is that my *hot* roommate just got out of the shower, and he used a different kind of shampoo than usual. The entire room is filled with this great odor, and it's really turning me on.

Too bad he's so homophobic, or I truly would say something . . .

Trust me, the smell of shampoo is the farthest thing from the mind of a heterosexual man. Do you really think he's too naive to know you're gay?

MollyMayhem

Thats a pity! (about that you cant have him!) but I'm glad I'm not the only one (I'm a straight girl)who loves the smell of shampoo on guys!!!

Why dont you just buy the same brand of shampoo and turn yourself on?! Oh and buy yourself some pride while you're at it. Just cos you're in the closet doesn't mean you should be living with a homophobic (if he really is one) - get a place to live with a more liberal roomy.

people who are homophobic are usually insecure about their sexuality . . . keep that in mind ;o)

yeh, don't say anything since you know he's a homophobe. y'know what kills me, the dorm i used to live in wouldn't allow people to have their bf's sleepover b/c they were trying to "guard out virtue" or some crap . . . but my lesbian RA has her gf over all the time & they had some noisy sex! so unfair

~Gambitgirl~

Aren't homophobics the ones that are actually scared of their sexuality? Maybe he's too afraid that if he accepts gay-ness he'll become gay . . .

Uh-oh! lol . . . .keep those comments to yourself! But most of all be happy for who you are, even if you are a "closeted" gay guy. (Besides isn't it nice to daydream, hehe).

You need a new roommate . . . that's just not right.

The Smoking Hypocrite

ew. that's gross. it's ok to be gay. it's not ok to use the fact that most ppl assume most other ppl are straight to be a peeping tom pervert.

Yeah, I lived in a jock dorm at Indiana University - and I loved every minute of the show! I wouldn't say anything to him - just enjoy what you get to see!!

gay men are so freaking hot. :(
lee(yeah, im a girl)

Obsession? Methinks Maybe

I have a professor at my senior college and I think she's great.

I'm not a lesbian, but I think I'm getting close to being a stalker. I watch out for her every day. I know where she lives and try to find out as much about her as possible. And I talk to her as much as possible without raising suspicion.

The thing is, I don't want to hurt or scare her or anything. When she's happy - I'm happy for her. It's just that I think my like for her is going a bit far - to the stage where I don't want to leave school even though this is my last year because I know I'll never see her again.

I don't know what the hell is going on in my head but I can't say I like it.

What if it doesn't stop . . .

It's fairly natural to want to spend time with someone you respect so much. Maybe if you told her this on purely professional terms and thanked her for the inspiration she's been to you, you may not feel the need to spend time with her in inappropriate ways. You could even become friends. Professors are really just people and not as intimidating as they can seem.

Seems to me like you are being attached to this teacher as an admirer. You think of her as an important person in your life, which in other case you might be considering her as a best friend, sister etc. But to me it does not mean that you are liking her. You watch over her, and know what she does only reveals that you want to know that she is safe.

OMG!!! I was that way like 2 years ago and last year w/ this girl that my (Then-boyfriend) liked. But then she went to another school and I don't see her anymore. I'm so glad I'm not the only person who has done something like that! I was jealouse of her and stuff, tho. She was kinda popular and that's why. Crazy cuz I'm friends w/ everyone, too, so it's not like she had that over me . . . I dunno. Well, just become friends w/ her is all I can say for you to do about it.

~Sarah~

That is really cool that you admire her so much, you don't want to leave school. But instead of obsessing over it if you think she is just such a great person try and follow some examples she has set for you.

~SheeptoHeaven

Distance is the painful cure.

I'm not sure but it sounds like your mother was missing from your life or something. Just a guess.

Dont worry about this. its probably not your first or last obsession. we are just humans. and it happens. sometimes when these people leave our lives, if they have treated us well, we remember them with peace and love. and if they have been less than fair to us we will say how stupid we were and what did we see in them. nevertheless, admiration is something to fill our heart. better full than empty. if this person can give u joy, then its worth the pain too . . including agonising whether this is normal or not. i have come to think it is normal - with me. i am a loving person and i am not harming anyone.

I feel ya. I had a teacher that I respect and admire very much and I was always interested when I learned something new about her. I'm not a lesbian either. I do know what you're going at, though. Don't have any answers for you, but you can always go back and visit her!

Raven

Oh my God! Me too . . . I've done that with various people through out my life. I'm glad I'm not alone.

Parental Surveillance

Every weekday I log on to grab a quick view of my 4-year-old at his day care center. They have a webcam interface via the Internet that you can switch from room to room until you find your child.

I confess that I have also been grabbing a quick view of one of the younger employees there. I have never seen her in person, my wife drops our son off and picks him up.

But I have fantasized about her from my desk . . .

I hope your kid doesn't go to the daycare I work at . . . . .

A bit creepy.

I work (single parent) and my 3 year old is in a day care with the same type of web cam viewing. It is supposed to give greater confidence to the parents to be able to see their child. You are nothing more than a hi-tech peeping tom.

Leave it to someone like you to pervert a good tool for parents.

Thats kinda scary . .

Uhhh, stop. You are married.
~Sarah~

Its kinda creepy that you are peeping on her, but I guess thats better than some low lifes on DC who acctually cheat on their wives with the babysitter.
~SheeptoHeaven

webcams at the daycare. what a brilliant idea. they should have them in all of them b/c of all the child abuse that goes on is some of the shoddy places
~Gambitgirl~

I suppose it's okay if you are just looking. Besides, your wife is probably tuning in to look at the hot dads that pick up and drop off their children.

Well, just keep looking and dont go out and find/hurt her . . . okay? ok! good job –
butthead

The Student Body

I'm sleeping with one of my students . . . Don't worry, he's eighteen.

I can't help it! He's just way too cute! He's athletic, and has a wonderful personality. And there is something about the sweetness and innocence of young men that makes them so much more attractive than exploitative older men. Older men are just large, hairy and overbearing.

I don't think he's doing it for his grades, though, considering I flunked him twice since we got together.

I'm only 23, come on . . . the age difference isn't that great. When I'm 70 he'll be 65, and no one will give a damn.

it's not the AGE you should be concerned about . . . it's the fact that you could be FIRED. either have him switch classes or end it, dear. your future is in jeopardy.

~barefoot & happy~

Well if you truly don't care, why are you so defensive? You could at least wait until he is out of school.

speaking of explotative . . .

That's just sick man. . .

No one would give a damn now if you were not his teacher. One of the two relationships has to stop.

i don't think it's the age so much as it is the fact that you're his teacher. as a former teacher myself i find you behavior disgusting & deceitful. i hope his paretns find out & get your ass fired . . . and by the way, older men RULE. only immature doofuses like BABIES

~Gambitgirl~

Ever wonder that when this relationship goes pear-shaped that he might tell your superior and you might lose your job?

There's definitely nothing wrong with this relationship, however keep in mind that you could lose your job if you are found out, not because people view your actions as immoral but because you are acting in a somewhat unprofessional way. Think of it like you'd think of a manager sleeping with one of his employees. But anyway, I'm not counselling you against doing this as it sounds like you have the right idea . . . just be careful as stuff like this gets around like plague in schools.

Where were you when I was in high school??

I agree the age difference isn't a problem. I'm 17 and my boyfriend is 22 and we have the most fun together! But the student-teacher relationship is.

If you want to risk ur job - go ahead. just so you know what you're letting yourself in for. I'm not giving out or anything like I'm sure many other people will . . . Sure whatever you feel is right is what you should do! Good luck!

Joey

But he's your STUDENT. It has nothing to do with age gap- your his TEACHER. TEACHER. he is sleeping with you so he can brag to his mates that he did a teacher!

---

watch out- highschool boys like to talk

It's amazing how someone with a college education, entrusted with the minds of our children, can be so stupid! What makes you think nobody knows? Fired for screwing a student will look great on your resume.
`Gramps`

I Don't Love Him . . .

I'm sleeping with a married man.

I've known him for about two years and he recently helped me through the breakup with my boyfriend. I don't have romantic feelings for him . . . he's just my best friend.

Whenever I need him, he's there for me. I don't even know how to explain our relationship. He didn't seduce me, take advantage of me or anything like that.

I don't want to have a relationship with him and he doesn't want one with me. I'm ok with that. He's my buddy.

My confession is I don't care about his wife. He's never lied to me about being married or anything.

Maybe someday, when it happens to me, I'll feel bad. But for now I don't.

Okay, so on an emotional level, you don't feel guilty. That's excusable since we can't always help how we feel. However, that doesn't give you any excuse to go on doing what you (at least intellectually) know can really, seriously hurt another person.

karma's gonna bite you in the butt someday. you know that, right?

No you don't care because you don't have an ounce of self respect and for that matter neither does he.

Great thing that you're ruining a marriage, and they probably have kids together.

Right now, you don't care. But one day you will, and you'll wish you'd never got involved. You sound like you're very selfish and immature, and so is your lover. Maybe you two deserve each other after all . . .

Wow, lucky you. You're f#%&k-buddies with someone else's husband. At some point you should understand that interferring with another woman's relationship, and feeling totally indifferent about it, is very self-destructive. What's more important to you, that you're getting laid, or that you're causing another woman pain?
MollyMayhem

So one day in the future, when you're married, it will be ok when your husband sleeps with another tramp like you?

Nothing is as emotionless as you make your setup seem. And there are other people involved. No good will come of this.
`Gramps`

So you know that someday, you'll get yours. That's good. So why not stop this affair right NOW? You don't want to get it so deep that you'll never come back up.

what happened to you to make your an emotional black hole? are you dead inside or something?

~Gambitgirl~

He's Persistent – And Kinda Cute

My 19 year old son brought home a "buddy" of his for this past Christmas vacation. I just received another e-mail from him asking to have a relationship (I am divorced).

I confess that between his physique and his mails, I am actually considering it.

Maybe you should make sure this is alright with your son first . . .
Nobleone

That would scar your son. Don't do it.
.:*Rachel*:.

You are an adult and you need to base your decision on a mature level. Talk to you son about it, see how he feel. If he doesnt like it, respect his wishes and go on your way. A fling isnt worth a relationship with your child.

Considering it to what end? Get up from your computer and start having a real life instead of this grasping at anything from your email box. Be the good mom, act your age, and allow your son to keep his dignity.
MollyMayhem

My mom did the exact same thing. My brother had a friend who she liked so she went for it. (She was 37 and he was 18) They've been together for 3 years and I think my brother still hates my mom. My advice is, if you think you two really have a future, go for it. If this is just a fling. NO. It will destroy your relationship with your son. It's not worth it.

dont do it. how would u feel if one of ur friends started dating ur son? i highly doubt that theres anything a 19 year old boy could do for a 36+ year old woman. whats w/all the MILF's, people?!?!?!
tb

One word — therapy.

Hey Chicky reality cheque!! He is your sons friend. YOUR SON. Do you not realize this also means he is your sons age? Do you really want to destroy your son like this?

Man I'm glad you're not MY mother.
Raven

This could work out great! Son pimps for mom!
`Gramps`

Hmmm sounds like your in MILF land. Your son won't be to happy if you go through with it. But his friend has serious cahones to be aggressively courting a "mature" woman.

If you want to destroy your relationship with your son, go ahead. If not, get a life! Find someone around your own age.

CHAPTER VIII.

Liar, Liar!

We all lie sometimes—every single one of us, either to ourselves or to someone else. It's human nature. But some people lie better than others. A few are such proficient liars they can beat the polygraph. Others, however, sweat, stutter, and fidget so badly that they may as well have the word "liar" stamped on their forehead.

The problem occurs when we start lying at a young age and get away with it. We learn that we can win friends, influence people, and get what we want by lying. Then it becomes habitual and compulsive. The answer is no longer perceived as a lie by the prevaricator; rather, it is simply the correct answer for the situation. This is when a person is classified as a pathological liar. Or a car salesman.

Then there is the person who wants to avoid conflict. Example: Wife asks husband if she is fat; husband knows wife has packed on a few pounds; husband knows wife knows that she has packed on a few pounds; husband knows that the truth means days or even weeks of involuntary separation, little or no conversation, and definitely no sex; husband does the only thing he can do; he lies. The husband is a teller of "white lies," lies that do no real harm and may even do some good.

Then there are the rest of us, who every once in a while say what needs to be said to do what needs to be done. We know it's wrong. We get caught from time to time. Usually we feel bad about lying, but when a buddy asks, "How are you doing?" We invariably answer, "Good, you?" For many of us, that answer is a lie.

On the other side of all this lying are the people who are being lied to. Most of them know they were lied to, but to avoid confrontation, they lie to themselves and just play along instead of shouting out Liar! Liar!

Honey, Do I . . .

Last night my wife of 11 years asked my if she looked fat. I told her no. Then she asked if I still loved her. I told her that I love her more today than ever before.

I confess that one of my answers was a lie. Being married can be treacherous.

(I do love her)

You did the right thing! (and I'm a women!)
knhw

I'm sure that is what she wanted to hear anyway ,so you did the right thing.

You win the million dollar prize. Next time when you say no to her "fat" question(keep saying it!), ask her how SHE feels about her body. If she tells you she feels fat, tell her that you want her to be happy. Support her in anything she wants to do to improve her feelings about herself and her health, too! :o) You're a sweet guy.

LOL . . . you get my vote for being the biggest sweetheart!
MollyMayhem

---

dont worry its just a little white lie . . . . no harm done
~*ounK*~

IF you love her tell her the truth. Then help her lose it

---

hahaha there was a guy on here who said "yes" when asked the first question. u can imagine what happened to him . . . whatever keeps the peace, i say. but if u think she should lose weight, or if she's feeling bad about herself, u should recommend that u two join an excercise program together, maybe a gym. ull both feel better and itll up ur health.

tb

It's best to get these things out in the open, If you don't do something about it, it could just get worse . . . Besides I tell complete strangers they're fat and my formerly fat friends couldn't be happier with my honesty.

That's okay. When we ask guys that question, we expect them to lie to make us feel better. If you told her the truth, she would've hit you upside the head and had you sleep on the couch. So don't sweat it.

Ahh, the things you do for love . . .

You're a good man.

Believe me, you said the right thing.

Raven

Maybe you didn't want to hurt her feelings, but you could have let her know the truth very politely, there's always a way you know. But you know your wife better, so if you think it was right then just smile :o).

Heh, as long as you love her then thats what matters, Good luck to you both and have a fantastic life together

Kieyza

Okay, folks! She wouldn't ask if she looked fat if she didn't think she was fat! And why would she expect her husband to say yes? And why would she accept a no? Game playing is stupid. And if Mrs. `Gramps` asked that question, she would expect and get an accurate answer. I can say that because at 5'7" and 130 lbs, she is all curves and muscle.

`Gramps`

Loves Them Just The Same

My girlfriend and I went to pick out some nice diamond earrings for this past Valentines Day, which really lightened my wallet.

I confess that the next day I went back and returned them, and bought cubic zirconias that looked exactly the same, saving myself $800 bucks.

What's wrong with this?

She's happy and she's telling all her friends. I'm happy because I saved all that money.

Win, win, right?

Can't you just admit to your girlfriend that you're a cheapskate?

Win win . . . but it's not what she wants.

LOL that is pretty funny . . . really, I don't know why chicks trip over diamonds (I'm a chick . . . and i don't get it. I don't want a guy going into the poorhouse for something shiny). Well it's wrong to lie but materialism isn't great either. I'll just leave you with this; you better hope like HELL she never finds out!

xx

haha . . . yea thats cool. better just hope she doesn't find out!
~bluefire

I think that you should have just bought her a cheaper pair of earrings. You could have still gotten diamonds, just a smaller pair you know. To me that seems really cheap of you to go and return the earrings that she loved so much. In the long run this will come back to you. She is lying to all of her friends . . . . one day she will find out and its gonna be buh bye to you!

~Maegan~

Why couldn't you just tell her that you really couldn't afford them and get her something less expensive? Lying to your girlfriend makes you a winner?

Why did you buy her an expensive gift in the first place if you are such a cheap skate? I hope you don't plan to do this with any other gifts, if you do please let this girl know. 800 dollars is a lot to spend on earings, but what you did was just dirty. Now she thinks she has diamond earings, something to wear on special occasions and to pass down to family. Not cheap chunks of glass. The first pair of earings were meaningful ("look how much my boyfriend loves me enough to blow this kind of cash for a special day"), the second pair just deceitful. If you don't want to give the girl expensive gifts that is fine! No one expects you to blow 800 on valentines. But to switch them was cruel.

The only problem with this is that you lied to your girlfriend and if she finds out they are only CZ's she will be unhappy I am sure. That said jewelery is over priced and over rated. For my engagement ring I insisted on a CZ. I really liked the setting, no one knows they are not real. Its such a waste of money on a little rock and a piece of metal.

Unless one of her friends is a jeweler].]

---

i hope she finds out.

Are you planning on getting laid or getting married? If this is short term, good for you! If you marry her, you'd better confess . . .

`Gramps`

. . . until she has them appraised for insurance. dude, if you couldn't afford them why'd you get them in the first place? if she loves you she wouldn't want you to go into the poor house b/c of her . . . and if you loved her you wouldn't be trying to trick her like that. you're lame

~Gambitgirl~

Wife Is Leaving Me

I have been trying to get a co-worker to sleep with me for four months.

Yesterday, I told her that my wife and I are getting separated and will most likely divorce. To verify this fact, I demonstrated that I was no longer wearing my wedding band.

Late night I finally hooked up with the object of my obsession.

I confess that I have never worn a wedding band, due to the fact that I have never been married. But it worked. She wouldn't give me the time of day until she thought I was married.

Yeah, I know. Very bad.

I never could understand the attraction of a married guy. Just don't get it.

No, not bad. Good for you, (and this is coming from a female), women like this deserve to be used. The only thing that made her sleep with you is thinking some other woman already found you good enough to marry. This girl deserves whatever she gets out of life with this sort of female vs. female attitude.

You both are trashy.

That is hilarious, I love you man! That is a kick in the pants to all those confessors who are cheating with someone. HAHAHAHAHA lol

She wouldn't sleep with you until she thought you were married? Wow, she sounds real classy . . . what a keeper, huh?

. . . serves the schemimg marriage-wrecker right!! And you can tell her that for me when she hauls you over the coals for lying to her to get her into the sack.

Skanga

This is the most pathetic thing I've ever heard! You're not married, but you think it's cool to sleep with a woman who thinks you're married but separated? No wonder the divorce rate in America is more than 60%. The sad thing is once this woman finds out you're not married, she will break up with you. I don't know which of you is more pathetic.

Woah. Totally kick ass. I have to do that. Thank you for your inspiration!

You caught the skank! You know what they say, birds of a feather . . .

that sounds like a long term relationship in the making.

Most people have a white ring under the wedding ring. Your sex object wasn't smart enough to notice that you didn't. Sounds like you've found yourself a winner!

`Gramps`

You two are the perfect couple. She's naive beyond belief and you think deception is an acceptable way to cultivate a relationship. Yea, this ought to work out reall well for you both.
MollyMayhem

glad i work in an office of mostly women. getting hit on the workplace is really annoying, especially by a LOSER
~Gambitgirl~

Wrapped Around My Finger

I am a woman. I draw nude women as a hobby. I have a subscription to Playboy Naturals, because I can't pay actual models. I don't even draw very well. Honestly, the drawing is only a cover.

My boyfriend doesn't know I'm a lesbian.

Why am I with him? Truthfully, he can provide for me. He has a good job, and makes a nice paycheck. We just moved into a house together - paid for by him.

Not only that, but I have him wrapped around my finger. He'll do anything I ask. I don't even love him.

And I'm never going to tell him any of this.

hehe whoops . . . lets just hope u don't get busted some day . . . just remember to never bring any chicks home. bad move. don't do it. all the best :D
~*Piper*~

Lets see, so in return for him buying you all kinds of stuff(like a house) you're willing to sleep with him. Doens't that sound like a prostitute?

i find your beahviour abhorent. if you want to be a kept woman, find a woman who is willing to pay for your pathetic little life. stop living a lie with this man - let him be free and find some girl who is going to love him! stop being selfish!

Evil, your just evil, like all women.

Could this relationship possibly be more disfunctional? I don't think they come anymore screwed up than this.

You, my friend, are scum. Have a bad day.

You aren't going to tell him that you are a lesbian just because he provides for you? So what are you going to do in the future, when you meet a woman whom you fall in love with. Your boyfriend isnt going to buy that she is your best friend until the end of time. Or, maybe he wont even notice. But I think you are denying yourself who you are for staying with him.

there are so many things that are wrong here its not even funny hope he gets somone better than you

=gringo=

I cant stand gold digging people like you. If you dont love him why not cut him a break and leave him. Youll be saving him alot of heartache and money in the longrun.

So you're confessing that you are a prostitute- you go girl!

Big Daug

Bob's Got Mail - A Lot Of It

Every time I need a bogus e-mail address to complete a form on the internet, I use "bob@aol.com".

I have been doing this for over five years now and have undoubtedly used this e-mail address more than a couple hundred times, it's just easy to remember in case the e-mail is the password.

Today, just for the hell of it, I looked up the screen name "bob" on AOL.

He exists. There is really a bob@aol.com.

Sorry.

BAHAHAHAHA . . . . that is the best thing i've heard all day i think.

Ha Ha Ha! That is hilarious! I never thought of that before, but it is a good idea. I just made an address on yahoo to do that kind of stuff.

Lol! There was this guy I used to hate. He was so mean to me for no reason. So one day, me and my friend decided to sign him up for as many porn accounts as possible. He wasn't the kind of guy who used them so it was a big nuissance. Hehe!

Don't worry about it. I'm sure 2/3 of internet users do that, I know I do (sorry blue at hotmail). I guess that's what they get for making such a generic email . . . right?

~Kittae~

---

hahahahahhahahaha!!!!!! thats hilarious! maybe we all should use that addy, then he'l be nuts with mail!

som

187

OMG! lol I bet hes really pissed at you! great thing this site is annonymous – Sunni

lol thats terrible, y dont you just create your own account somewhere so you wont be sending OTHER people junk mail?

~dream~

Right off hand I'd say that Bob repeatedly tells his friends "If I ever catch the son of a bitch who's doing that I'll pull his heart out!"

LOL! That is so funny! Sorry for the poor Bob though. Why not just set up some free email account that you use just for filling out forms etc.? That way poor Bob can stop wondering where all this spam is coming from.

Hobbit Queen

And I bet "bob" is wondering where in the Hell all this mail is coming from!

awwww poor bob!! :(

That is YOU who is doing that?!? You really tick me off.

bob@aol.com

I Faked It ?!

I joined the US Army as soon as I graduated High School ('98). The only reason was because I needed money for college. I enlisted to be in the Infantry. I was in boot camp and was finding out that it wasn't exactly my thing . . . and I wanted out!

Now, in boot camp there's about 10 out of 55 people trying to get out, trying anything and everything (claiming homosexuality, purposefully hurting themselves, assault) but I beat the system and I don't regret it.

I faked sleepwalking.

I would get up in the middle of the night and crawl under my bed, other peoples' beds, into the bathroom, I even went down some stairs and scraped my head on the ground so that it looked like I got banged up.

I had many meetings with my drill sergeant saying I wanted to stay but it just got too bad. I never changed anything about my performance so it seemed totally legit. I got an Entry Level Separation for "Failure to Adapt" 3 weeks before Boot Camp was done.

Now I'm in college fulfilling my dream, I'm HAPPY!

That . . . is AWESOME!!!!
elegantly_wasted

I faked manic-depression!!!! Don't you just love separations division?!

Well the government uses you and you beat the system good on ya.
~DarkGirl~

My boyfriend said that if he ever went back in and wanted out that he would feint insanity. I might have to share your idea with him, it sounds safer=)
*L*K*C*

Good stuff outta you! I like it . . .

That is an AWESOME story! Seriously! Hopefully no one military will read it, though, . . . cuz you're probably the only one who did it. =)

GOOD FOR YOU! You got out of a situation you realized wasn't the right

---

Are you my ex? He did that- oh no wait that was '94 . . . How lame . . the army has such an easy boot camp too. Go to the Marines and try that crap.

Too bad for you and all of the other men/women who want out of the military - because those section 3's, section 8's, etc . . . stay on your records for LIFE! Oh yeah - thanks for helping the U.S. Army when we need it the most in this time of crisis.

---

thats pretty good, i've got to say. your mother would be proud.
Confucious

You gotta do what you gotta do! I applaud you on thinking of something that slick. But now I know what to look for in my division. And I think I remember hearing about you.
Sgt Baxter

---

thats a waste if you ask me-
pib

That is just WRONG!

I Sent Him To Jail

I'm 22 now. But, I did something very wrong when I was 15. I needed money and asked my uncle for it. He said NO.

I was so mad at him that I lied about him. I said he touched me, he never did. My mother was so mad she called the police. I did not want to get in trouble, so I kept my lie going.

He went to jail for 2 years. My family has nothing to do with him. I feel so bad, I think about it everyday and have trouble sleeping.

I can't tell everyone I lied, because I don't want to go to jail. I wish I was not so stupid.

[Webmaster's Note:

You have done something wrong and realize that. You were a child, and although you should have known better, you may not be legally culpable for what you did. I do not know what state or country you live in, but if you are living in the U.S., DailyConfession.com would like to help you and your uncle.

We will provide legal counsel at no cost to you, so that you can come forward and right the wrong. Our concern is not to see you punished, rather, it is to set the record straight so that your uncle can have his good name and dignity restored. We would also like to give you the opportunity to regain your self-respect. After all, that is what this web site is all about. We will also offer counseling, at no cost, to you, your uncle and anyone else in your family affected by this incident.

Please contact me at greg.fox@DailyConfession.com.]

You are pure evil. You have ruined a mans life over money. You can't even tell anyone that you lied because you are weak and pathetic. You have wasted my time.
~Queen Bee~

That's just wrong you disgrace every women that has been sexual abused for real you should be in jail in his place. And I would'nt cry if it really happen to you in jail.

Tell the truth. If you don't, this will follow both of you for the rest of your lives. It's true you did a terrible thing, but you have a chance to at least help him clear his name now. Every day you keep silent you are doing something just as terrible as when you first told the lie — maybe worse, since at that time you were just a kid. Now you're an adult. To allow him to continue to suffer for your own wrongdoing would be cowardly and self serving. And by the way, you'd better hope you never go under anesthesia, have too much to drink or find yourself in any other situation where your guard is down. I somehow doubt you do the right thing, but hope for both your sakes you do.

YOu are just pathetic. IF theres any justice, one day you will be abused for real, and no one will believe you. Payback is hell . . .

That is one of the cruelest things I have ever heard. Think about how your uncle feels! That's just sick, how someone's life could be destroyed because you didn't get a few measly bucks.

Wait, I see a trend, you evil, selfish little turd! You didn't get whatever money you needed when you were 15, so you sent your uncle to jail. Now, at 22, you are again too selfish to come clean. You feel "bad" and stay up at night because you feel so guilty. Boo-hoo. Think about your uncle, the person whose life you've ruined. Not only did your disgusting sense of entitlement put him behind bars for two years, but he probably has had to add his name to some sex offenders list kept by the government, which will follow him through life. Tell your parents, the police, and the court that you lied. You can't make this hideous situation right, but you can do something to make it better. If you're worried about legal ramifications to yourself, which I'm sure in all your selfishness you probably are, don't fret little liar, you were a minor when you committed perjury or otherwise caused your uncle's wrongful incarceration. You (unfortunately) can't be prosecuted now.

You are a pathetic human being who is a disgrace to the female race . . . i hope u do go to jail!

You have NO choice but to tell your family what happened!!! You can't let your uncle live the rest of his life in bitterness and anger over what he's been through. He served time in jail for something he didn't do . . . and now he's going to spend the rest of his life in an even worse version of jail. Ostracized by family, friends and the community!!! The only way you will EVER be able to move on from this and live a happy and complete life is if you make things right. It's going to be hard . . . it's going to SUCK so bad . . . but you have to do it. You have to.

"Blueper

You send someone to jail just because you can't get your way? Psycho.

Dude at 15 ur'e old enough to rationalize between good and bad. It's never too late to come clean but I know a no value selfish chicken $hit like u won't do that. I can only say may ur uncle and God forgive u.

Jac

You need to come clean and tell the truth. You ruined a mans life cos you wanted money. Since you obviously have few morals why didnt you just go turn a trick? Its people like you that makes it harder for woman who have actually been raped to be taken seriously. Its gonna cause you pain. I doubt you'll go to jail tho. But you MUST come clean about what you did. Otherwise karma is gonna take a giant chew out of your ass. And you full on deserve it.

---

being 15 means you were old enough to realize what you were doing. that's just aobut the most vindictive thing i've ever heard. i hope the guilt EATS YOU UP. your poor uncle, prison is so horrible & he didn't even do anything

~Gambitgirl~

KARMA is for sick people like you. You deserve what is coming to you

---

First of all, you were 15. You're not going to jail for something you did at that age. And you OWE it to everybody concerned to set the record straight. You know it was wrong, you feel rotten, and you need to get right with everyone.

`Gramps`

Telemarketers

Yesterday I was eating dinner and I got a phone call. I excused myself to the table and got the phone. I picked up and heard, "Hello I'm with AT&T and I was wondering if you would change your phone service?"

Outside of my teenager's range of hearing I asked a very simple question. "Do you know how to get blood out of carpet?" The confused telemarketer asked, "Excuse me?" and I repeated my impending problem. Then I said, " Oh shit it's everywhere!" and hung up.

Unfortunately the telemarketer then promptly called the cops and within minutes I was being questioned by the police. I told them what I had done and that I was only venting frustration at the telemarketer.

Then they did the unthinkable, they laughed, they actually told me that was good and they asked me to have a good night and left.

I confess that I probably scared a telemarketer out of her wits and for that I'm sorry. :-)

Man, I'm a college student and I don't know how they got my number but last week I got 4 calls in 2 days from the same telemarketers in Las Vegas. I was trying to wrote a bio lab but instead I argued for an hour with the manager. Then I discovered the key (yes, I am a little naive). Just say I don't want any, and they say "thank you, bye". This was on the second call, and the 3rd and 4th calls were much shorter.

HAHAHAHAHAHA. I was drinking some juice while reading that, and nearly spat it out. That was great!! Jerry Seinfeld would be impressed.

Lol!! We have loads of them phone up our house. Maybe i should try something like that!! Haha!!

~?~sam~?~

It makes a nice change from personal insults I'm sure. I shall have to remember that for when they get me the next time.

SugarSpun

Hey, that was a good one. When I get those calls, I tell them that I have someone at the front door and ask them if they mind holding on for a minute. Then I set the phone down and leave it there for 10 minutes or so and when I go back, they've hung up. I wonder why they would do that? :) I've only had one that called a second time, and since I repeated the same thing, I haven't heard back from them. How about other people's funny ideas as to how to blow off a telemarketer . . . let's hear them!

---

lmfao thats hilarious!

I am so doing that, next time someone calls

---

i used to get call all the time from psychic hotlines advertising their services . . . i'd just say, "Oh, really you're psychic? Then I guess you saw this coming" and i slam the phone down

~Gambitgirl~

LOL! it's especially annoying when they call during dinner! how rude! Here's a way to make the telemarketers themselves hang up. Last time one called during dinner, my dad said "and what did you say your company name is? I'm writing down all the names of companies that call during dinner to make sure I never buy anything from them" and the guy said "um . . . well I guess I'm one of those companies! bye" and he hung up. Hahaha

---

Ha ha ha!!! That was funny, but not nearly as easy as just telling them not to call back.

puokgirl

I ask them if they could call back later, since I am in the middle of having sex, and I have to hurry, because my wife will be home in 15 minutes.

---

thats awesome!! i have to remember that! what i do is tell them i cant talk right now but ask them for their home number so that i may return their call. when they refuse to give me their home number, i ask them "why, dont want to be bothered at home?" and then i hang up!!

Drew

Its always fun to keep them on the line for an hour or two by asking them stupid questions about their product . . . "I am calling from AT&T . . . " my response: "What exactly does the second 'T' stand for? Then they continue and so do I. At the end of it all they ask me if I want the product and I say 'no thanks' it gets them really angry! :)

1040

I just filed my income tax return.

I must say that even Stephen King would marvel at my amazingly convincing blend of fact and fiction.

Now I have to sweat for the next seven years to see the IRS audits me.

That will come back to haunt you, guaranteed. Lying always does. Stay sweaty . . .

Tornado

LOL . . .

DontKnow_DontCare

Thank you for helping to raise my taxes. Why is everyone so dishonest?

Boainmypants

We had a confessor previously who said he killed for the govt. I assumed he worked for the IRS. But don't worry, he was retired . . . Besides, they may actually let you pay.

`Gramps`

There was one year I did that - not a good idea I can tell you. Honesty is the best policy! BTW, do you folks realize when you turn in a tax cheat you are eligible for a percentage of the recovery? And, I might add, in complete anonymity?

unluckyatlove

I don't know what is worse, cheating on your taxes or turning your neighbor in to the IRS for a reward. Don't dictatorships operate this way?

Cheesehead

I know exactly what you mean! I've done that too. Luckly my seven years is almost up! hehehehe Good luck!

Anonymous Talkbacker

The wheels of justice turn slow but I'll catch you . . . . . . Uncle Sam.

BookemDano

i hope you're proud.

heather

Living The Lie Till The Bitter End

I married you when I knew you were not the one.

I confess that I only married you because "It was the right thing to do". I was 23, just out of Annapolis Naval Academy. You were 30 and pregnant and as it turns out, not with my child but I married you anyway.

You were so in love with me that you couldn't even admit to yourself the child wasn't mine, not then and not now, 20 years later. I find it the ultimate insult that you can't even face truth between us.

Well I made the child mine but I never loved you, never.

I've wasted 20 years of my life, most of it hating you. If for once in my life I'd not done "the right thing" and walked away . . . . you'd be in a trailer park and perhaps I'd be in love.

You still say you love me but I can't stand to be in the same room with you. I've never been so alone as when you are at my side.

This is so sad. I lifetime of hate. I don't think that "the right thing to do" was, in fact, the right thing. Now is the time to truly do the "right thing". Time to end this life of constant hate and begin your new life free of it. Good luck to all involved . . .

---

20 years is a long time to be married to someone you hate. However, you're 43 and have time to make up for your mistake and live it for a while. Phatboy.

Oh peel me a grape. Nu, get a divorce! If you've been lying for 30 years, you can lie now and say you want a divorce for some made-up reason. But by all means, you've been cruel enough to lead your wife on all these years, don't you dare tell her that you "never loved her". Prove to the world that you've managed to mature a bit in the past 30 years.

VIII. LIAR, LIAR!

That is one of the saddest posts I have ever read on here. Do yourself and her a favour and divorce her! Living in hate is no way to live!

Well dammit break up w/ her! HELLOOOOOOO thus, another lesson is learned. Don't marry people because it is "The right thing to do." The right thing to do is marry out of love!!!
~Sarah~

Why does it have to be to the "bitter end"? You married her, she'll get child support if you leave her and not live in a "trailer park", and you can find true love . . .
Leigh

Except for the school you were attending, I could have written that one. Folks, pay attention - don't marry in haste and wait to have sex!

it sounds to me like this isn't working at all. if you hate her so much and feel like you've wasted your life end it. stop stringing her along, you're only hurting the three of you- end rant

Oh my god, Um . . . . . Maybe you should have told HER this a long time ago instead of wasting 20 years of her life.
XdivineXtragedyX

If you did your best to help raise this child, then it wasnt 20 years totally wasted. However, that doesnt mean you should stay married to him. The bottom line is, would you be happier with her or without her?

Youve put up with being there for her for long enough. Leave her, and be your own man.

Boy, some people really like to wallow in it! It's been 20 years, the kid is grown, why haven't you gotten out? Or did you have more kids? (As much as you hate her.) Sorry, but you've made your bed and you don't seem to want to crawl out of it.
`Gramps`

Clear Cache

Let me start off by saying that I don't know much about computers.

I was sleeping over at my mother's because the next morning was my niece's 1st birthday. I couldn't sleep that night so I went online and looked at porn . . . out of boredom. I shut the computer down and went to sleep after.

The next morning the house was crowded with friends, family, and even some co-workers of my mother's. Tons of kids from ages 1 to 8.

My sister went on the computer because she wanted to show everyone a cool web site she knew of. As soon as she popped a web site up . . . my porn show from the other night came up too.

Jaws dropped . . . children's eyes were shielded . . . . and adults literally threw themselves at the computer to prevent eyes from seeing.

Then my mother looked at me.

I thought I was busted. My face bright red, I stared back. Then she calmly told me not to let my boyfriend use the computer again.

I let her believe it was him to save my own butt.

Oh god! I would do that same thing!!!!

So then, those computer classes at school are looking better and better now eh? Its not the cache, its the prefs on the browser program . . . set to go to the last visited site when opened . . . open the browser program and look in the 'edit' drop down menu . . . the prefs link is usually at the bottom. Scour that puppy and fix it, then you won't have to lie again. Some day, you'll tell her about it. She might not laugh, but I'll bet you do.
MollyMayhem

Good job. So let me ask you a question: if there was something so bad about it that this chaos happened . . . then what were you doing in the first place? Jeez, no one has control over their stupid hormones these days . .
Raven

Everyone is going to be talking back and saying that you are a horrible person and stuff. But listen, there's not a very good chance that anyone in your position would do anything different.

haha well as far as i can see no harm done, as long as u dont marry this guy. if u do ull have to tell ur mom the truth so she wont unfairly judge him. although u should have fessed up anyway . . .

Think how he feels, thats the cruelest thing you could do . . . Just imagine if you married him, how your mother would always think it was him . . . Just tell her it was you and tell her some lame excuse about it.

Moms aren't as stupid as their kids think they are! She helped you save "face"! Now stop looking at porn on other's pc's or at least learn how to use internet tools and delete those tell tale "cookies"!
Big Daug

LOL I know exactly how you feel. I used to do exactly that all the time. My only question was how did she know it was you? She must be psychic

I'm sure your boyfriend appreciated that!
CoolJerk.

Fabricated Fiancé

I bought one of those $7.99 rings from Wal-Mart that look like an engagement ring.

I proceeded to go to several bridal shops and try on a ridiculous number of dresses. I told the sales people about my "fiancé," the proposal, the wedding plans. etc. for hours.

I put a couple of the most expensive dresses on hold, after accidentally getting lipstick on a couple others.

I am a sad, sad single girl.

Either you were just really bored, or you have some serious issues with having someone in your life. I am leaning more towards the latter. Please, just talk to someone about this, like a counsellor or something. It could make you feel better.

Have you seen "Muriel's Wedding"? She did that and took photos too! I don't think you are sad, weddings are made out to be such fairy-tale like things it's understandabel you'd want to pretend. I'd try not to let it become an obsession though.

Wow! That is sad! Why are you doing this? What would you do if people you know found out? Better cover your tracks but good.

OHMIGOSH! This is too cute! Although I'm not single and won't be getting married for quite some time, this sounds like sooo much fun. I might just try it myself. Fabulous idea sweety!

---

ummm I guess you shouldnt be sad for being single, many are, but you can be sad to know that you need Therapy . . yes a shrink will do . . .

Someone has WAY too much time on their hands. Course, I am also sitting here reading this confession. Guess we should both get out more.

Haha . . . don't worry me and my friends go into Walmart and sit there trying them on fantasizing about our "would be marriages" . . . . however we've never actually bought one or went wedding dress shopping. Oh well . . . have fun, you're a kid!..its your job :)

It's ok . . . I wear a wedding band sometimes to pretend I'm married.
Bomba

Yes, yes you are.

Yes you are. The fact that you would ruin an expensive gown just to play your game speaks volumes. Get help.
`Gramps`

I was just told that anybody who wants to can walk into those places and try on dresses any time they want to.

Hold All Calls

Every Thursday at work I have a conference call scheduled with all seven regional managers.

The purpose is to go over the past week's performance and review strategies for next week. This sounds involved and I block three hours every Thursday to accommodate this meeting.

In reality, it takes us about 30 minutes tops to complete our business.

I confess that I spend the rest of the time in my office behind closed doors just goofing off. I surf the web, call old friends or just take a nap.

I love working on Thursdays!

That is awesome. I want a job like that. Definitely nap time for me.
BostonGirly

Hope you created a sleeping area under your desk like George Costanza
so you get caught like he did but hopefully you get fired for being decietful
chicago_guy

Ah, you smartass. Good work.
smartass

I know there's no way you can hear the swell of all of us sucking in air to
say all together at once a big collective, 'So?' I guess we'd all like to think
that if one day the call actually required the entire 3 hours you'd do your
job. If you take only 2 and a half hours a week to screw around at work
I'd say you're about the average employee. Now if you're the boss, I'd
say you're far and above most others for only screwing around that little.
MollyMayhem

Meetings - the practical alternative to work!
Unluckyatlove

I would love Thursdays too, if I had your job. :)
Sparkle

And I bet if you saw any of your lower employees doing that every
Thursday, you'd fire them. Clever management.
eve_attax

I can't understand any of the people who are talking back and being
extremely righteous. Get over yourself. You know everyone screws off
and, heck, if you only screw off 2 1/2 hours per week, you're amazing
dude. I'm sure a lot more people screw off more than that. I know I do.
Leigh

You know I can't judge you cuz of that cuz I'd be a hypocrit of I did. ~Alya

Alya87

---

where do you work at? im gonna apply to it.

UncleCharlie

Well, as long as you spend that time on Daily Confession, you are forgiven! (Is my nose brown?)

Megxxx

To all of you people who call him a bad manager for doing this . . . you know, he earned this. He was probably a lower-level employee, but he worked hard and got promoted. Maybe if you worked hard, and got promoted, you could have a little break every thursday too.

Mr_DNA

I want a job like that, way to go man!!!!!!!!!

My Dirty Little Secret

I am secretly obsessed with gay porn.

I am a 20-something female and love to watch two men together . . . it is a real turn on.

I have been with my hubby for 10 years but he doesn't have a clue about my obsession. He likes to watch 'straight' porn and I am always telling him that I am adamantly against all porn . . . but I am obviously two faced because of my secret gay porn stash.

I wish I could come out in the open, but then I'd just be a hypocrite.

---

i'm a female and gay porn does not turn me on at all. it's just plain nasty.

saphire

HA, you should tell him that you want a threesome . . . but forget to mention that its with another guy . . . that could be quite the event!
Prozak

i hate to tell you this, but you're a hypocrite whether you tell your husband or not.
god_chic

Your husband has probably found your 'secret' stash by now . . . .
Bootylicious

I think there are quite a few women out there who like to look at gay porn, as for the issue of being a hypocrite, i guess it was just your way of trying to hide the fact that you like to look at it. It's not very accepted for a woman to look at porn, let alone gay porn. And to be honest i don't know many men who would like their girlfriends/wives looking at it. I know my boyfriend wouldn't like it. There are such double standards, i mean guys love to watch 2 women, what's the diffference if women watch 2 men?
lylya

You're still a hypocrite—it's just a matter as of whether you choose to admit it or not
Kittae

I'll never understand why people feel the need to keep secrets about their sexuality. Regardless of whether you tell your hubby or not, you're still a hypocrite, telling doesn't make it so, doing makes it so. I sincerely doubt your husband would think less of you if you revealed yourself.
MollyMayhem

You're a hypocrite anyway. Just no one knows it. Except us.
mypeepsnme

i'm a guy and i rarely if ever look at straight porn. lesbians all the way :)
dysfunction_ptr

You don't wanna be a hypocrite, then for christ's sake just stop preaching to him about it!!

MissDemeanor

Yes, you are being a hypocrite and a liar. By telling your husband one thing and doing another you are not only being a hypocrite but you are going against the marriage vows you made ten years ago . . . in my opinion you should let your husband know you watch it and you should both stop looking at porn. It is a very gross and controllable thing. It would also show better your commitment to each other, and would show trust.

princess_of_words

ME TOO!!!!! GAY MEN RULES!! hehe. there's nothing wrong with liking gay porn. i'm sure ur hubby will find it quite kinky and nice :)

gelly123

gay porn does nothing for me, male or female . . . i prefer to see straight porn, or group sex, especially 2 or more men with 1 woman . . . everyone's got their prefernces, you just like what you like . . . no biggie

~Gambitgirl~

A Good Day Off

I'm told my boss I had doctor's appointments last Friday so I needed the day off. My company pays for the occasional day off for health related things.

Just between you and me, I actually went a bar all day and watched the Atlantic Coast Conference men's basket ball tournament and got hammered.

The only doctor I'd be seeing would be because I drank myself stupid if we won.

That is awesome. Everyone needs a day like that sometimes. Even though you didn't really have doctors' appointments, you really were doing something for you health.

BostonGirly

Yes, that's called a mental health day and some employers actually endorse that. Now get back to work.

MollyMayhem

Drinking not required. Stupid things are happening anyway.

mypeepsnme

Better hope he doesn't ask for a doctors excuse. You'll be screwed.

Jenapril

Don't sweat it. :)

MissDemeanor

Those are called 'mental health days' - enjoy them.

indym22

Good on you, man. People need to be a little more spontaneous and just take a day off for themselves.

Otter

Hope you had fun while 'I' was at work.

Deilphandkhor

CHAPTER IX.

The Fear Factor

Nature gave us fears as a means of protecting ourselves. Psychologists have taken those fears, renamed them phobias, and turned them into a multibillion-dollar business for themselves and pharmaceutical companies.

What we fear most is the unknown. How we deal with that fear defines, for a large part, who we are.

One of the more perplexing adjuncts to the topic of fear is the insane names they have given to fears. Here are a few:

Agyrophobia—Fear of streets or crossing the street

COMING CLEAN

Bogyphobia—Fear of bogeys or the bogeyman
Coprastasophobia—Fear of constipation
Dutchphobia—Fear of the Dutch
Emetophobia—Fear of vomiting
Ergophobia—Fear of work
Gamophobia—Fear of marriage
Genuphobia—Fear of knees
Helminthophobia—Fear of being infested with worms
Kathisophobia—Fear of sitting down
Leukophobia—Fear of the color white
Oneirogmophobia—Fear of wet dreams
Panophobia or Pantophobia—Fear of everything
Phobophobia—Fear of phobias

Some fears, like nyctophobia—fear of the dark—are fears that we usually grow out of. Then there are fears like agoraphobia—fear of open spaces or of being in crowded, public places, which can be a lifelong handicap if left unchecked.

So if you find yourself uncomfortable on Friday the 13th or just can't stand high places, relax. You're not alone. You are just another a victim of The Fear Factor.

Not At Any Price

I don't know if it is true or not. I do not want to find out first had.

I am flying to San Diego next month. I have only one fear with regard to flying.

This will be a four and a half hour, non-stop flight. I know that I will have to use the lavatory at least once during the flight. I confess that ever since I heard that if you are sitting on the toilet and create a pretty good "seal" (I am pleasantly plump . . .) that if you flush, it will basically disembowel you.

I am a college grad, I'm not subject to irrational fears. I know this cannot be true.

However, I confess that you could not pay me a million dollars to sit on the toilet seat of a plane at 30,000 feet and flush.

Don't worry . . I'm terrified that if I lick an envelope and it cuts my tongue roach eggs will get in (that supposedly happened). Sounds completely irrational, but since I heard that I use a sponge

---

Who flushes the toilet while still sitting on it?

---

uh most of us stand up before we flush. I think that would eliminate this problem.

That *did* happen to a woman . . I think the word is "vacuum"? I'll be careful on 'plane loo's from now on . .

---

who the hell flushes while they're still sitting anyways? Even if you don't want to sit you can "hover". Besides, there is no way thats true.

Why would you be flushing while you are sitting down anyway?

Just stand up when you flush.

You're accustomed to flushing while you're sitting? Get up dear, then flush. Trust me, if you're plump you'll be more worried about how you're going to turn around and fit on the seat in there. Airline restroom accommodations are smaller than Barbie's Malibu Beach House.

MollyMayhem

so do ur stuff, stand up, and then flush . . . ur insides will be fine!

That is a urban myth!

haha ok, that is a really sad fear. if you really have to go, stand up before you flush and you will have nothing to worry about.

dinkus

how about $100,000,001.00?

(Dr. Goldfish)

no it is not true . . the only thing i hate about plane toilets is that when it flushes, it's so loud it scares me

Taken By Surprise

I'm am still at work. Ten minutes ago a roach walked over my naked arm while I was eating a burger and fries.

I confess I screamed, jumped up from my seat, the roach fell into my fries, I screamed some more and literally ran around in circles.

This wouldn't be so bad if not for the fact that I am a 37 year old male and manager of my department.

I just can't believe me.

I did receive a standing ovation . . .

I hate those things . . . my parents, me, my brother, grandfather, and uncle where on the back porch when one crawled up my pants leg . . . they all got to see my pink drawers when I come out of those pants

LOl that was just way too funny, eso for 12:54 in the morning! Aww that was great. I can picture that and it really does crack me the freak up!!!
~Sarah~

Hehehe :) I suggest that you find another place to eat.

You go girl! Heh, roaches are gross . . . on your arm, in your fries. Ick.

:) I wish you were MY boss.
clonedkitty

OMG that was the funniest post ever!! I love this post

ROFLMAO!!!! LOL! That's about the funniest damn thing I've ever heard!!! . . . Only because I would do the same thing . . . LOL.
_

Don't feel too bad. Roaches are among nature's most disgusting creatures. I hope you took your bows, then complained loudly to maintenence or to whoever handles sanitation in your building.

BWAHAHAHA~!! I just about fell out of my chair laughing at this one . .

hee! i like you.

I do the "roach dance" too!

Having a fear of bugs does not make you less of a man. We all have phobias and we should not be judged by them. I once watch three men run away from a mouse. I didn't and I killed the mouse. I don't think better of myself or less of them for it. In fact maybe I'm just a cold and heartless bastard or maybe I just hate mice. Good luck

LOL. That's awesome. At least people appreciated your theatrics.

seriously, you coudd be Colin Powell & still do that . . . roaches are horrible, vile things that should all die die DIE!
~Gambitgirl~

Clowns

I confess that I'm deeply afraid of clowns. It started in eighth or ninth grade. It's just something about them.

I don't know how to describe it. Please tell me I'm not alone . . .

I hate them too - yay Im not alone. they give me the creeps

---

same here they freak me out
.:me:.

I agree with you. I hate clowns. They look evil. Holla back
airforce1

I am too.

I've been afraid of clowns for as long as I can remember. My mom made me dress as one for Halloween a long time ago, and I have been traumatized ever since. It's terrible. So, yeah, I feel your pain.

Im not but that is a scary ass picture the webbie put up.
jj

---

the clowns made me do it!!!! ahhh!!! they said they would eat me otherwise . . . don't be mad . . . please . . . i am so very afraid of them!!!
seriously i am

---

omg! u r not the olny one! the scare me shitless!!
~!~Stoner Chick~!~

OMG! i am scared of them to! i dont know why, but i just do not like them. who would trust a clown?

Hell no, pennywise is real, and they all float

You're not alone! I hate clowns and they scare me too. It must have something to do with the fact that they have a mask and you can sense that they are not what they pretend to be.

Cosmo Kramer, is that you . . . . ?

You're not alone. I've hated clowns since i was 8. I hate them so much that i started crying last year when i saw a production that had about 20 clowns onstage.
~PurpleMunki~

You're not alone! I saw the Stephen King film IT and I'm scared too
~ali~

Did you watch IT? That Pennywise the Clown really made me change my views about clowns too.

Things That Go Bump In The Night

Okay, I know that this is really lame of me, but I am finally ready to fess up so here goes.

I am 18 years old and really afraid of the dark. When I tell my friends or mom this, they just laugh, but I am really serious! I even have to sleep with a night light on or I get really freaked out.

For example, sometimes at night my mom will ask me to go out to the shed and get the laundry. I really hate that! Even though the shed is only like thirty feet away I always have to bring a flashlight, and then sometimes I get so scared that I end up running back in the house with my heart racing.

I don't really think that things are gonna jump out and get me, but I guess my mind just plays tricks on me. Somebody please tell me that I am not the only one with this problem!!!

---

you are not the only one with this problem. i get the late nite willies too, dark is scawy!

The mind is an amazing thing. It makes you see things that you don't even normally think of in broad daylight. I'm not saying that you're being paranoid or anything close to it. I think you're being cautious and this is a good thing. It keeps you ready for the unknown. I do the same thing. I guess you could call it heightening your senses so to speak. So to answer your question, you're not the only one. There are a lot of people out there that keep themselves aware of what goes on around them. I know things will be alright for you.

~~Jazz

ahh thats crazy, cause i am totally like that!! I used to share a room with my sister, but she has since moved to college, and now i have to sleep with the light on, but if anyone else is sleeping in the room with me im fine, but if i have to go to the bathroom in the middle of the night i run all the way down the hall and back!! its great to know im not the only one!!

Wow, you remind me so much of myself! I am 21 now, and I can't sleep with the light off either. I don't think anything tragic happened to me when I was younger, but It freaks me out to be in a dark room alone . . . even my own. I'm fine if I'm not sleeping alone. When I get married that will probably help.

Okay I also have the same problem and I'm 18 so don't worry. I'm actually starting to think that my fear of the dark has something to do with a past life. Might wanna check that out see if possibly that's what the problem is

KoRn AnGeL

U aint alone, especially after a scary movie!

~AH!

Well . . Im just starting to get over this but i'm the same way. The mind is an amazing thing, can do all sorts of things if you let it. Im 23 and up until this past Christmas, I always slept with a nightlight. It doesnt help that I live alone. I recently just bout a chocolate lab, his names Scooby hehe. lol anyways, your not alone. There are tons of other people like this so dont feel bad. Just keep reminding yourself that theres no one there and that everything will be alright. Eventually you'll get to be OK. I dont think you'll ever fully get over this. I dont think I will. I just hope my future husband doesnt like sleeping in the dark . . .

~- Ashley

Don't worry about it at all! In the dark, I go crazee!!!

~Michelle

i have a slight variation of that. such as if i'm going upstairs i have to either run up them or constantly look behind me. also, i catch myself straining my eyes in my darks room to see if anyone is in there with me. guess i better lay off

hey, it's alright . . . I've got a lamp that i've had for at least five years, it's a nightlamp, i will always use a lamp because the plugs in my house are in such obscure places that a nightlight would be useless. I like to be able to see

there are times when i'm afraid of the dark myself . . . and i'm 23. my 19 year old sister confesses to the same thing.

kaykay

All ya have to do is think of something else and take your mind OFF of it. It worked for me!!! Just whenever a thought like that comes into your head, push it away and replace it with a new thought!!!!!! It works i promise!!!

Of Course I'm Circumcised . . .

I'm not circumcised. I always hear girls, and society in general saying, "If you are not circumcised, you can't pleasure a woman as well as someone who is."

Well, I haven't been far enough with a girl yet to find that out. It is something I fear - I don't want to screw anything up.

I could get circumcised if I really needed to, but now that I have a choice, I don't think I could let anyone cut me up down there.

LOL . . . don't worry so much about it!! If it bothers you, go ahead and get it circumcised. They will put you under anesthesia and you won't feel a thing. You make it sound like some hobo's going to whack at it with a knife while you're wide awake! LOL. As for pleasuring a girl, I wouldn't know about that. Just don't worry about it bud :)

Don't worry about it. You can pleasure a girl just as well, as long as you know what you're doing. I'm surprised you even know what that is. Most guys I know look at me funny and ask what's that when I ask them if they're circumcised (to get the reactions, lol) If a girl cares that much about your penis, she doesn't care enough about you.

§hadowkiller

Being circumsized can actually de-sensitize it. I was with a guy who wasnt and he seems to get a lot more pleasure out of it than circumcized guys Ive been with.

I don't think it matters. I've had guys who were circumcised and guys who weren't. Honestly, the only factor is if the guy knows what he's doing. (well there is another matter of SIZE . . . but that's not the issue). Just know how to please a woman and you'll be just as good as any "clean cut" guy!

My boyfriend is, but he is my only, so I can;t compare.

angelface

You do know that people with un circumcized penis's expierence more pleasure then guys who are circumcised! Just thought I'd tell you :) And I don't think it would matter to a girl if she really wanted to do you. I mean, I wouldn't be sitting there STAIRING at it for gods sake, I think I'd be a little distracted. So no worries!

~fragelistic~

actually i've heard that there is not all that much of a difference during sex.

Well, I'm excluded from society or whatever. just because a man is circumsised does not mean he's a better lover. That's absurd.

Being circumsized has nothing to do with being able to pleasure a woman. They feel the same while erect. The only thing I dont like about uncircumsized penises is when the man doesnt keep it clean, it gets all smelly.

Dont worry- I haven't gone far enough with a guy to figure out what the difference looks like!

From what I understand, the foreskin allows motion without constant rubbing, which can cause soreness for the lady. As far as satisfying the lady, remember, it's how you use it ;). If a woman did not see or feel "it" before the deed, she probably couldn't tell you one way or the other.

Its a myth. Just be sure to keep all your little folds of flesh squeaky clean and there'll be no trouble.

SugarSpun

Never Seen One Like That Before

I confess I told my boyfriend we couldn't have sex because I wanted to take things slow. But that's not the case.

I am 21 years old and I have never seen an uncircumcised penis (he has told me). I am afraid I will laugh or something worse.

Since he knows I have never been one to sleep around he is completely cool with waiting.

But I love him and I am afraid that I will never be able to do anything sexual with him because it looks like a hot dog (or so I have heard)

dammit now us guys got another reason to be insecure around girls? what the frig is wrong with the uncut version? i got it. it don't look like a damn hotdog.

the_captain

nope it looks like an elephants trunk ewwww

HA HA . . . . . . boy am i glad i'm circumsized!!

Unless you're both a very playful mood, laughing during sex is not a good idea so until you gain some sexual maturity its probably best you wait anyway.

MollyMayhem

It looks fine and the skin rubs up and down making it better

If you really loved him you would accept that that's how he is, and be okay with it. I hope he breaks up with you

---

I really don't know what to say.

It's no big deal really. The first guy I ever had sex with was uncircumsised. it scared me at first cuz I had never seen anything lik it and I thought somehing was wrong with him (he din' tell me at least your man did) but Hotdog?? Not quite . . . More like a pig in a blanket. ;) LoL

Sounds to me like you are in some desperate need of growing up.

Looks like a hot dog??? ROTFL Sorry. I'm uncircumsized and it doesn't look like a hot dog to me. He seems like a great guy to wait for when your ready! You'll be fine!

Oh grow up!

Believe it or not, it actually looks better,

Passive Pee-er

Whenever I go to a public bathroom, I cannot pee if it's too quiet.

I'll just sit there until someone flushes a toilet or turns on the sink or makes some other kind of noise that will masquerade that peeing sound. Sometimes, I'll wait until nobody else is in the bathroom to relieve myself so I won't get embarrassed.

I'm 29 and won't acknowledge the fact that everyone pees.

I do the exact same thing! you're not alone!

me too!! i just don't like it when other people can hear me pee . . . it's totally embarassing!

If you aim it forwards, it will hit the basin before it hits the water, therefore making no noise. =)

I'm the exact opposite, I have a hard time going if its too noisy, its worse at concerts and stuff and I goto a lot of huge concerts like ozzfest and New england Metalfest and i HATE bathrooms where there's lines of like 20 people and only 2 urinals and 3 stalls (one of which is always trashed and overflowing if you get my meaning), its gross. But I have one hell of a time trying to pee with too much noise.

I know how you feel, I cant pee when its quiet either
~*~Littleone~*~

I put toilet tissue down the toilet so that the peeing trickle is muffled.

why dont you just flush the toilet yourself??

haha this happens to me all the time . . . the only thing i can think of is if there are automatic flushers, then press the lil button to make it go off and kinda quietly but loud enough for ppl to hear say: "damn automatic flushers . . . " haha it works!

~kelcey~

You are weird????

I know exactly what you are talking about!

I do that too!

Do you still not pee if no one is not in the room? All these little phobias seem odd, but then, my old science teacher was deathly afraid of dead fish . . . .

Default

It's called bashful kidneys. You're not alone. Of course, I've never had that problem . . .

`Gramps`

No worries . . . I can't pee if someone walks up the urinal next to me . . .

áéíóú

Night Light

I'm a clean person but there are roaches in my apartment (if there are roaches in one unit, they spread to every unit in the building).

I sleep with 100 watts worth of lighting directed at me because I'm paranoid that if I turn out the lights, the roaches will crawl all over me while I sleep.

Move. Or call the people at Fear Factor and see if they would like them to use in an upcoming episode.

---

they probably do crawl all over u when ur asleep cuz u can't even feel them on u when ur asleep!

Ummmmmmmmm . . . . MOVE!!!!!!!!!
CommonSense

Honey, roaches aren't afraid of the light . . .

It's called "Surface Spray" Use it on all the joins and gaps around your flat. You'll be roach free.

Aren't all types of bugs attracted to light???

Who can blame you..I would MOVE as soon as possible . . . ewwwwww

---

The house next door to mine had raoches when I was younger and they spread to my house my mom says they actualy like a cleaner place to live in and you should get some roach motels and such

---

you do know that roaches are attracted to the light . . . . Hello, Terminix?

one word . . . moths

agh . . . i would just move . . . . screw the deposit & MOVE
~Gambitgirl~

Never Catch Me!

I'm 41, married, three kids and I have a great job. I would consider myself an intelligent, well-rounded guy.

Last night my wife made mention of the way I get into bed. She said that she has noticed since we got married, that I always stop a few feet short of the bed and almost leap into the bed.

I never realized I was still doing that.

I thought about it for a while and then it hit me. When I was six or seven, my older brother scared me with the story of the monster that lived under my bed. The night he told me that, I started leaping into bed, always careful not to get to close to the bed so that the monster couldn't reach out and get me.

I confess that I have been doing that ever since then.

hahah that cracked me up!!!!
kcsgrl

ROTFLMAO . . . this is the funniest confession of the week! Thanks for the laugh . . .
DontKnow_DontCare

heh. i do that sometimes still.
prettyflower

that's hilarious . . . . old habits are hard to break . . . I'm almost thirty and still sleep with my baby blankie . . .

TheQueen

People don't realize that the stuff they say, although no harm is meant, can linger for a long time. I have things similar that have happened when I was little and that cause me to react and act in certain ways.

TheFugitivePsycho

Awww, that's cute . . .

pettyfan

That is too cute.

dazie

When I was small the monsters also lived under the basement stairs (courtesy of my older brother). I am 42 years old and STILL run up the basement stairs at my parents house! Bill Cosby says 'monsters won't get you if you have your music with you.' I simply can't take the chance that it might not work!

Amazon_Troll_Babe

That is so adorable!

immise

hey, it's cute. It shows you're still childlike in a way, that's a good thing.

Fitz_Freak

Ahh bless - that's quite endearing

Skanga

HAHAHAHA! i dont even think a monster could exist under my bed with the smells i make!

gregthomas02

I figured out a long time ago that there was a board along the length of the bed at the foot of the bed. I don't have to jump, I just crawl up from the foot of the bed. Now making the bed is another problem . . .

`Gramps`

CHAPTER X.

Body Works

"What speaks with one voice, yet in the morning walks on four legs, walks at noon on two legs, and in the evening walks on three legs?"

The human body is an amazing thing.

But when we are toddlers and youths our parents and society at large teach us that many of our bodily functions are yucky things that must be hidden. At some point, we develop our level of modesty. And from then on, if someone hears us fart we are shamed; we no longer run around naked; we learn that going "number two" is a very personal and private thing. Some youths and adults cannot use a public restroom if someone else is in there who could smell, hear, or see them. We are taught that a very natural, universal bodily function is shameful and must be hidden from the world.

But when sexual maturity hits, all bets are off. Some of us (most?) compromise our modesty, ethics, and religion as we explore our bodies and become curious about the opposite sex. To make things even more interesting, some of us learn that we don't have a strong curiosity for the opposite sex but rather are attracted to our own gender. All this goes on while we gain weight, lose weight, get zits, grow taller, and get stronger. Then the granddaddy of them all. Something special saved for the fairer sex—menstruation.

If we survive puberty, we start to judge the things that make us unique. Being taller, thinner, shorter, fatter; having birthmarks, moles, bad breath, body odor, sweaty palms, smelly feet; snoring, nose-picking, farting, belching, and you know what they say about a man and the size of his feet.

But did you also know that by age twenty-five, the average American has five pounds of undigested meat that just sits in the large intestine? (That's not true, but many of us believe rumors and myths like these about our bodies.) The truth is the body is a fascinating, confusing, complicated piece of machinery. We know a lot about what makes it tick, but many of the things we hold as truths are just not so. So the next time you are sitting in a crowded restaurant and let loose a S.B.D., be proud! Let everyone at the table know it was you. Don't be ashamed about how your Body Works.

Hey! I Do That Too!

Earlier today my girlfriend laughed so hard she peed her pants.

We were in the kitchen and she just stood there as the puddle grew around her feet. The look on her face was priceless, somewhere between complete shock and complete humiliation.

I saw the "crying eyes" start to make an appearance and I told her not to worry, It happens to everyone. I then proceeded to pee in my pants.

I confess we looked very weird standing in the kitchen with pee all over the floor, but I love her and would do anything for her. Even pee in my pants to make her feel better.

It worked.

You ROCK dude! I almost want to tell you I love you, but I love my own boyfriend too much already. :)

---

that has got to be the sweetest most amazing thing, your gf is so lucky

---

aww, how romantic . . .

---

aww . . . that is so cute ;)

::princess blush::

Aww I wish I had a guy who would pee his pants to cheer me up! . . . or do I . . .

That is soooo gross and sooooo sweet!!!

---

you're the best boyfriend anyone could ask for! now who cleaned up?

Omg that is the cutest thing ever. There are three of us girls here and we all wish we had boyfriends like you!

---

awww . . . that was so sweet of you. i hope you stay together.

llamatron

AWwwwwwwwwwwww . . . . . that is so sweet and funny at the same time. Reminds me of Billy Maddison where Billy puts water all over his pants so the kids think it is cool . . . your a sweet guy!

---

oh . . . my . . . god! that is so funny! sweet & senstive but also royally wacky! what people do for love! *falls on the floor laughing*

-Grumble-

---

aw thats so sweet! if a boy did that for me when i peed my pants i would love him forever haha

---

There's something wrong here. She pees, you pee, everybody thinks it's romantic. Why am I the only one who thinks it's stupid?

`Gramps`

Mine Are Innies . . .

This is probably gonna sound weird. Here goes. I'm female, 21, and my nipples are what can only be described as "innies" They're always inside my boobs. The only time they come out is when I'm cold or turned on.

It's one of the reasons I'm afraid to let a guy go too far . . . . I'm embarrassed.

I confess that I'd give anything to have normal nipples, that were always sticking out.

Am I a freak?

---

im a guy and my nips are innies too. but i guess i dont have to worry about that. well u arent alone.

~InnerChild~

You and me both, Im 20 year old male and I have the same problem . . . I wouldn't mind your innies :)

You're not a freak. It's perfectly normal. At least you don't have torpedo nipples that make bumps even under a thick sweater.

---

you must be southern honey. they only stick out when your turned on or cold? thats normal. "our bodies, our selves" good book check it out

---

no your normal a lot of women are like that ur not alone!

.:me:

No way! you're so not a freak. my s are flat until, like you, i get cold or turned on. just get a pump that they have for breast-feeding mothers! it works

Yeah, but if you got to the point where a guy would see your boobs, you'd probably be turned on, so it's a moot point. So enjoy em!

Nope . . . mine do the same thing! They only "come out to play" when I'm cold or extremly aroused. Don't worry . . . nipples come in all shapes and sizes.

Don't be embarrased! There are alot of women with innies. If you treat it like a game and challenge the guy ahead of time to see if he can pop your buttons, it will be more of a turn on for the guy than a turn off. Trust me, us guys are freakie like that.

my nipples are in unless im cold or turned on too . . . am i a freak aswell???

My first girlfriend had that. I think it's really sexy as you always knew when she was turned on:)

omg same with me!!!!! its perfectly normal don't worry about it! i think they look so much better than outies anyway!!!!!!
-Innie

they are inverted nipples - they are reasonably common, no you arent a freak you just might have a few problems breastfeeding is all

I Like Sex, Butt . . .

I can't have it for at least 3 weeks because yesterday I sat on a hard wooden stool for an hour.

Anytime I sit on a hard seat with little or no padding for more than 10 minutes (church and park benches, bathtub, bus or subway seats, wooden kitchen chairs) I wake up the next day with ugly, excruciatingly painful, swollen red things that look like big boils or pimples, right where my butt cheeks become my thighs.

I'm too embarrassed to be seen in my birthday suit in front of my wife until it goes away. The only way to "cure" them is to wear boxers and carry a cushion around for the next three weeks or so and avoid sitting on anything hard at all costs.

I think my butt is either allergic to hard surfaces or has a mind of it's own and loves to torture me.

There is a saying among naturopaths that goes like this: if a person feels inclined to become embarassed, he is likely to develop skin problems.

You should just get over it. She's your wife, if she leaves you for a boil on your ass, I'm gonna guess it wasn't meant to be. We all get them (I'm an attractive 22 year old chick, I get them too) and it doesn't stop most of the population from enjoying a normal life.

speechless

Go to the doctor. It's that simple

Thats odd, anytime I sit on anything wooden, my butt itches uncontrollably.

I think you should probably go see a doctor about that . . .

Sinner

I am a girl, and that happens to me sometimes. Don't know why, I haven't related it to the hard surfaces, but maybe I will look for that pattern! It is embarassing. I hate it, it looks like I have an STD, or something. Which I don't - I've been tested. But, they go away quickly, and I haven't been to the doctor. Let me know if you found out how to fix it!

LOL!!! That is funny and sad at the same time!Mabey you should try to put some petroleum jelly on that area before a sit.It's probably caused by perspiration.

~S~

Ouch . . . . . that really sucks! I feel for ya man! At least it won't take very long to go away!

~F~

I believe those are called "Hemmorhoids".

Dude, see a dermatologist! This condition could be cured with a cream or pill—or it could be the harbinger of a major illness!
CoolJerk.

Why not try the boxers full-time? Go see a doctor who can offer real advice.

First, I think you should start carrying a cushion around with you all the time. Maybe one of those ones you can get at football games or something. Second, she's you wife. I doubt she's going to care about some bumps on your ass. Doesn't she kind of wonder about these three week dry spells?

brainie

Stop The Car . . .

My bride of seven months and I were on a road trip from Orlando, FL to Key West. About two hours into the trip my beautiful, innocent honey announces that she had to pee. No problem I told her, I would pull over at the next rest stop. She looked at me and in the sweetest voice said, and I quote, "just pull over now."

It's 2:45pm, broad daylight, not a cloud in the sky and we are south bound on I-95 with a ton of traffic whizzing by. I pull over and my demure, modest bride hops out of the passenger door, drops her shorts, squats and whizzes right long with the traffic.

I don't know if it was because In all my 29 years I have never seen a girl answer the call of nature whilst in nature, or that she would do at roadside what I would go behind a tree to do.

Just when you thought you knew someone, you marry them and a whole new person walks out of that chapel . . .

Hey,lol,when you gotta go,you gotta go :). Ikkins

When ya' gotta go, ya' gotta go. Suggestion: keep a nice big cup in the car so that doesn't have to happen again.

~~~Eagle Girl~~~

---

in defense of your bride, holding your urine for more tha 20 mins not only doubles the amount og bacteria in the urine, but slows blood flow to the heart by 20%, and increases chances of getting a uti, which means no sex for a week. besides, men pee all the time on the side of the road, what's so different about a woman doing it?

~Ravaan~

dude you shouldnt condemn her for that . . you should be sayin " wait let me get the camera" . . . it things like that that makes people unique . . . and its somethin that you ll always remember too . . . so chill out and learn to laugh
josh

Yea, I know the feeling. My wife took a crap along one of the interstates in Tennesee a few years ago. Daylight, lotsa traffic and everyone honking thier horns. Wanna trade?

lol . . . . wait 'til she starts farting in bed.
-bk-

if u had to go really bad and there were no trees would u go?
~sk8r dude~

soemtimes when you gotta go, you gotta go.
~DarkAngel~

Hey dude ur woman has guts! Lol

omg dude that hilarious, i would be so embarresed, should,ve just drove off and let her be the next to the rode peeing with nobody around driving off down the highway,

Sounds like youve never been camping . . . . where else do you think we'd pee? And isn't it a bit of a double standard to be amazed at a woman relieving herself on the side of the road and not to even bat an eye at a guy doing it?

Just goes to show you: you can never know everything about anyone except yourself.

whoa. your wife has a great sense of humor.
KamikazeX

your wife is my god

I Need To Get Something Off My Face

I have a mustache.

This wouldn't be so bad if I were a guy. But I'm not, I'm a 20 year old female.

I'm fairly attractive and I know getting rid of it would boost my self-confidence 1000%, but I don't want to do something that would leave a chemical burn, nasty odor, or some other gross/painful side affect.

I'm also concerned about how hard the "stubble" will be to get rid of.

one word: electrolysis. :) hope that helps:)

Bleach it and the guys wont care. I am a guy btw

Shave it, use a little water and maybe some soap. Or wax it
MO

I'm 16 and i've got one too. i'm female also. i use nair hair removing cream. i have had no problems with that whatsoever, it leaves no burns or redness. you should try that. if you're a bit nervous then you can try it on a small bit of your arm. good luck

NAIR! Or go to a beauty salon and get it professionally waxed.

May I suggest lazer hair removal? It is permanent, and painless. Look into beauty therapists in your area that can do that for you.

Dont worry-just shave it of and keep using immac-this makes your skin really smooth and non-hairy. I sometimes use it and its really good and not painful at all. Good Luck!!

get it profesionally waxed. & don't believe that b.s about how shaving makes it grow back faster. how does cutting hair makes the internal mechanics of follicle production grow faster. it's just an old wives tale. it only feel like it's growing back faster b/c you get stubble. honey just WAX it
~Gambitgirl~

Wax it!
~gagirl~

Seriously, just Sally Hansen (Nair) it off. It doesn't grow back thickly, and its painless

Dude you sound HOT

treatment is probably the only affective treatment for ur problem, however, it is expensive and won't guarantee a result, also, its well known that it can leave tiny but visible holes on the surface of ur skin. Waxing leaves stubble, the only real option u have is to learn to accept that beauty is from within.

Not That Kind Of Gas!

A couple days ago I was about to take my 4-year-old nephew to the park when I realized the gas tank was empty.

I simply told him that the car had no gas and we couldn't go. I proceeded to go inside and saw that my nephew wasn't behind me.

When I went back outside to get him, I confess that he had his butt pressed up against the car and he was straining as hard as he could. When I asked him what he was doing he told me that he was giving the car gas.

I have never laughed so hard in my life.

That is soooo cute!!!! :)

Aw..that is adorable. Now I want your nephew. Can't I have him? *steals*
~die-AnA~

I wish my newphew where as sweet as that

Aren't four year olds great? Thanks for making me laugh!
~@Cazz@~

LOL!!!! AHAHHAHAHAHAH . . . wow . . . brilliant . . .

---

snort kids!
~Gambitgirl~

Wouldn't it be great if cars actually ran on that stuff? We oldies could be on the road constantly.
`Gramps`

that is so funny hey but can you do they are all so cute at that age

lmfao, Tell your nephew that he made my day . . . I don't think I laughed that hard in a long time

~Mara~

Kids are so funny!

Working Late

I called my wife to tell her that I will be late getting home tonight. I called my production assistant in the outer office and told him to take off now to start his weekend early. Now I'm waiting for my partner to leave.

I confess that I had a little accident sitting here at my desk about an hour ago. I'm not even going to stand up until I know that everyone else has left.

I have never been so embarrassed in all my 37 years.

at least you're not a girl . . . blood is more visible than wetness. You can claim you sat in something with wetness . . . but blood is harder to explain. Especially when wearing a white shirt . . . so I feel your pain, man.

Awww, that could happen to anybody. But I'm glad it was you and not me . . . and that I'm the one sitting here chuckling about it.

MollyMayhem

oooohhhh that sucks

um . . . haha maybe u should keep an extra pair of pants at ur desk for one. another thing, how the hell are u 37 and having an accident? i couldnt fathom . . . lol

tb

---

good way to handle the situation.

LOL

H

Awww . . . I feel for you. But you got to admit that is pretty funny. LOL. Don't worry about it. Walk it off, walk it off.

Good thing you didn't panic! Hehehe . . .

Raven

You handled it well. But at least you didn't get your period.

NOT what I was expecting after reading the title of the confession. I feel bad for you, I really do. That's gotta suck.

"Blueper"

Liquid farts are hell! And the older you get, the more you have to watch out for them! Now at least you're on guard . . .

`Gramps`

You handled the situation well. If this happens again, you should see your doctor about the problem. If not, hopefully you'll be able to look back on this and laugh one day - I already did!

Wyn

---

oh well don't worry about it. hold your head high and keep on walking! at least you're not a woman. you would have to deal with a more noticble problem EVERY month!

Oops! Sh*t(p*ss) happens? *_*

I've been there before. Hope it doesn't occur again.

I am laughing so hard after reading that, I just might pee my pants!! Sorry, that's not funny.

Farty Girl

I'm a fairly good looking 23 year old mother - without being immodest, I tend to turn heads, but what those guys don't know is that I stink!

I've always tended to drop farts quite easily, and I confess - I've always found farts funny, and I 'entertain' my young son with a toot and a parp here and there, until even he got sick of it.

Anyway, we agreed that every time mummy farted, she would put 50p in a jar on the mantelpiece. That was a month ago. We counted it up today, and saved £32! So I took him out for a film and a burger.

Its such a good way to save for our days out, we're going to keep emptying the jar every month - but I'd just like to say, about the ozone layer, I'm sorry . . .

im not even going to comment on this
K

God.

I will steer clear of the house with the ochre cloud over it.

LMAO, that last line made me crack up. If I did the jar thing, I'd probably be a millionaire by now. Farts have to be the best tension breaker in the world, they're so funny. I can't understand those people who find them unfunny—they haven't experienced the joy of spreadin' the cheeks apart. ;)
~~LilBaddy~~

Get a Hobby, thats just as entertaining!
*m

That's a novel idea!! I think I shall suggest this to my dad . . . .

haha! that's hilarious, but oh well, at least you get to spend time with your son, it's a good thing to do . . .
????® ?????

lmao . . . so cute!!!! you're a great mom with a great sense of humor!!!!

Feeding your son with your fart money . . . something very disturbing about that.

That's an entertaining little family group you have there. Just be prepared for the kids entry into the smelly world, as he follows your guidance and lets go at the wrong time. Personally, I always blame the dog . . .
`Gramps`

lol thats sweet. spending time with ur son. but if you dont like farting that much try Beano. but i think ur idea about the money.taking ur son out somewre every month is really sweet also :)

My mother is a VERY farty person too. Eventually everybody gets used to it.
B

lol . . . parp!
~Gambitgirl~

You sound like my hubby. He can let one rip at a seconds notice. I think hes 50% gas. The other 50% has got to be something heavy enough to keep his little body from flying into outter space :o)!! . . . Thanks for this giggle too!!

---

that is pretty raunchy . . Maybe you should take some gas-ex or something. It's offensive. I mean you seem pretty proud of it. Your fascination with your own bodily gases is disgusting. Seek help.

You pay, you play. This is what I thought the confession about being Ass-imilated was going to be about.

MollyMayhem

Oh That Smell

I confess, my husband disgusts me.

He waits until he can smell himself before he'll go take a shower, he rarely brushes his teeth, and he never changes his socks. His socks are so dirty, and so stiff from sweat that I swear they could get up and walk around on their own.

I have repeatedly asked him to clean himself up before but then he gets offended. This didn't start happening until after we got married.

I love him, but I can't stand to be within five feet of him.

Here's an old saying : "Distnce makes the heart grow fonder." Of course, Abraham Maslow disproved that one.

Loo

That is disgusting. How can you sleep with this guy?

I feel your pain . . . That is so disgusting, you should explain to your husband that you do love him, however you are repulsed by his unhygienic ways . . . Let him know how you feel whether you hurt his feelings or not. He should at least care enough about you to clean himself up.

So now is when you pull from all the other reasons you love him. Surely there has to be more important redeeming qualities that will allow you to let this one slide. No? Then tell him straight up just like you've told us, only this time make sure he understands what the consequences will be. Then be ready to follow through on what you've decided the consequences will be.

MollyMayhem

This is soo-o disgusting! And how do you guys ever make love? This must totally destroy your sex life. Well, there is just no way around it, girl — you're gonna have to divorce him.

He needs to see a doctor.

Move out. Tell him, "I ain't coming back till you get your act together and clean yourself up. I can't believe he doesn't get fired from his job. And if he doesn't have a job then divorce his ass.

You need a new man, that has better cleaning skills . . gross . . you're just as sick being in bed with him every night too! Ew. Brush your teeth especially . . . EW! Gross

Eww that's really gross, but if you love him then you should talk to him. Don't just say "eww you stink go clean up", but sit down and tell him how you feel.

~Czar~

At least you know he's safe from any other girls

men are like puppies, you gotta train him. only have sex with him after he has taken a shower. make him think . . . clean=sex. dirty=no sex. it's really a simple solution.

I used to work with a guy like this. By the time I met him, he had two teenage daughters. His wife dealt with the problem by becoming an alcoholic. As bad as he was, she was really a mess.

---

if gets acts all offended when you tell him he literally STINKS, then tell him his lack of hygiene & b.o. offend YOU. i mean, gawd, tell him he's making himself about as unaatractive as humanly possible & then withhold sex if that's what you need to do to get the man to bathe! EW!

~Gambitgirl~

Start doing the same thing. He'll come around. They always do.

First of all, he was like this before you got married. You just never noticed. So what do you do now? You're going to have to hit him over the head to get his attention. Declare your intentions, then start hammering at him. Sleep in another bed. Comment on the smell out loud in public. Spray disinfectant profusely around the house, letting copious amounts drift down on him. You've got a long row ahead of you.

`Gramps`

So unless he takes a shower, tell him no more sex and make him sleep on the couch. That's just gross . . .

~Cristi~

Over-Shaved

I hate shaving!

I don't understand why women are supposed to be totally hairless . . . None of us are! So we are all striving to look "female" when in reality, females have hair!

I confess, I haven't shaved in two weeks. Fortunately, my boyfriend is in the army and doesn't know about this new development. I guess I should shave before he gets back.

Still, I'm nice and soft and furry now!

---

all the more power to ya!

Malenkaya

LOL . . move to Europe, and you'll fit in!

LoL Good Job girl! I hate shaving too! As soon as my boyfriend left for the marines, i chunked the razor in the trash can!

---

dear lord thats gross. im sorry but if i had a girl id expect her to be hairless in the right places . . maybe thats just me, one guy, talking but thats how i feel.

the_captain

Im a furry girl too :)

Congratulations, you've finally figured out what every normal woman does when her man's away (and some when their guys are right next to them on chilly winter nights).

MollyMayhem

You get 'furry' after ONLY 2 weeks??????
~Kat~

Before women didn't shave. It's not until more recently in history that it became popular. Personally I do not like looking at my legs when they are hairy, but when winter comes hairy they go!

If your boyfriend loves you, then he will accept who you are, hair and all. I too hate these ridiculous rules that are placed on women in society today. I say GO HAIRY and LOVE it.

AMEN sister, I hate to shave my legs allthough I have to keep the pits hairfree. I go up to a month without shaving my legs in the winter. Its quite common I do believe.

---

i can see not wanting to shave your legs . . i shave my legs but its annoying . . but i do hope you shave your armpits . . that would be gross, excess hair can make them smell more you know . . .

Hey . . . no biggie. Face it, we're human. We're born with hair. What you do with it is your own problem. I don't shave much either. And for guys who think it's gross, you shave down there and then i will. keep it up girl. girls rule.

---

wait and see if he likes it. Alot of people do, if nothing else it provides a new sensation for him. If he doesn't like it, let him watch you shave.

I am soooo-oo-o with you on that one! It's such a double standard when guys don't have to shave! This plus periods, it sucks being a girl!!!

Guys hate hair because hair represents testosterone. Sure girls have hair but it just makes them look manly. it's the way of life

Not Gonna Do It

I am engaged to a wonderful man who takes care of me in every way he can.

I have a six-year-old son from a previous marriage, who my fiancé is raising as his own. He treats us both like royalty and I love him. He has no children of his own and wants at least one or two.

Problem is that he says if we have a child together that I WILL breastfeed it, no questions asked. Now, it doesn't bother me to see someone else breastfeeding, but the thought of me doing it turns my stomach and I'm ready to throw up.

I confess that there's no way in hell I'll EVER breastfeed a baby. I know it's better for the baby and the mother, but it's the grossest thing I could ever imagine doing.

I'm considering telling him that I don't want any more kids, when actually, I'm dying to have one.

My son turned out fine on formula. In this day and age, we don't have to act like a bunch of wild animals anymore.

I have no desire for leaky boobs and chewed up nipples. And I'd be going back to work, so it's not happening!

Here's how to make everyone happy: just pump your breasts and give your baby a bottle of your milk. Good luck to family.

Excuse me, act like a bunch of wild animals? And what do you call the act of mating? That's right, sex! Should we stop that aswell? Fine if you don't wanna breastfeed your baby, but don't you dare put other women down for wanting to do so, in public or not! (yea, so I'm against the american insanity with locking yourself and an inncoent baby in the loo to breastfeed. barbaric, if you ask me!)

It is a good idea to breastfeed at least when the baby is very first born because your milk will have needed nutrients. However. Not every woman is suited to breastfeeding and not every baby will take to breast-feeding. It is more important that you are bonding with your child which can be done in other ways than breastfeeding.

You should breast feed your baby. It's ok if you don't but try to make a deal with him like you'll do it on and off or something. Kids are smarter when you breastfeed them. I'm sure he'll understand your feelings.

Jordan

you know, they have breast pumps so you can "get" the milk in the privacy of your own home without "chewed up nipples" good milk for the baby, and healthy nipples for you, its going to be there you might as well put a use to it.

I've heard that breastfeeding makes you lose weight faster . . . . .

Tell him he can choose how to nourish the children he carries for 9 months. Do what you want it's YOUR body!

There is a much more serious problem than breast-feeding or not. This is a control issue and his complete inflexibility scares me. DO NOT marry this man - run the other way!

Can you say Selfish?????

I understand that breastfeeding isn't for everyone, but you sound like one of the most selfish women I've ever heard of.

tell him how u feel. you are the one who would be feeding it not him!

.:me:.

---

wow. You have to look at all the benefits of breast feeding. There are about a thousand. Your breasts are there to feed your child . . . that is their purpose. You need to talk to your man. If your unconfy with it, then ok . . . maybe you can use a breast pump.

I get the impression you haven't been quite as frank with him as you are here. I'm sure you realize you're among a very small minority of women who feel its animalistic and truthfully if you're using terms like 'grossest thing', 'ready to throw up', 'wild animals', and 'chewed up nipples' there's something amiss. Most people view it as a very loving, natural thing, a way to bond with their baby. Could be your husband has very strong feelings when he sees a woman breastfeed, his reason might be a little more selfish than just leaky boobs, which you won't be able to avoid anyway, until they dry up.

MollyMayhem

---

your choice- tell him he can breast feed the baby if he wants- men can be given the chemicals and hormons to do so now. If he wants it, let him do it himself.

Have I Broken It?

Since I was 10, I began exploring my body. I enjoyed it so much that since then I've been using unusual utensils to feel good, and "lost my virginity" to it.

Now 21, haven't had sex yet because I want to wait til marriage. My boyfriend is pretty strict with things like that and is expecting me to bleed on our first night

I am to embarrassed to tell him what I used to do and I bled because of it.

I'm afraid he wont believe me, and will think I slept with someone before him. Even though I didn't.

---

that doesn't count as losing your virginity . . .
Malenkaya

Not all women bleed the first time they have intercourse. The hymen can break playing sports and such. Explain that to him. The whole bleeding thing is old-fashioned and blown out of proportion.

---

tell him that you broke it putting in a tampon. simple as that.
Kawzmik

I think you need to find a new man if this one is so uptight all he worries about is whether you bleed on your wedding night. Before you marry this guy, think this through some more.

---

so tell him, he'll understand that when ur young you're curious. he's a guy, he should totally accept it or at least forget . . . . kind of.

---

so many other things could have broken your hymen . . . if he won't believe you then he doesn't trust you and you shouldn't be with him.

You don't have to go into details . . . besides whether or not a hymen is intact is NOT a thoroughly reliable test of virginity. If he is so distrustful maybe you should look around for someone else.
xx

---

tell him you went horseback riding as a little kid. accidents do happen.
the_captain

That's silly. Hymens can burst from many different causes. Riding bikes or horses, tampons, falling, etc. Some girls don't even have enough hymen to create blood to begin with. I wouldn't worry about it.

Have him talk to a doctor, its actually unusual for a girl to bleed alot her first time. Girls are much more active than they used to be and the hymen usually breaks through regular wear and tear anyway. Let him talk to a doctor to learn this and he wont be any wiser for it.

If your boyfriend is such a medieval prude that he want you to "Bleed" on your wedding night, than he'll probably be more horrified that you actually explored yourself than if you were "tainted". Dump him and find someone who doesn't have 12th century views on women.
~Blondie~

Well not everyone bleeds their first time. He's ignorant if he's expecting that. So don't sweat it. Your still a virgin

---

When I lost my virginity, I didn't bleed.

As you get older, sometimes your hymen breaks without sex. Maybe you should explain this to him before your wedding night to prevent any problems from occuring.

And you're sure he's never masturbated his entire life? Fore sure there should be more trust in your relationship or the marraige isn't likely to work well. I'd tell him, but if you just can't seem to come clean, tell him you rode horses as a child.
MollyMayhem

Something Else

I am sitting here, nine months pregnant with my first child, and was just about to confess something else. Now all I can confess is that my water just broke.

My husband will be here soon to take me to the hospital, and until them I can't move from this spot.

I am just way too excited.

CONGRATULATIONS!! go you!
kazz

---

congrads!

Very cool! GOOD LUCK!

That's weird . . . Congradulations though! =)
SafetyPinned

---

wow, that has to be some wierd coincidence

COngratulations! =) COme back and confess the other later hehe.
mudpuddleplayer

Eww!

Congrats! Good Luck! ;)

---

yay ur havin a baby!
.:me:.

What were you about to confess????

I sincerely hope she didn't mean her water 'just' broke and she's still sitting the chair with it. I wonder if we'll ever hear the details.

MollyMayhem

Congratualtions! I hope you had a safe delivery :-)

::grin::

. . her water breaks . . . and she thinks of DC . . . this place is just too addicting

---

hope you have a wonderful baby!!

Wahooooo! Congratulations to everyone involed! I felt all funny when I read that . . I didn't even feel like that when my baby brother was born 5 years ago. lol Aww.. I'm so happy for you!

Gasp - *Shudder*

This is very strange, but I really, really hate kissing my husband. I tell him it's because I don't like kissing while we're in public, but, seriously, I shudder at the thought of his tongue in my mouth.

He has developed a chronic case of "halitosis" and no matter how many times I offer him gum or ask him to brush his teeth, He just doesn't get it.

Have you tried talking to him about it directly? Sometimes guys are a little dense (no offese any guys reading this :P), just tell him, he's your husband, you should at least be able to talk about something like this. He probably doesnt realize and is wondering where the romance is . . he'll probably THANK you

---

Just say it!!

Try being a little more direct. A dentist could probably help him figure out why he has halitosis
MollyMayhem

Ok, that is disgusting. Tell him what you just told us, and for heaven sakes, tell him to brush his teeth!

---

you are married, for petes sake. if you can spend the rest of your life with him, you can tell him what the issue is.

I know exactly what you're talking about. I ride around with mine in the car with windows rolled down in the winter because of the smell. He's oblivious because he always asks me if I'm hot

---

Tell Him That!!!

---

just tell him - if he gets mad at you then you need a new husband all together!!

---

since you're married, i assume that you two are comfortable enough to discuss matters like this. so do the obvious thing and talk to him about it. it's not you're purposely hurting him feelings . . so he has some mouth disease. you'll benefit him and yourself if you tell him to get to a dentist . . . asap!

Did you not know this before you got married? He's your husband - TALK TO HIM!
Jainya

---

for yours and his sake tell him!!!. I have a work mate whose breath is actually left wavering in the air even when she leaves your personal space. My gosh i gag when its on me,, tell him for everyones sake
kiwi bloke

---

tell him as soon as possible . . . . wouldn't it be so embarrassing if you were told the same thing, but it was too late . . . . you kissed people all the time but no one told you until then?

---

beating around the bush with guys never works . . you have to beat the info into them. Tell him no sex til he takes care of his breath.

Lace

Just tell him! Youre MARRIED to this man and you can't even tell him his breath stinks? i bet he'll be grateful, most people don't even realize they have bad breath. he probably thinks your attraction to him is diminishing, im sure once you tell him its just his breath, he'll feel a lot better. PS. if your gonna be with this guy for the rest of your life, you have to be way more open about these things

---

Dont worry sweeite. My husband is the same way. What I did was, everytime he brushed his teeth, I would go in and brush mine, and then kiss him as romantically as I could. He would try to kiss me and I would say, "I want to brush my teeth first, care to join me?" He got the hint after about a month or so. Try that, or just tell him his breath is offensive. Good luck ;)

There is a GREAT line of products called therabreath - they are WONDERFUL. My ex-boyfriend had the WORST breath EVER and if he used it every day it was fine!

Between My Legs

One morning I woke up with an itching sensation between my legs.

When I went to the bathroom there were small ant size bugs crawling all over my nether regions.

I showered many times to get rid of them but they wouldn't go away. I though it was lice.

I was too embarrassed to ask anyone about it. So I went to my garage and sprayed my private down with raid and other bug repellents.

---

ooohhh bad move . . . those are crabs. you need to go to the doctor cause you can't spray raid down there. i think one of the only ways is to shave it.

chocobo

Eew, eew, EEW.

Ummmm, they were probably crabs. You should really see your doctor because bug spray wasn't meant to be sprayed "DOWN THERE"!!!!

OMG!!!!! OUCH!

Oh. My. God.

HAHAHA this has to be one of the funniest confessions that i have ever read! did it burn when u sprayed? i bet it did . . . hunny it sounds like u had crabs. u should have just gone to the clinic and gotten it taken care of.

tb

You used bug repellent on your 'nether regions' wow man that is not healthy see a doc about them and don't use the raid there again!!

That is oh-so gross! How could you not ask someone about it? Ew, you absolutely make me shudder. You must have absolutely NO hygiene.

Ew . . O_o

O M G how did it feel?

Sounds like crabs to me!

EEEW that is REALLY gross, I think you should see a doctor about that . . . or an exterminator . .

:S

Not too bright there are ya ohnie. You don't say whether it worked or not, my guess is no. You're infested. They're in your bed, your clothes and on your body. Just go see a doctor, like everyone else and get the right bug killer before you pass your little friends on to everyone you know.
MollyMayhem

Oh my, that is sad. Very sad. You really needed to go to the doctor rather than spraying yourself with Raid and other insect killers. You may have CRABS? You should really get that looked into and now that you've sprayed yourself with all that crap no telling what you've done. Ew I can only imagine the horror of spraying myself and finding bugs crawling on me, that is so nasty, get it looked into immediately.
PEACH

EWWWWWWWWWWWWWWWWWWww that almost made me sick . . . . . . and you should have shaved off your pubes. YUCK and bug repellent was NOT a good idea!
hunnybunny

Are you crazy! Why in the world would you spray bug spray there. You are lucky you did not end up in the hospital. If you are old enough to fool around then you are old enough to go to the doctor and get checked.

Grow up.

Only one way to get rid of crabs. Shave one side. Pour gas on the other side and set it on fire. When they come running out, stab them with an ice pick.

`Gramps`

COOTIES!

~Gambitgirl~

CHAPTER XI.

The Kitchen Sink

So now we come to the "everything else" category—the confessions that intrigue and entertain us but don't quite fit into any of the specific categories. The fact that they can't be categorized certainly makes them no less entertaining. In fact, given the responses these confessions elicit, they are some of the most entertaining to appear on DailyConfession.com.

So rather than attempting to summarize what you are about to read, let me just suggest that you take the phone off the hook, sit back, and get comfortable. Because just when you thought you heard it all, it's time to make room for what's circling the drain in the Kitchen Sink.

You Animal!

Throughout high school, I was shocked by my friends when they would talk about it.

I couldn't believe that they would engage in such activity. I even stared to think that maybe I was missing out because they were all doing 'that', and considered doing it myself (as embarrassing as it is to admit now).

I confess that until my third year of college, I thought that 'wild animal sex' was sex with animals.

I further confess that I lived a very sheltered life until I move away for college.

I was (am still) such a dweeb.

---

that's okay . . . I used to think that oral sex was just talking dirty.

Fitz_Freak

That's funny, but don't worry. I catch on to stuff slow too. My life was also sheltered. Embrace your dweebhood. I do. Not everyone needs to be a sexual dictionary! That's still funny though.

Mandolin

I did not know how humans reproduce until high school. I asked my parents once when I was 12, they refused to tell me. So don't be embarrassed. And my parent's attitude might explain why three of my sisters had children before marriage.

unluckyatlove

---

haha . . . that is way TOO funny . . . don't worry about it, some people take things literally all the time

sapphire

LMAO . . . I'd love to hear what you think 'animal magnetism' means . . .

DontKnow_DontCare

Dear G_d. Here's hoping some butthole doesn't make fun of you for admitting this. P.S. As in the case of the animals, I do not refer to ACTUAL buttholes.

MadEsquire

imagine if you had followed with what you thought the in crowd was doing. dolphins may be the only other consenting species.

artichode

ah the naievete of youth . . . lol

~Gambitgirl~

Hahahaha! *points at you* Ha!

tieyna

Eh, at least you didn't do it. Though, I can just imagine it: 'Hey, guess what I did . . .'

ElVaron

Are you trying to tell me it's not?

`Gramps`

It's ok I didn't know what 69 meant until last year.

Alya87

Your confession is sooo sweet lol. Its nice to know that ppl can still be innocent =)

Woody

I've heard of people who didn't even know what sex was until they reached college. At least you weren't that naive.

~Sage~

That's nothing to be ashamed about . . . being pure is good.

Flygtning

But It Says So In The Name...

I am recently married to a great guy. He was very understanding of my desire to wait until we were married before we had sex. He is also extremely patient with my lack of experience.

None of this helped too much when he explained after my first attempt, that, "...it has nothing to do with "blowing" . . . "

Three days later and I am still very embarrassed, but a little more experienced.

Some day I will be able to laugh it this . . .

You know there is a lot of books on this subject. Some homework really would have paid off.

I never understood that either. They should call it suck instead of blow. Things would be less confusing for the inexperienced. You will learn to laugh at it . . . . . I did. ;)

angelface

Well if you'd like to learn more, you can get books on sexuality (not just any sex book . . . one that helps and describes what to do), and if you can't get a book on that then you can go to websites where they also talk about sexuality. If you decide to do this I'd recommend this: get your hubby into this also, he might find some useful information that even HE doesn't know about. :) just my 2 cents!

Good for you because you waited until you were married. You have my respect.

—9—

You're so cute!!

xx

---

laughs awww ;) you must've felt so silly! this is the cutest thing ive heard in quite some time!

Kari

---

you know I was thinking about this the other day . . . Had me curious too. Maybe the 'blow' refers to HIS part in the endevour . . . not yours. *ahem* Just a thought. :o)

---

ha! At least you didn't injure him. The first time I pleasured my boyfriend I pulled the wrong way. He spent most of the rest of the night locked in the bathroom. You'll get over it ;) good luck!

Some 30+ years ago I made the same asumption. But hey, I didn't know either LOL. My husband didn't know, and he'd been married for 6 years to his first wife, and she never even tried. After we did that blowing thing he'd heard so much about, he wondered why all the guys thought it was so good; he thought it just felt cold. LOL LOL Live and learn.

Don't worry . . . . just laugh it off. You know if you blow it, an air bubble would end up inside your husband's penis. Its called Air embollism. Anywayz, have a great life together!

LN

So what do you think guys should think, if their girl really can "blow" - How did they get that way? I am sure he is in love with the thought that you can learn together, and probably has bragged about it with the guys . . . . . .

That's pretty funny . . . As for the inaccuracy of the name, "blowjob" is a more euphemistic than "suck job."

That is just too funny! true, the name does suggest some blowing action. But still . . . I can't imagine doing that!

You would be surprised how often that happens *lil smile*.
HitBear

LMAO . . . you actually blew on it? gawd, that is priceles. also, where have you been? i mean i knew what a blowjob was YEARS before i ever actually had sex. it was just common knowledge
~Gambitgirl~

Why is it that a man will take months when he's seducing a woman, but let him get his wife into bed the first time, and he wants the full treatment. Done right, "blowing" would be something you wanted to do, not something he asked you to do.
`Gramps`

So That's What Oral Means . . .

I confess: As a kid, I used to think that oral sex meant talking dirty. You know how for an oral report you have to get up in front of the class and talk? Well, in that line of thinking, I thought oral sex must involve talk.

Imagine my confusion when we learned in sex ed you could get STD's from oral sex . . .

don't feel bad. i didnt know what a hermaphrodite was till i was 16 . . . i was like the only one in my entire grade who didnt know.

hehe, bless ya, that's so funny.

LOL . . . this is why parents should NEVER, EVER hide any aspects of sex from their children.

Hahahaha! I thought the same thing until I was like 15 or so . . .

How cute.
~DarkGirl~

Ha Ha . . . thats hilarious

lol, thats funny. you have a good point though on that oral report thing . . . hmmm

Ha ha ha . . . my friend thought that too when we were ten . . . I didn't believe him.

Hahahahahahahaha now that's gunna make me laugh for a loooooooong time. Thank you :)

hehe when my dad would catch me talking about sex with my friends he would always say, "talking about sex for 3 hours doesn't make it oral sex!" I thought we were the only ones who had that pun!

MUAHAHAHA! That's hilarious! I've had similar experiences, though . . .

lol, i used to think the same thing! and i thought i was the only sheltered child out there . . .

How funny! Thanks for sharing that with us.

And i thought i was the ONLY ONE!!! You're not alone . . . . i was in the same boat till I was in high school . . . then foudn out what it really was!!!

Why I Pull You Over . . .

I'm a state trooper in upstate NY, and I have a confession: sometimes I pull over good looking women just to look at them. I'll tell them they had a brake light out, then I'd tell them to try all their lights, then say something like "it's working now" then let them go.

A friend of mine from the interstate patrollers also says that he pulls young people over sometimes because he likes the looks on teenagers' faces when they think their going to lose their license so soon. We've never done anything like taking favors of any kind from drivers, we're human, but like having fun too.

I don't think it's so cool to pull people over and lie about the reason. I'm sick of getting harassed by cops for lame excuses. Your job is to serve the state, not to get excited about scaring a bunch of high school children or drooling over girls such as myself.

Im sorry but you might think thats fun but its defently not the right way to go about it, esp the teenager part! Do you even remember how sensitive you were when you were younger? They dont need that extra stress! Talk about getting off on power trips.

I am so angry! Yes, I understand you are human bc this good looking woman is human too. And I want to trust the police. If the police pulls me over just to check, that's the right we have given you. It borders on abusing power. And piss off about 'your lights are not in order' when they are. That is also confusing ppl.

I suppose you have to do something for fun because it seems your type of people don't have many friends in the 'civilian' world to have fun with.

~rantgirl~

Just some harmless fun. I guess if you enjoy your job your will be better at it. I don't think you have to be a saint to wear a badge.

You like having sadistic fun. If you are ever talking with your buddies about how the public views cops, remember the terrified look on the faces of innocent people you've decided to have fun with, trooper.

I think this is a good example of why we all hate cops!

LOL . . . dude, that sucks! I bet you have people wiggin out and like chompin down on all kinds of drugs to get rid of them. LOL maybe you should look in their teeth next time. ha
faerie

That's all well and good, but stop using the siren when you're just going for donuts, okay?

Oh Great. My parents live in upstate New York. I'm a young and good looking female so I'll be sure to mind my manners the next time I'm cruising out to visit them in my nice 97 Corvette. Thanks for the warning!

I just want to say that I am a new driver and that is NOT funny. You get some sort of sick pleasure out of making young people all paranoid? I'm so glad I live in Canada
~DJM

That's the meanist thing I have ever read. I am a young teenager and my best friends dad is a popo. So you know what, if you want to be the pervert cop and go pull over women like me and just look at them be my guest, but one time you won't know it and you're gonna get in so much friggen trouble you sick perv.

I'm 20. In the past, I've had police officers pull me over for 'my brake light.' Let me tell you, it's the scariest thing to get pulled over by you guys. I bet we don't look too good being scared to death! :)

You have a special job. You are supposed to be an authority. People are supposed to look up to you and listen to you. You do stuff like this and wonder WHY so many people hate you guys. Geez!

Oh goody, you like to have fun. That makes me sooo happy! I mean, there's nothing like pulling someone over and scaring them to make life that much more wonderful. You guys are human too? Who would have thought? Hey, get a fun hobby, look at porn, eat pizza. But stop practicing cruelty and sexual harrassment. This is why people don't like police officers.

Just A Trim

I'm 24, a single male. Two years out of college with a great job - life is great!

I just bought my first electric razor. Being completely fascinated with it, I throw out my "low tech" razor and celebrated the new, high tech marvel. It does it all; shaves, trims, is battery powered – simply amazing.

About an hour ago I was looking in the mirror and noticed the little bridge between the eyes was becoming more pronounced. I want to get rid of my growing "uni-brow", so I whip out the New Braun and selected the trim blade.

I had a plan.

I started with the center and moved towards the right eye. Next, I returned to the middle and raked towards the left. I stepped back to review my handiwork, and noticed that it was just the slightest bid uneven. No one else would notice, but I would know.

So I made a small adjustment with the trim blade and re-evaluated. Damn! A little too far the other way. No problem. With trusty blade in hand I even them up . . . almost.

By the time I realized just what was happening, half the brow was gone from atop either eye! I sport a striking resemblance to Britney Spears now.

I have stopped. I have sat down. I have returned seven times to the mirror to assess the damage.

I have called sick at work for today. All my years of college never prepared me for this. I look like an idiot – hey wait – I am . . .

---

hahahhaha that is so funny! you could always just draw them on w/and eyebrow pencil!! (Joking) just say you got drunk and passed out at your friends party and someone nailed you with the razor!

Thats why you always have to pluck your eyebrows, never shave.
~SaL~

---

one word: PLUCK! if you need to, get an ice cube and numb the area. Never pluck more than one or two hairs at a time. That way you wont have this happen again. If you want to get technical . . . take a pencil, line it up with the bridge of your nose up towards your eyebrows. You shouldnt pluck PAST where the pencil sits, that should help.

LOL!!!!! I bet this will get Pick-Of-The-Day! Wow i did that too once with my brows (only tweezing and i'm a girl) and i ended up with like a strip over each eye. boy did that suck when the stubble grew in . . .
Killi

ROTFLMAO!!!!! This has got to top all other confessions I've read. LOL From a girl, it's VERY nice that you cared enough to trim your unibrow, however, tweezers usually do the trick better than razors . . .
IndianPrincess (my dog is looking at me so funny b/c i'm laughing still!) :)

It's ok man. Just realize that most people are too busy looking at themselves to really care, and all will be better.

that is the funniest thing i have ever heard. good luck on growing your eyebrows back out. maybe you could use some eyeliner to undo the damage. lol :P

mina

LOL! oh, that is FUNNY! I'm sorry but it's just SOO funny . . . . that's what happened when i cut my friends hair . . . . she looks a little butch now . . . .

This is sooooo funny!!! Hahahaha

Hehehehe that is so cool . . . see a beautician for a wax next time - even Britney Spears knows that you shouldn't shave your eyebrows.

~Starlover~

ROFLMAO . . . you poor thing . . . but geez that's really funny. I kinda did the same thing once, except it was with my fringe, I decided one day to give it a trim. It was wet and after cutting it to the desired length, I noticed that it wasn't quite level. So I gave it another trim, and it still wasn't level, and another and another. By the time my fringe dried, and I'd finished trimming, it was only about 3 cm long from my scalp. It looked so awful, and everybody kept commenting on it and staring. Oh well . . . the things we do . . . *sigh*

Hahahaha . . . Lol, Dude thats kinda funny, it'l grow back soon though so don't worry!!

~?~sam~?~

LOL!!! It all started in fun and games . . . when good razors go bad! don don don

[Casey]

Poor guy! You have my sympathy. I've done the same thing with my moustache!

LMFAO!!! I did the same thing . . . in 7'th grade!

i'd rather date a dude with no eyebrows than one with mono-brow. LMAO you poor

Tried To Get My Dog . . .

Last night I tried to get my dog high on marijuana. I lit up my pipe, and breathed in a huge lung-full of smoke. Then I grabbed Molly, our English Springer Spaniel, by the nose, put my lips around it and blew.

A lot of the smoke just came out of her mouth, but she breathed some of it in I believe. I did this about three times and I became pretty high myself.

I couldn't tell if Molly was high but she became really hyper, ate all of her dog food, and then chewed on her bone for about two hours.

hilarious, some people might consider that cruelty to animals but those are the same people who eat beef and chicken and wear leather. I think it's just plain funny

Hahaha!!! Dude. Your dog was totally stoned. Showed all the typical signs of an animal that's high. LOL I have done that to all of my friend's houses that I've smoked at that have pets . . . so far, I've gotten high dogs, cats, rabbits, guinea pigs, a snake, and a rooster.
IndianPrincess

People like u don't deserve to have animals

I know the animal rights activists are going to be screaming, but we did that once to my cat, we put half a gram of hash in her food (quite alot for a little cat) and she went mad it was really funny, she also ate all her food, and then slept for nearly three days, my sister (it was her cat) still doesn't know what happened.

That's sick. I hate when people do that. Your pets are NOT asking for blackened lungs thankyouverymuch. Grow up!

Hey! I used to have a english spring spaniel named Molly. Maybe its mine reincarnated. Anyway, its all good, not like you gave her anything majorly dangerous. Me and my suitemates try to get my hamster high and drunk all the time.

I got a frog stoned once. We put it in a jar and blew smoke in it till it was wacked

~ali~

LMAO! My friend has a dog who eats his stash on a regular basis . . . and apparently if u breathe it into a cat's ear (where all the blood vessels run close to the skin) the cat gets stoned. Heh heh heh . . .

If you care anything about your dog, dont do that again. How would you feel if she died? That could happen . . .

That is sooo cruel!!

Dogs love pot! As much as cats love catnip. I did the same thing to my dog. Didn't know if she liked it. But then every time I toke up she'd come begging!
CoolJerk.

I worked at a small animal hospital, the sheriff's dept. brought in a dog who was tripping big time. The owner have given it a hit of acid. It was really pitiful. The owner ended up on disability before he was 30 because he was so messed up and died a couple of years ago. What a future you have to look forward to. Mess yourself up - LEAVE THE ANIMALS ALONE!!

---

getting an animal stoned is just CRUEL. just b/c you like getting stoned & acting like a doofus doens't mean your dog wants to. we hardly understand what effects pot has on the human brain, much less a canine. you might actually be hurting your pooch
~Gambitgirl~

---

lmao! I went to my friends house for dinner & he smokes ALL the time. Well he asked my boyfriend to pass him the mull bowl, I was right near it so I said I'd get it, I picked it up and started walking over to him, his dog went totally mental at me . . . barking and nipping at my feet!! He then proceeded to smoke his pot, with the dog sitting on his lap. When he asked the dog if he wanted another, he'd look at the bowl of pot, then at the bong then at my friend, LOL! It was hilarious! I've never seen a dog so hooked on dope in my life!

You monster! How dare you abuse your poor dog like that??!

Oy Vey!

I have an interesting uncle. When I was a kid, My uncle would take us kids to baseball games, coach our little league teams. He even taught us Yiddish – well, he taught us the words but never their meaning. We're Jewish and I spoke some Hebrew, but Yiddish is a Germanic derivative and I only picked up a few of the words.

I am now married and last weekend we had a family gathering bringing together folks from my side of the family to meet my wife's family. My wife's grandmother was there and through the course of my conversation with her, I found out that she spoke Yiddish.

To impress her, I began reciting the Yiddish that my uncle had taught me many years ago. Well, the look of shear disgust came over her face and she let lose a Yiddish diatribe and stormed off.

My uncle, who was not only in attendance, heard the whole thing, and was doubled over laughing. I asked him what the hell I had just said. It was something to the effect of ". . . her 'female anatomy' looked good enough to eat."

Thank god my wife has a since of humor.

Can't say the same for grandma.

Still not talking to me.

Write her a nice apology letter, telling her you were trying to make her feel welcome and be a part of the family. She will get over it, and elderly people are impressed when a youngster writes a well-written letter. Oh, make sure you hand write it neatly, e-mail and typed letters don't make as much of an impression.

LMAO omg thats funny. Well not for granma perhaps. It is funny tho. I knew a guy who had a simular experiance but s/o was teaching him Spanish. Except for excuse me they subsituted a more colourful expression inviting the person to have unnatural relations with their mother. It didnt work out well when he bumped into the huge Mexican later that day and said what he thought was Excuse me =)

Lmao!! Nice job.

HAHAHAHAHAHAHAHAHAHAHA!!!!! That is absolutely precious!! Poor grandma!!! I only wish I could have witnessed that, hahaha!

---

heh heh oy vey!
-Grumble-

I can't believe a grown man would do something like that. You are so naive! But you're not alone. There's a lot of innocent children who have been taught "words" by their relatives. Of course, they have enough sense not to use them later on in life.
`Gramps`

Oh god, that's funny . . . but disturbing.
Mr. E

I love it!! That is priceless. Of course your uncle has issues teaching dirty phrases like that to kids, but now that you are an adult . . . no harm, no foul. I am still laughing hard though.

ROTFLMAO!!!!!!!

Your uncle is twisted. I never speak foreign words unless I know what they mean or I'm asking for the definition.

---

rofl! omg that made me spit out my toast . . . dude, you seriously need to get back at your uncle!
BlueMonkey

That's so damn funny, thanks for sharing.

dirty old men certainly do instigate some interesting situations . . . . my tummy now hurts from giggling and thus ends the night!
j

Thats very very funny! I wish I'd been there to see it.
Phatboy.

I Did It For A Bet

I was in the pub, I'd had a few beers, you know how it is. Gary bet me £50 I wouldn't do it, so I did. I had my manhood pierced. I now have a shiny silver Prince Albert ring dangling from my old chap. I rather like it.

Funny thing is, Gary never coughed up the £50 and it actually cost £55 to have it done.

meep, doesn't that hurt?
Malenkaya

Gary, if you're reading this: COUGH UP!

i bet girls won't.
BlueMonkey

So how do you get through the metal detector at the airport? And what do you do if it gets caught in your zipper? And do you take it out for sex? Do they let you walk around with it hanging out now? So much I don't know . . .
`Gramps`

haha . . sounds like lord of the ring dings if you ask me! :)

I think Gary owes you your money or you owe him an ass kicking.

---

i don't think you should be worried about the money, he's paid you back enough already! it makes sex so much better! by the way, happy infection

---

Ewwwwww. Ouch.

At least you didn't get breast implants like that other guy that made a bet with his friend . . . . . except . . . .uh . . . . but he got like $1500

LMAO @ "gramps" . . . He always knows just what to say . .

I think the breast implant guy got $50000 for it

---

jeepers!! did that not hurt like hell? i think you might not be so keen on it when it goes septic . . .

Well you just kissed goodbye forever safe sex. And as for getting it done OUCH!

You musta been a ring-a-ding-dingbat to have that done. Goodness, it must have hurt! –

Gidget

Yuck, why . . . nevermind I don't want to know, what I do know is that you can't "preform on yourself" for 2 - 3 months till it heals . . . that sucks.

---

holy cow . . . you got a whole punched in your wang on a bet for only 50 quid? yikes! i might pierce my nip for 5000, but only 50? no way!

~Gambitgirl~

Wow that's pretty cheap compared to here. It's like 80-100$ here. I hate piercings but some girls are into them. Be careful for infection, and be very Careful during sex because it's easier to catch something . . . . But Wouldn't the piercing rip a condom? Uh oh! There's a lot you should have considered before you did something on a bet.

~*LaDy~*

Lights Out

The confession from my point of view:

I was standing at the bar counter to order coffee (???), leaning on "something" when WHACK! The lights went out . . .

From an on-looker's point of view:

I was EXTREMELY drunk, went to the bar counter to grab another beer. I waited too long and put my arm up to lean on something, not realizing it was a short, angry bald man's head . . . .

WHACK! I was floored by a man half my size!

Ha ha ha now that's funny!

Umm, heads up? Sorry, too late.

---

this was the best! . . webmaster poease make it a keeper!

---

simply priceless!

---

okay . . . u would have to be very drunk to do something like that . . . i feel sorry for someone like u!!!

---

lmao! i bet being short gets real old for that guy . . . heh heh.
KamikazeX

---

lol!my mom did that! she was in a theater and she was getting yup, (it was really dark)and she reached for a handrail and accidently started rubbing this dudes heead! he looks up and says, 'oh i liked that, i thought it was a head massage' while my mom turned like BEAT RED!;)LoL!;)
~sTARdANCER AKA chels

LoL!! That's hilarious! Never underestimate the power of a short person ;)

Short, angry and bald! That is a lethal combination. Funny story.
~~~Sparrow Boy~~~

WOOO!!!! tHAT was priceless! Gives a new meaning to heads up, huh?

Disgrace To Manhood . . .

I confess I have betrayed my masculine instinct. I live with my wonderful girlfriend and for some reason - could be out of love for my her - I have started to put the toilet seat down afterwards! Sorry brothers!

YES!! You rock! We girls LOVE you for that! Thank you! I'm sure you are appreciated.

its ok. it happens to the best of us, I too have recently fallen.

awww thats sweet . . . . i wish more guys were like you!
~]kittiecatjen[~

Put it down FIRST! Sprays 20 ft when you flush. Toothbrushes, towels, shower curtain . . . . . all that crap! Yuck! Watch Oprah, its a sad and disgusting thing.

Aww sweet . . . Here's a doogy treat for you. Now you go and fetch me newspaper. LN (sarcastic and not impressed)

Better whipped than lonely, right?

i am not ur damn brother!

As long as you retain authority over the remote and the searing of meat with flame . . . I don't have a problem with it. It's one of those not-really-important things that could interfere with harmony in the bedroom, he he. Wait . . . you're withholding info: are you holding her purse while she shops? Do you?!

Next thing you know, you'll be reading Cosmo. You are on a slippery slope my friend.
HitBear

Bah! If girls are too lazy to put the seat down when they have to go and expect us to put it down then phooey to them . . . put both the seat and cover down so they have to do some of the work at least.

it's funny how putting the toilet seat down is viewed as the ultimate male sacrifice
~Gambitgirl~

Sell out!

THAT IS A DISGRACE! I solved that dilemma long ago by putting down both seats! This bit about it being ready for her to sit down on is garbage. Make her lift the lid too! Best part is, she can't complain! After all, you're being neat about it.
`Gramps`

hey man, it's cool . . . I do it all the time - but to prevent the dog from drinking piss water.

Oh man . . . extra lovins for you!

EVERYONE should put not only the toilet seat down, but also the lid. Every single time you flush, tiny particles of your urine or feces spray into the air. NOw think of all the things you use in the bathroom. Towels, bar soap, and your toothbrush. Happy brushing if you don't put the lid down!

Hey man, I wouldn't worry about it. Speaking as a 20 year old guy raised in a household of three females of varying ages, I know the consequences and terrible wrath which rain down upon you, should you forget to put it down. However we can be obnoxious to them in other more "tolerable" ways . . . heh heh.

yay! perhaps more will follow . . . .
memyselfandi

That is not a disgrace! My boyfriend does that for me too! :o)
-Shorty-

Aww!!! That's auctually relly sweet and shows your man enough to REALLY love a woman! Way to be!
knhw

The Only Reason

I confess: The only reason I'm going to college is to find a husband.

They don't call English 101 "Marriage 1" for nothing . . .

what century are you living in? thats a waste of money and really stupid. this confession really depresses me..

Um . . . ya, okay. Good luck with that. (I geuss)

That's funny, I'm in college, and I found my fiance' at work.

LOL . . . at my school there is a motto: "A ring by spring or your money back." heehee, hasn't worked for me yet, hope you have better luck than I am having! :)

You are joined by the majority of your peers. Sure, we may say we are career oriented, but let's face it, when push comes to shove how much comfort are you going to get from a career with a soulless company.

So you're going to college for your MRS. degree? Focus on the ones who are Juniors, Seniors, or grads. A lot of the Freshmen and Sophomore men still have "issues".

Plenty of women go to college just for that reason. I just went for my Phd., so I won't need an Mrs. poetic-chaos

going for your M.R.S degree huh? do you know it's the 21st century? ~Gambitgirl~

Awwwwwww you're getting an MRS degree! At least you're honest . .

At least you're not bottom fishing. But aren't you too young to get married yet?
`Gramps`

That's an expensive way to try and find a husband don't you think? Maybe while you're there, you'll learn something about common sense too.

Drunk horney frat guys good luck!
short_nsweet

I guess that is a good place to find them. But, I've found that you can't find them when you are actually looking.

Ahh, another person working on their MRS.

Don't be surprised if you don't find anyone. College guys are there to party and learn, not to find a wife. Grow up, learn a skill, go to work, and don't worry about marriage until you are 25.

Going for the 'ol MRS degree. The only problem is most people that marry at 21 get divorced.

Biker Girl

At my university, almost everyone bikes to class. I'm a freshman who, like many other students here, had not touched a bike since fifth grade. As time went by, I gained confidence in riding . . . as well as a bit more.

Here's the thing — I've discovered that leaning forward slightly presses my lower regions in just the right way, making my rides to classes VERY enjoyable! Although I haven't quite orgasmed while riding, I almost always get to class very much aroused. It's getting better now that summer's here and the seat's warm . . . ;)

For some reason I don't remember liking bike riding so much as a kid!

I just wanted to say more power to ya. oh yeah to the webbie where do you find such great graphics? You seem to have one for almost all confessions.

Duncan The Stout

Hehe . . . nice;)

Sounds like a ton of fun, i would ride more than is necasary!

Interesting - Is this common I wonder?

I do the same thing! Ever straddle the arm of a couch? Heavenly!

If it worked that way on an exercise bike, there would not be a single overweight woman in the world.

firstly if you do it for long enough(and you can now cuz schools out)maybe you could have an orgasm and seconly your a little sick

You go.

HAHA lmao . . . that is great . . . lol i'm gonna have to dig out my bike and give it a try . . . hehe shhhhh!

LOL good for you I have to try that

can't wait to try

That is the most amazing thing I have heard all night!! I am impressed.

couches don't vibrate! what on earth are you talking about?!

Well . . . thats . . . interesting. Ciao babe.
~*GhettoBooty*~

Power be to you, everyone needs something like that.

Well, that's not something you hear everday, but hey if it gets you off . . .

Growers Delight

I have over 150 marijuana plants growing in an isolated safe location. When September comes and my precious little girls are done growing I get about 3.5 to 5 ounces of dope per plant (or more pending how I chose to grow the plant).

Let's do some math and I'll show you what I'm getting to here. I'll even round the average DOWN.

3 x 150 = 450 ounces

450 ounces divided by 16 ounces per pound equals 28 pounds.

I sell a pound for $2800 or $3000

So average of $2900 x 28 = $81,200.00

81,000 dollars = average of what my extra earnings have been yearly for the last 5 years.

I also have a real job too. $$$

So thank you Mr. Government for being so god damn intolerant of drug substances that you give little old me the chance to make so much money every year with the black market you created.

Having so much $$$ in cash and not in the bank is a little freaky at times cause you don't know where to put it all . . . but that's why I turn it into diamond rings and new cars.

That's awesome!! Watch out though . . . you'll get investigated because they IRS or gov't is gonna notice all your stuff and wonder where your gettin the $$$

knhw

---

i am building a new house, want to wire me some money, i only need 2 years of your extra income to pay off my house,

sits and waits obediantly

I hate you!! Not cuz you're doing somethilg illegal, but because you're making so much money doing it!!! I hope they catch your ass and put you to jail!!!

That's . . . great. I never had much respect for potheads and drug dealers . . . until now. You've turned my life around. Hell, why don't we all just go to our own little isolated safe spots and grow 81 thousand dollars worth of weed a year? Oh, I know! Because it's illegal, that's why. And it's harmful. I'm glad there are people like you to keep our children doped up all the time. Now they don't need to do anything except sit around the house all day, smoke your weed, and eat chips. Oh, and let's not forget when they go out and kill each other to get more. Or when they get caught with it and go to jail. It's nice to know that America's future's well-being is in the hands of such a stand up citizen like you.

don't count your chickens before they hatch . . .
Christina

ya, my wife and i do the same thing. how the hell else are ya gonna get ahead in this f***** up world? being canadians, (meaning GREAT pot) we average about $20,000 every 3/4 months. great set-ups (we have people all over that were in with) allow us to do it free and clear! have fun and save too, we all get old and ya can't do this forever.

Careful cupcake. Have you watched the news lately? With the restructuring of the FBI, they have passed new legislation allowing them to monitor the internet more extensively. There is a very good chance one of them just read that. Do you think that if they contacted the owners of this page and demanded your ISP that they would say no to them? Me neither. Yes it is an invasion of privacy, and no they don't care.

Way to go brother. If I had the balls and a place to grow it, I'd be doing the same thing. Weed: God's way of saying "lighten up".

Be careful- but the way I see it as is, if it grows on Earth, then it's ok to smoke! :)

You are truly a god! If you lived anywhere near me you could be my new friend :) and I'd pay ya! LOL — keep them plants growing bud :)

In this state growing more than 5 plants is a felony. If you get caught you'll never have a chance to spend that money. Also, you could get shot by a thief over the plants, or the money.

hook me up man . . !!!!!

My god i want someone from the govenment to see this. I;ve wondered for most of my life why they don't sell the drugs themselves- thereby enabling them to control the whole world. hmmm i think smoking this stuf is just making me paranoid . . .

Dude, keep that shit coming and send some through Wisconsin . . . we're a bit dry up here right now.

Hooray for the enterprising farmer! Just watch out how you spend that money. Cash transactions over a certain size have to be reported to the government. Of course, you could always pay taxes on it. Call it gambling winnings. Then you'd be home free.
`Gramps`

Sounds more like a lobbyist's ploy than a confession. Anyway, I agree. Pot should be legalized.

rock on with your bad self. if i had that kind of money i pay off all my student loans & buy a new truck. but whatever makes you happy
~Gambitgirl~

He's A Jackass!

I was at my son's hockey game last weekend with my wife and her friend whom I hadn't met before that day.

We were in the stands and the referee made a bad call against my son's team, I stood up and yelled, "You're a jackass for making that call . . . " or something along those lines.

I sat back down after my tangent, and the woman with my wife leaned over and said "That jackass is my husband."

Guess I made a bad call too.

I don't think they should let parents watch their kids play sports anymore. You are a prime example of why.

---

whooops! maybe you should have found out a little more about your wife's friend. lol

~h~

That's when you should have replied, You have my sympathy. ;-) But really, it's a game with children, calm down and act like an adult. You probably embarassed the heck out of your son.

---

lol whoopsies LOL

---

haha oops! maybe next time ull keep ur mouth shut. u never know who's gonna be around. and hey, if it makes u feel any better at least u didnt say/do anything worse!

tb

---

i would have thought that your wife would have told you that she was the refs wife, so i think you souuld try and blame her.

I think the jackass is that woman for saying that. She could have just kept quiet and let it go. Like you knew.

Oh no!!! I hope you apologized. Sure, you were caught up in the moment and made a mistake, but you can at least try to make things better. Everyone gets loud at hockey games so I'm sure she'll understand, although it will probably take her a little while.

Daisy

Oh no . . . you're one of THOSE parents?? My son plays hockey too. There is nothing more annoying than you. You take all the joy out of this game for the kids and for their parents watching. You, my friend, are the jackass.

"Blueper"

The problem with situations like that is that the best reply doesn't come into your head until the next day. Work on a good one in case either one of them ever mentions it again.

`Gramps`

Instructions: Place foot in mouth. Keep it there.

Now, I'm guessing that your son's hockey team is not playing for a title, so maybe you shouldn't have made the comment. Especially if it was at a KIDS game! Parents wonder where language comes from . . . sheesh.

Bwahahahaha!!! God that's funny!!!

Lord Elwood

Oops. Hopefully she has a sense of humor and forgave you.

You're the one who sounds like a jack ass. What is with you blood thursty parents who go to thier kids games and shout obsenities and threaten coaches and referees. These are just kids! It's just a game! They should be having fun, not worrying about thier daddy killing someone if they lose the game.

Sounds like you and he have a lot in common, being jackasses and all . . . .
don

A father is supposed to set a good example for his child. Do you think it's
OK to yell the word "jackass" in public, under ANY circumstances? I don't.

DOH!
~Gambitgirl~

Missed It By This Much

It is February 17th and I just remembered I missed my eleventh
wedding anniversary.

It was February 14th.

How could I forget that Valentines Day is my anniversary? I'm just a
wee bit of a loon.

My bigger problem is figuring out if my wife also forgot (doubt it) or
if she is just counting the days until I confess my stupidity (most likely).

hahaha how cute! ur in big trouble. just tell her that ur sorry and it slipped
ur mind, however thats no indication of how much u care about her. but
then, did she do anything for the anniversary? if not then dont beat urself
up too bad. next time ull mark it on the calander wont u? lol good luck guy!
tb

Hmmm . . . a wee bit? Perhaps you should rethink that one . . .
*~*princess*~*

um, yeah. i think she's just counting the days until you realise that you
missed it. you are in trouble matey
~h~

ok . . . your wife remembered. Im almost positive she did. I mean come on, how could you forget. Its your anniversary! And Its also on valentines day! I think you really messed up. You should go apolagize to your wife because she is probably really hurt right now.

~*~Littleone~*~

The only thing she's counting the days to is when those divorce papers come through!

~~Mia~~

There's a billboard near my home that says 'Make her forget you forgot'. I dont remember if it's for jewelery or a hotel, but boy, you better get moving on the groveling ;)

LOL . . . you will be paying for this for some time, I bet. If you haven't already gone out and bought her a FABULOUS present, I hope you do it now . . . before you confess your stupidity. I'd be a lot more forgiving of a husband that came bearing jewelry. :o)

"Blueper"

She's counting! Confess, and take her out for a lovely dinner! Quick!!

Buy a gift, and hang on to it. Then, if she finally says something about it, you can then present the gift and ask her what she got for you. Hey, I've learned a few things over the past 46 years . . .

`Gramps`

Yup . . . you're dead. Might as well 'fess up now and get it over with. (Did you at the very least get her a nice V-day present?)

Eviltwin

Most likely the second one. See how long it takes her to mention it to you, and when she does, act like you have been testing to see if SHE remembered and pull out the gift from the closet.

Jainya

Don't let her punish you! You're not her son OR her dog.

---

you better buy her something really nice!!
kim

Give her a card and then tell her how upset you are that she forgot your aniversary. Tell her you have been counting the days but just can't take it anymore! Wedding anniversaries are not just for the women you know. Two people were married. Don't give in to that sexist Bullcrap!

HA! god, how hard is it for people to remeber dates LOL. i know all my family's birthdays & anniversaries, it's not that hard to recall something like that . . . but for some reason no one else in fmaily remembers that stuff. my sisters are always asking me when my birthday is & i'm like, "Hey I remember yours! What's your problem?" guess not everyone is as date-anal as i am heh heh
~Gambitgirl~

Women's Bodies

I am a straight 23 year old female. And I confess that I find the female body to be beautiful.

I enjoy looking at nude women on the internet because I think they are so beautiful and sensual. For some reason, I also like seeing two nude women's body intertwined or caressing.

And I'm not talking about lesbian porn, because porn web sites are absolutely disgusting. I mean it in an artistic and natural way.

I also find that these things turn me on, but I would never want to experiment with another woman because it doesn't sound very appealing to me.

I totally know how you feel . . . I am straight as well but I think that we feel this way because the female body is generally so much more beautiful than a males'. I don't think it means anything in terms of our sexual preferences.

you know what? there's nothing wrong with u, and i don't think that ur a lesbian.i'm a female myself, and i find the female body much more interesting than the male's because of all the perfect curves it has. as for having sex with another woman, i'm sorry but i just think it's discusting. it's against my religion(not that i'm very religious , but still)and i think that it's also not normal. i don't mean to disrespect any homosexuals, but i just don't get why a female would sleep with another female when there are millions of guys out there!!!

um . . . ok ill just respond w/my phrase of the day: "whatever rocks ur socks"
tb

Are you trying to convince us that you're not gay, or yourself?

"It is unthinkable that God would do wrong, that the Almighty would pervert justice."
(Job 34:12, NIV)

Totally understand what you're talking about. I'm the same way.

I think you are a very confused uhm bisexual? lesbian? Who cares, but you are confused. If you were 100% straight the imagery wouldn't turn you on. Straights are attracted to the opposite sex, bisexuals to everything and gays to each other. Not that titles really matter though. I think you can be straight and appreciate a piece of art work, but without uhhh enjoying it the way you are.

Your appreciating the human body for the beautiful and complex machine that it is. Enjoy!

COMING CLEAN

I enjoy looking at naked men, it doesn't mean that I am gay! Oh wait, I am gay!

---

i'm a 22 year old straight man and i feel exactly the same; women are gorgeous.

dw

There is nothing wrong with that - the female form is a beautiful thing. And it does not mean that you are lesbian because you enjoy it. I enjoy it to, and I am female!!

---

there is noithing wrong with how you feel. I"m sure most woman feel the same- I know I do. The female body is very beautiful.

I have to agree. I've just gotten into photography and I'd love to take pictures of a nude woman. Not porno, though. I find the female body to be absolutely incredible, though. It appears to be so frail, and yet it has this incredible ability to give life. I don't find you strange at all. ^.^

There is absolutely nothing wrong with appreciating the female form while being "straight." The female body is softer and has more curves, which is undoubtedly more sensual than the straight lines of a man . . . Not to say that a defined chest and stomach on a man is not also very hot, but I completely understand what you are saying, and agree in many ways!

Womens bodies are beautiful, so are mens, taking time to appreciate them is not lesbian or sexual at all, you can love beauty in a pure way. We all can. To label it as gay would be like saying those who look at a beautiful field of flowers are inclined to have sex with the flowers.

Hey, she didn't say it turns her on, she said she thinks it's beautiful! There's a difference. Not EVERYTHING involves sex!! People's minds these days are lost in their hormones and rotations around a single activity.

Raven

B Line

I'm a bus driver been one for twenty years.

The other day, a young well endowed lady bounces up the stairs to my bus, showing an abundance of cleavage, she showed me something which I took to be a bus pass.

But now I must confess, she could have been holding up a piece of toilet paper, for all I noticed. My eyes were buried somewhere in her lovely bosom.

And the sign reads: Beware of Big Beautiful Bosoms Bearing Bus Passes.
MollyMayhem

And if every one who hopped on your bus showed a bit of cleavlage you would probably have no job . . . . Ha Ha

---

Ha! It only what every man would do! i think thats hilarious!

I'm trying that.
~Rina~

Don't worry about it. In another 20 years, you'll be able to check both passes and bosoms.
`Gramps`

---

thank god for big boobs lol
~Gambitgirl~

Ha, all women are probably getting on buses for free!
H

Heehee, that might've been me. If it was, that wasn't no pass, I flash my library card to male bus drivers while wearing distracting shirts. I've saved enough so far to buy some new shirts to show them. :}

Rexie

I've done that before. I woore a push up bra and a very low cut shirt, man I was about to fall out of it but anyway, I showed the bus guy my school id. Heh he wasn't looking at it though. Yeah good times . . .

Lunatic

I Remember Feeling A Slight Breeze

I am completely dumbfounded.

I am 26, married - no children. I was just surfing the web while my husband was at work and I came across one of those cheesy Spring Break sites.

Lo and behold, who do I see a photo of - Me! A full on beaver shot.

I was wearing a dress on the dance floor at a club in South Beach and my dress fliped up to reveal - well the fact that I was not wearing any panties that night. This was four years ago. I never knew anyone was taking pictures.

I'm not sure if I actually like my special moment of fame on the internet or if I am feeling completely crushed and violated.

Weird.

You may have to walk away from this one, unless you're willing to spend a lot of time and money tracking down and litigating the culprit. And the moral of the story is?

MollyMayhem

XI. THE KITCHEN SINK

Gasp.

lol omg if you were wearing a black dress I saw that picture!

ummm try writing the site and telling that you are embarassed and to please remove the picture. Can't hurt to ask.

Lessons to all! Cameras are everywhere nowdays. Unless you own the house, they could even be in all rooms of your home. Big Brother is coming!
`Gramps`

She's going to have to walk away, #1 because the court has ruled many times that you don't have a right to privacy in a public place. Ask the girl who sued the producers of "Girls gone wild" and lost on those very grounds. So, if you don't want pix taken of it, don't wave it around in a public place.

oh lordy. you should contact that website & tell them to remove that picture of you. i'm pretty sure that by law they can't display that photo of you after you've expressly told them not to
~Gambitgirl~

Uh-Oh, I saw that one too. Look at it this way, it is a spring break you will never forget! And, oh yeah, next time wear panties.

. . . uh, if you were wearing a denim dress, I think I saw that one. Or the black one mentioned above. Thanks.

Molly, Molly, Molly, loosen up! BTW what was that sites adress again?

hey, there is no such thing as a "special moment of fame" on the internet - it's out there till the end of time baby! at least your grandkids will know what a party girl you were :)

You forgot to tell us at which website the picture is posted show your hubby when he gets home and maybe he will like the idea and dcide you should have your own private photo shoot. Just make sure you keep the pics so they don't end up on the internet.

Lmao

I had some friends - that was there entire mission this past spring break. (to capture on film 100's of females flashing) they tried, but got nothing!

Trading Places

My wife and I were going to a party the other night. The invitation said "Cocktail Attire".

She thought it meant that I had to wear a suit and tie. I thought I could get away with a jacket with no tie. I told her I didn't want to wear a tie because I wear one all week and they are so damned uncomfortable - they must have been invented by women. I was adamant about not wearing one.

She said that's the same for pantyhose, must have been a man that invented the damn things. I said they couldn't be as uncomfortable as a tie . . . so she proved her point.

She said, forget the tie then, wear some pantyhose!

She ran to the store and bought me a pair and told me if I didn't wear the tie, wear the pantyhose. So I did, and she wore a scarf tied tight around her neck.

I tell you, they felt kind of erotic, holding everything in place and the silky smoothness rubbing against my thighs when I walked.

But by the end of the night, she was right - I was ready to pull them off. But I didn't tell her that!

That's right. Never, under any circumstances, admit that she might have a point.

MollyMayhem

---

this marriage sound frickin' hilarious. stay together for a million years LOL

~Gambitgirl~

Good for her - and you. Glad to see at least one man knows what we go through. She should have made you wear heals when you got home, too!

The stuff we have to do to look good, OMG!

I completely agree with you!! I can't even wear turtle neck sweaters because I can NOT stand something around my neck. I think you were right in standing your ground . . . but pantyhose? I don't even want to think about my boyfriend in pantyhose. If I do . . . I might never have sex with him again.

"Blueper"

---

exactly . . . but the question is . . . how did your wife feel witht he tie wrapped around her neck-

PWB

Ever think she might have bought them a tad too small?

`Gramps`

---

you think a tie is uncomfortable? try being on your period! or try wearing 4 inch heels, panty hose, a strapless bra, and a thong. i have no sympathy for men like you.

---

you dont need to tell her. she knows what they feel like.

kafer

---

lol women are always right!

Wet Girl Walking

I confess that in my dorm at college, we sometimes like to play pranks on each other.

So the other night, while I was in the shower, my friends thought it would be funny to steal my clothes and towels and take them back to the room.

When I got out of the shower and realized they were gone. Since I live in an all girls dorm, I figured it would be ok if I just ran down the hall back to my room.

So I turned the corner out of the shower room and I ran smack into one of our starting (and very good looking) football players, who was there to pick up a girl he was taking out. I stood there dumbly for about 5 seconds, frozen in shock, and then I ran like hell.

As if things could get worse, my roommates locked the door, so I had to stand outside naked and wet until they let me in.

I confess I have never been so embarrassed in my life. They are going to get a major pay back for this one . . .

---

wow id be pissed!! haahaa yeah it was funny but i mean . . locking the door?!? its bad enough that you had to be naked in front of ppl running down the hall but then to be stuck outside your door naked . . . haahaa and cold . . !! haahaa it is quite funny but id to have that happen to me . . howd that football player react? haahaa maybe hed change his mind and want to take you out instead..haahayeah get your roommates back good!!!

---

hahaha ur gonna have a hell of a time topping this w/out someone getting hurt or really angry. good luck. i think this was a little much though, if u wanna know the truth. next time u see mr. football guy just smile and wave and act like its no big deal. haha did ur roomates know that u ran into him? haha now im getting too curious so i bettr wrap this up. good luck!

tb

hahahahahahahaha!!! couldn't you have just locked the door on your bathroom?
@h@

lol..thats sooo funny, Id be embarressed too
~*~Littleone~*~

Hahahahahaahahaha! I am laughing out loud right now! Oh that is a really funny story, but I'm sorry that you had to go through that. All I can say is that you should get revenge!

You should have ripped the shower curtin down, that's usually what people around here do when someone does that to them.
namegirl

Oh you crazy college kids . . . . .

Cute college trick. Just don't kill them. Your only consolation right now is that they're probably sleeping with their eyes open.
`Gramps`

Oooh, stories like these make me not be able to wit for college. Hee Hee Hee Hee . . . PS I'm just a puny highschool freshie.
Default

That just made my day! Thanks for the laugh!

Tell them they went too far and ruined your reputation. Tell them your moving to another dorm.

In Need Of Anatomy Lessons — Wacky

My significant other and I had unprotected sex last month when we were a bit on the wasted side.

My buddy and I were smoking some bud the other day, and I realized I couldn't remember my last period. In fact, I couldn't remember ever having a period at all.

I called my significant other and told her I was afraid I was pregnant. She was very angry and told me she disapproved of my marijuana use.

I don't think I will be smoking for a while, considering I am a male and I believed myself to be pregnant.

---

haha omg that cracked me up so much THANX 4 MAKIN MY DAY

---

hahahahahahaha

I am laughing so hard! That stuff had to be laced with something! I've never thought that I was the opposite sex when I've been smoking.

---

lol that has to be the funniest thing ive ever heard!! ROFL!

OMG, That is quite possibly the strangest, funniest thing I've ever heard in my life.

Lmao! Heh, that was good . . . thank you for the laugh.

---

lol, yeah that's probably a good idea . . .

"No more soup for you!"
/Seinfeld.

BWAHAHAHAHAHAHAHAHA!!!! Thank you . . . . I really really needed that laugh . . . . . whew . . . . .

OMG! That's great. I had to read it a few times before I got it. But, after I finally figured it out, I was laughing my a** off. But yeah, that might be a sign that you need to get a grip on your habit. Thank heaven you're not pregnant though! That would have been really harmful to your "baby."

LMao LMAO!!!

That was the funniest thing I have read in a long time . . I think you need to put that stuff away for awhile . . or even better forever

HA HA HA HA HA HA HA HA HA HA HA*gasp*HA HA HA HA HA HA HA HA HA HA HAAAAAAAAAAAAAAA
~Gambitgirl~

You have issues.

Possibly the funniest confession I have read on this site!!!

Abandoned Car — Abandoned Brain

Six months ago, I began to regularly drive to work.

For years I had taken public transportation. About two weeks after I began driving every day to work, I was leaving work, was walking to the garage and saw "my bus" as it went past.

I completely forgot I had driven that morning, ran after my bus, got to the stop in time and boarded the bus for the 10 mile trip home. I realized too late, when I was almost home, I had left my car in center city.

I began to laugh out loud on the bus and everyone looked at me like I was an idiot.

I confess that I was, especially that day!

That is hilarious!!! That also sounds like something I could've done.

It is so true that old habits die hard . . . I hope your car was in good condition when you finally got back to it. :)

As humans, we are creatures of habit, good one though.

lmao that's so funny and just the kind of thing i'd do! It could be worse, i know someone who did the same, except she didn't remember and reported the car stolen!!
~iylya~

I did something similar. One time in college, where I usually walked to school, I drove, and that afternoon I started walking home, and was almost there before I remembered my car at school.

LOL, that was way too funny. Reminded me of the guy who forgot he had moved and he drove home to the wrong house!!!
~Sarah~

Why would you drive when good bus transportation is available? Not an SUV, is it?
`Gramps`

heh heh sounds like something i would do
~Gambitgirl~

that is hilarious!
sal

They're called Brain Farts. I get 'em all the time.
Qwerty

Hey, once you get yourself into a set scheduel, it's hard to break it. I probably would have done the same thing if I were in your shoes.

That is soooo hilarious

Aww, I hope it worked out okay.

Haha . . . I've done something like that before. I don't know too many people who read the owner's manual for their car though. Don't feel too bad.
The Angry Midget-

Sure I Would

I confess that my secretary just showed me her pierced nipples.

I didn't ask to see, I didn't even know that she had them.

I am happily married for seven years and haven't seen any other women's breasts for over nine years. I have worked with "Lisa" for ten years, she is twenty-nine.

Today she came into my office and was obviously excited. We have always had an honest, open, platonic relationship. When she asked me if I would like to see her nipple rings, I said, "sure!", thinking she was just kidding.

Next thing I know, big as life, two erect nipples with silver rings through them were staring back at me.

I confess that not only am I embarrassed, but I also feel that I have in some weird way "cheated" on my wife.

Just guessing, but I'd bet these rings are new acquisitions . . . I had virtually the same thing happen to me. I'm a guy, my female sec (for 7 years) got a boob job. She was so excited when she came back to work, the first thing she did was offer to show me. There was nothing sexual about it, she was just showing off her new goods. Bet that's the case here. Don't worry, no harm - no foul

Maybe if you tell your wife she'll understand. I don't think she would be too understanding if you did go all the way. I like the phrase look but don't touch if you have a significant other.

Shake it off. Don't think about it again. This situation isn't out of control . . . yet!

you didn't cheat on your wife, but the path you can go down now is very steep. You can gain speed or put on the brakes.

I wouldnt stress it to much if you werent really interested in seeing them. All the same though I wouldnt tell your wife.

Ah, you're all right, man. Just as long as you don't touch her in any form or fashion, you'll be fine.

aéíóú

You didnt cheat. Unless you were lying to us that you were just joking when you said Sure then you are innocent. You might have a chat with your secratary though and let her know that that was not appropiate.

Well now we know why she's 29 and just a secretary.

Liked it, huh? Window shopping is not against the law or your vows. It just proves you're still alive.

`Gramps`

Everyone gets off the hook once in a while. I had a secretary give me a big red lipstick kiss on the my bald spot for my birthday a few years back - I'm _still_ hearing stories about that one! I'm NOT recommending this for you, but I told my wife about it, and she thought it was hilarious.

Face it - Lisa lives in a world where that's not a big deal. It's not like the world you and I live in . . .

Don

As long as it doesn't go any further, dont bother telling your wife. Even though I say I'd want to know if that happened to my boyfriend, Id rather be in the dark — ONLY if it never happened again AND if it never went any further. Oh, and consider getting a new secretary!

Don't feel bad, you did less than someone who went to a strip club and that's not cheating!

You did absolutely nothing wrong. But if you feel like it's somehow cheating on your wife, then why don't you tell her the story of what happened? I'm sure she'd forgive you.

at least you feel bad, but you should tell lisa you were only joking. many complications can come from this, including lisa telling your wife. you'd best explain everything to her- end rant

noo you didnt cheat. She sounds a pretty skanky.

Dont worry . . . you didnt cheat on your wife. Even if you might have feelings for this girl now, you arent cheating. Just dont act on them.

Wish someone where I work would do that . . .

-_DANMAN_-

i think getting your nips pierced is GROSS. seriously makes me want to cry just thinking about jamming a piece of metal through the ta-ta *cringe* but i have tattoss so what do i know LOL~

Gambitgirl~

Five Second Rule

I'm sitting in my dorm room, killing time before class, reading confessions and eating a bag of cheddar goldfish, when I suddenly sneeze and drop the just-opened bag face-down on the floor.

I just opened it. I'm a poor college kid. I can't afford more food.

I confess, since nobody was around, I ate every single goldfish! Ugh, and I haven't cleaned my floor in ages . . . .

I'm sick.

Hey, Goldfish are dry food. They are less likely to retain germs that food like ice cream or fish fillets . . . especially in five seconds. We've all done it.

I'm a broke college kid too, and man that is sick. Just think of all that crapt that's on that floor!

Hey . . . . haven't we all done that at some point?:)
B

My brother was in the army and he told me that one time he dropped his spagetti Bolognase in the mud - he picked it up and ate every last bit. So to you my friend, you are far from disgusting. My brother is disgusting it was full on MUD. He said since joining the army nothing really turns him off . . . The Australian Army that is.

---

so what? i eat anything that falls on the floor. no big deal.

Uh no, you're right, there is a five second rule. Well okay - its a three second rule, but sometimes it takes longer to pick all the little buggers up so its a five second rule only if you also blow on them (to dislodge and send to the wind any hair, dirt or otherwise unknown cooties). Don't sweat it.
MollyMayhem

i totally understand, rules like that dont apply anymore if you are in college :) hehe as long as it doesnt fall directly in something nasty

Ok, I confess, I do it too. God made dirt, and dirt don't hurt, right? But if you haven't cleaned your floor in awhile, I hope you at least dusted them off or something. I keep my floor clean, and my shoes never go on my carpet (I know it's clean, I bought it for this room and I clean it about once/week) so, as long as you're ok with eating a little dust/sock fuzz, ok. But thanks for makin me laugh.

I've definitely done worse and definitely didn't worry as much as you do . . . bank on fire

Oh my god that is something I have done and would do again . . . it's ok as long as it isn't a messy food, that is a little disgusting. I understand I am a poor college student as well.

you're a guy aren't you typical.

5 second rule if it's in public, 10 second if it's in your home . . . after all, it's just your germs at home!
~Gambitgirl~

As long as nothing stuck to the fishies . . .
`Gramps`

Never Got One - Never Will

I've been pulled over by cops six times in my life, and never once got a ticket. The reason because I'm a cop too. The truth is I'm just as guilty as the next guy.

I confess, it's not fair at all. I really don't feel guilty at all about it though.

---

dont feel bad. i know alot of people who benefit from being a cop or being related to one. moi included.

~~ReD~~

Do you think that you can't kill anyone by speeding just because you're a cop!? It really pisses me off when I see a cop run a red light also!!

---

hey, you put your life on the line for a bunch of ungrateful jerks on a daily basis. you deserve some perks.

My father has talked his way out of every single ticket he's ever been pulled over for. He's going to teach me, hopefully I will be in your shoes without the free ride.—

misanthrope Panda

No way will you ever get a ticket! My ex boyfriend's dad is a cop, and his mom worked with all the cops in our city. They even made the address that is connected to his liscense plate the cop shop . . . every time, all you hear is, "who do you know in the police department?" and you know everything's good.

---

share and share alike. why dont u spread the joy and spare some poor sap a ticket. barring of course if theyre drunk or under the influence of anything.

tb

I hate that . . . . cops don't get tickets, yet you are breaking the law just the same as the rest of us . . . . . we have to pay fines, and waste our time at traffic school while you don't suffer no consequences . . . . . . cops are pompus a-holes.

Ah, but the egotistical, stick-up-the-arse, unfair, do-anything-to-get-someone stereotype of cops isn't fair, either . . . oh wait, yes, it is.

---

so whos benefit was that for? wow, im impressed and shocked . . . not.

Your probably the only guy not to get a ticket because you're a cop, you are in fact quite lucky that you don't have to make "sultry eyes" and flash a bit of leg or breast like us women to avoid a ticket.
~Jen~

Do you also . . . steal from the drug dealers you bust, lie while under oath during a trial, rough people up that you encounter during your day, and cheat on your wife with hookers, eat free meals wherever you go . . . stuff like that?

But I thought cops were supposed to pull over and cite a designated number of off-duty cops per month . . . .

Thats because youre a pig and think you are above the law.
Potrick

Don't worry dearest, I'm sure the LORD has a special place for you . . . in Hell!

I understand that you do deserve some perks, but I don't like they way you flaunted it on here. No one's impressed, it's not like we didn't ALREADY know that you never get a ticket for anything.

This isn't a confession, it's just confirmation of a well known fact. Every job has its perks, but I sure as hell wouldn't want your job just to avoid tickets. Live high!
`Gramps`

yes it's not FAIR & it pisses me off! my sister used to be a cop & one time she got pulled 3 times on a six hour car drive for driving like mario andretti. she also drank a beer while driving on that same trip, got pulled & didn't even get a warning b/c she always wore her police department t0shirt with the logo on it & flashed her badge. i swear to god, i thought she was going to kill someone one day & i'd wind up on Hard Copy or some shit as the sister of the "Drunken Killer Cop" . . . it really annoys the shit outof me that some bad cops break the laws all the damn time & then turn around & act flippin' holier-than-thou & bust someone else for doing the exact same thing

~Gambitgirl~

Rewind — Reverse That

Today, I was cleaning up my apartment before some friends came over.

In one hand, I had a glass of water I wanted to empty into the bathroom sink. In the other was a pair of shorts I was gonna put into my dirty clothes hamper.

So I walk into the bathroom, empty the water into the hamper and put my shorts in the sink, then walk out of the room.

About five seconds later I realized my mistake.

I feel like an idiot.

That's not bad. One time I was clearing the table after supper and I scraped the leftovers into the sink and threw the forks, spoons and knives into the garbage.

Malenkaya

Lol I have done something like that. I took out a glass and a carton of milk, I put the glass on the table and poured the milk on the floor. That same week I tried to turn the tv on with a calculator.

I do that all the time! I'll put the remote in the fridge, and bring the milk out to the living room . . stuff like that. It's like . . . dyslexic thinking or something.

.:Allikator:.

Awww . . . . . . shit happens . . .

UniSoL

Some people just weren't born to multitask.

---

u and i should start a club for people like us. i've done more things like that then i care to remember . . . but don't worry, incidents like those make great stories to tell others once u get over the embaressment of being stupid enough to do them.

Oh man, I know how you feel! I did the same thing in school yesterday. In one hand I had my wallet and a glass of water, in another I had my empty plate. I put the wallet in the glass bin and the glass in the food bin and I walked out carrying my plate. My friends burst out laughing, which then made me realise my mistake and I had to take my wallet out of the glass bin which was full of water and orange juice. Ugh!

Ha ha ha. That's really funny!

I do that kind of stuff all the time. I often put the cereal in the fridge and the milk in the cupboard. I think that why I am poor I keep having to buy more milk.

Hmmm . . . there are two major things that indicate the mind is aging; one is forgetting what you're doing . . . I can't remember what the other one is . . . oh yea, its doing what you did . . . . lol

---

thats like when i sit down with a drink in one hand, remote in the other then continue to drink the remote and change the channel with my glass. didnt work . .

o_O

At least you realized you did it.

~Crow~

---

hehe it happens. A friend of mine eating nuggets took his coke and emptied it on his food when he meant to pour honey on them.

Jac

LOL, I once did something silly like that. I had chips and ice cream out for some friends, and when I went to put them away, I put the chips in the freezer and the ice cream in the pantry. The pantry sure was a mess to clean up a few hours later.

Welcome to my world. This happens on a regular basis to me. I just put Tylenol in the fridge the other day. And where did my glass end up? Yep, in the medicine chest. Wait until you try answering the phone with the remote.

---

one time, i was eating. i wanted to put salt on my food and take a sip of my drink. i picked both up and did it wrong

---

do you walk around with a tampon behind your ear saying, "Now where did i put my pen?" sorry, old joke

~Gambitgirl~

It's going to get worse. You're going to start walking into rooms and forgetting why you went in there. You'll show up at work on a holiday. You'll call the kids by the wrong names. In fact, you'll run through a list including the dogs name before you hit the right name.

`Gramps`

This Is My Gun — And This Is My Weapon

My husband is a former police officer. He sleeps with a gun in a safe under our bed.

Last night the burglar alarm went off and he jumped out of bed, popped open the safe grabbed his Glock 23 and proceeded to crouch and cover the entire house looking for the breach (I love his police jargon!). He shut of the alarm and came back to the bedroom where I was laughing hysterically.

He asked what was so funny and it took about five minutes to calm down enough to confess that the image of him with the gun, crouching, naked as he walked out the door was too much – I then explained that if he did find anyone, they would burst out laughing and give themselves up to the gun toting, naked madman without a fight

He didn't find the humor in it.

I love him anyway.

I knew a guy who did something sililar but with a sword replica. And there really was a burgler. The burgler ran away. I think the sight of a naked sword wielding madman was too much for him to deal with.

Lol . . . great confession.
BlueMonkey

This is cute. I think one day he'll laugh about it.

---

heh heh, that made me laugh out loud. Thanks for the laugh.
Malenkaya

LMAO!!!!!!!! That is so funny!

Hehe, lol . . . the mental image . . . lol . . .

~*M*~

---

lol come to think of it, it's a good strategy, distracts the attacker and gives u an extra second or two of action.

Jac

---

rofl! ha ha ha . . . . *falls off chair*

BlueMonkey

You're pathetic. When your husband responds as he has been trained, protecting his family without concern for himself, all you can do is laugh at him. You had better hope he responds the same way each and every time the alarm goes off. With all the home invasions, you should be happy you have someone to protect you.

BOB

SOOO FUNNY!!

^Evie^

---

oy BOB, laugh a little, might help that stick slide out of your butt easier. confessor, that was great! unfortunately i got a mental image of my cop brother-in-law doing the same thing. ewww todd naked ACK!

~Gambitgirl~

Hey BOB, get a freakin sense of humor.

Excellent. I like playing Rambo when I'm at home too.

Phatboy.

So did he leave two tracks or three?

`Gramps`

Could You Please Sit On A Towel

If my roommate walks around naked one more time, I might kill him. I'm not prude or homophobic. If he has to go from the bathroom after taking a shower to his room in the buff, no big deal.

If he come out of his room at night, slouches on MY couch, and watches an hour of TV, then gets up and fixes his dinner - and eats it – all while being completely naked, I take exception to that.

The worst is when his girlfriend calls, and I can tell what they are talking about by his "response" . . . I guess I should consider myself lucky that when the wood strikes, he take his naked self into his bedroom.

I must save some coin to be able to afford my own place. School is tough enough without having to deal with "naked guy".

You should leave some Nudist Colony brochures on his bed or something.

Get yourself a video camera and threaten to put the pictures on the net. Or send them to his gf.
`Gramps`

Inform him that you don't appreciate seeing his junk all the time and ask that he at least throw some shorts on. If that doesn't work, snap a polaroid while he's wandering around sans clothes and tape it to the front door of your house/apartment building. Em-bare-ass-ment will cause people to change behaviors in a hurry.

---

that's gross . . . just tell him something, i am sure he'll understand. and if he won't just take a picture, copy it and put it all over the school, hehe-hehe just kiddin.
~CAPOEIRA RAT~

That is so gross, tell him to stop if it bothers you that much.

Evidently he is not a minder reader or he would have known a long time ago that his nudity bothers you. All you have to do is tell him. He is assuming that you don't care because you haven't protested yet. Don't let a couple of loose balls ruin a friendship.

^Evie^

You have every right to be thoroughly disgusted. Are you sure he's not gay, or bi, and trying to impress you? I would wonder . . .

You have one weird roommate. I feel bad for you but have to admit that I laughed my ass off at the visual, as well!

That is so rude of your roommate. He should have more respect.

---

hey you pay 1/2 of the rent you get a say in what goes on around there. just lay it out for him. tell him his strutting around naked & rubbing his bare crotch on YOUR sofa is pushing the limits of roommate acceptance & it won't kill him to throw on some boxers. if he doesn't like it he needs to get a place by himself where he can be naked all the time . . . eating in front of you naked? EXCESSIVE

~Gambitgirl~

It seems like to me, he's trying to tell you something. Maybe he wants to get down with you, so he walks around naked to see if you will do anything to him sexually. I mean im a guy, and i will never walk around naked in front of another man, not in less i wanted something from that man. Got it.

GOod

---

just pretend like you're gay and he'll stop

Go gramps, and I agree with the talkback that was in the daily newsletter thing- point at them and go "are you getting smaller???" Maybe one of those things would do the trick.

~Cristi~

lol call the police, its illegal to do that last time i heard.

som

Why don't you print all of the above responses for him and hand them to him. Also you could make up a sign to post on your gate or window/door, saying "Beware of Nudist".

While At Home . . .

My best friend's husband doesn't wear clothes when he's at home.

I have known "Shelly" all my life. I love her husband, but I confess that I still can't get used to going over to her place and seeing him naked. It's nothing sexual, he has never come on to me and he does "shift" when he notices that I am turning red.

I guess it's just weird and after three years of seeing him like that, you'd think I'd be well over it by now.

Tell "Shelly" that you don't feel comfortable around him.

Jelly

---

well . . . there's nothing wrong with being shy. but if he refuses to put clothes on when you're around maybe you go over there when he's not home. it is his house after all.

rachie

WTF!?!? Um, thats just gross. Its her husband, not yours, he shouldnt expect you to be okay with him being naked around you AT ALL. Sorry, im not one for exibitionists . . . not like that, anyways.

~*MG*~

So, you really think it's nothing sexual, even when they're aware of how uncomfortable you are? It's called exhibitionism. Wise up. (Before every one blasts me, yes, some people are less inhibited than others, but most people will cover if they are aware they are making others extrememly uncomfortable. Exhibitionists enjoy this reaction.)

Can I suggest you ask that they come to your house from now on?

You'd think.
MollyMayhem

No way would I accept seeing some nekked dude besides my husband.

Um, I dont know what 2 think . . . hehe
bad thoughtz

Every time you see him at home, point at "it" and giggle. Soon enough he'll be covering up for you . . .

Thats gross. Just because he does that when he is at home does not mean he should do it when he has guests at his home.

Someone who doesn't even have the courtesy to put on his clothes when you are visiting . . . .hm. If I were you I'd seriously question whether or not he wants me there.

Have you ever actually talked to "Shelly" about this? Try sitting down (just with her) and telling her how it makes you feel. (It should be an easier subject for her to bring up with him.) Tell her that it makes you uncomfortable and you can't come over if he's going to be naked.

Tell "Shelly" that you don't fell comfortable when he is naked. Maybe she will talk to him and then he will put on clothes when you come over?.

Worse Than Men

I am married, my wife is the "bread winner" and I work part time at home. Yesterday I went to the annual "cookie party" the ladies in or neighborhood throw.

I confess, women talk more trash, and talk in much more detail about sex than guys ever do.

Women are pigs! And I loved being one of the "girls" and talking trash with them!

You should hear the stuff we talk about when men aren't around! Teehee!
~*~PRPrincess

Women may talk more trash, and you may love being part of it, but I'll bet you didn't match them in the trash talking. Chicken! Did you share the conversations with your wife?
`Gramps`

Count your blessings,for you are truely a gifted man.
Arkie

---

maybe they will get you an apron, and a cute dress, so you guys can do bake-offs

---

That's why all my good friends are men. (From a woman.)

That is why I enjoy hanging with guys more than girls. Girls are the meanest, nastiest, cruelest people on this earth. Sometimes it makes me sick to my stomach that my own gender is so gross. And then girls wonder why I have only 2 female friends. Well, girls, maybe if you'd stop being so critical and stop talking behind our backs I'd let you in my life a little more.

you are right . . . women are the biggest trash talkers around. I am a woman and I always find it much more comfortable and pleasant to be around men.

shhh your not supposed to let every other man know that we r just as bad as them if not worse.

hahahaha yeah us girls like to gossip =) i think the main things we ever talk bout is who we hate and fine guys

Good for you bro. Just for the record though, everyone knows that women are much more piggish than men.

Men do it, too, you guys just usually don't speak of your sexual conquests beyond "she was hot so I nailed her."

Yes, we women are more fun than guys!

LMAO!!! Nice work! Now write a book about it and us guys can say their pigs instead of the other way around, i knew it!

isn't it fun?

Damn, you're on to us! :D

xx

LOL, it takes you fellas so long to figure that shit out . . .

A Hole In My What?

My wife of 11 years has several body piercings.

This past weekend we were "downtown" and walked past the tattoo and piercing shop she has patronized. She told me that she wanted me to get a piercing, a "Prince Albert".

I told her sure (I was feeling no pain at that time). The wait was over an hour, so we decided to go to another bar, but only after I promised I would come back next week for my piercing.

I confess that I just found out what this piercing is. There is no way in hell I will do this.

I love my wife, but . . . .

---

haha a word to the wise: never agree to something if you dont know what exactly your consenting to do!

tb

LOL . . . I wouldn't be getting drunk with your wife anymore.

MollyMayhem

Don't do it! I bet the hurts like no other! hehehe

Look you can't force someone to tell you what to do. If you don't want to do it don't. Even people you love, such as your wife, shouldn't be able to boss you around. Just tell her how you feel.

---

it should be your decision. its your body, not hers.

---

i don't blame you mate. Some things just aren't meant to have a bolt put through.:-P

Don't do it - You'll be scarred for life.

listin it will hurt like hell but you wife will love it iknow from expirence yur lookin at a full 3 weeks of pain but its its not too bad except the enitial needle thiong go for it

I actually have a PA and I made a confession about it a couple of months ago. I suggest you go for it, it's great. I have no regrets at all.

yeah, you cant have sex for, like . . . four months . . . ug.

So don't. She should not have a problem with it. If she does . . . I hope you say too bad. For your nerves' sake.
Raven

Barf? That's supposed to be attractive? If I saw one of those, _I_ would double over in pain out of sympathy.

I heard that if you get it done that you can't have sex for 6 months or so after it is done. Just something to think about.
~CJO~

go ahead and do it

Doesn't it hurt to go to the bathroom? I mean, what if it got infected? That's just gross!

oh it doesn't hurt that bad, and it's sexy. Go for it, you'll be surprised . . .
Lace

o God. That's be so awkward! Don't do it. and besides, I never really understood how a woman could stand having a pierced—erm—up . . . there.

Gotta Go!

I work late at night. I'm am usually the only one there.

Now, I'm a guy, and if I feel the call of nature (#2), I confess that I use the women's restroom. The men's room is dirty, it smells and there's pee all over the floor.

I am only confessing because no matter that I may be the only one there, and the only one who will ever know, I feel that I have:

1] Violated the sanctity of the women's room

2] Violated the male covenant which states that ". . . a man shall never be caught dead in the woman's room"

Please forgive me.

---

meh your forgiven, the toilets are only going to be shat in anyway.

I used to clean office buildings for a living, and while the women's room was no problem, I would always gag when I had to go into the men's room.

Just don't stink up our washrooms. Ladies don't like pee on the floor, if you're clean enough and no one else is there . . go for it.

If management is too lazy to get up off their asses and clean up the men's room they have no one to blame but themselves if men want to use the women's washroom.

I have also worked in a place where the ladies room was available late at night. You are right, it is MUCH cleaner. And exactly how is it the women rate a COUCH in their bathroom?

Jeez, lighten up! Heck I've been blocked out of the men's restroom by women when their line was stretched around the corner! You know they were desperate!!!

Big Daug

Sounds cool to me! I have seen the women's restroom, and it is much much cleaner than the men's.

You fellas have a convenant? I never knew. Your reasons are valid, your employer should be keeping the men's room cleaner. Explain it when they call you upstairs to explain what they've discovered on the video surveilance tape.

MollyMayhem

What kind of workplace keeps the men's restroom like that? But heh, you gotta do what you gotta do.

-massasi-

As a Nation, just how anal retentive are we? When my wife and I are out and the ladies room is busy I'll stand outside the Mens room and guard it, so she can use it. She feels no guilt and neither do I. The wierd thing is when will we grow up as a nation and only have unisex bathrooms? As long as we have stalls and screens, who cares?

lol I'm never using a public restroom again

Well, you haven't broken number 2 yet until you get caught . . .

Well, I'm a girl and I have used the men's room when the line for the ladies was too long. Of course, those restrooms didn't have urinals . . . .yuck! I forgive you.

That's cute. Don't worry, it's no big deal! As long as you're not peeing on OUR floors and seats.

Raven

No such male covenant! I would use the cleaner restroom everytime!

Grins I remember the first time I went into a guys bathroom— I was so nervous and excited and so afraid that I'd get in trouble (I was in 2nd grade). Now, I use them whenever the ladies' room is full— I just go in (knock first) and use it. I have no problem with what you're doing. None at all. In fact, I may do the same thing now (go to all womens college, in basement they house a department and have mens restroom). You go!

Kytana

I admit that I too have visited the lady's room

You Didn't Really Just Do That?

I'm a father of two boys, 8 and 16. The oldest likes to massage feet. I never thought anything of it until today.

He asked if I wanted my feet rubbed while I was laying on the couch watching TV. As always I said sure. While I continued to watch the tube, suddenly I felt something soft and wet on the bottom of my foot.

My son was licking my foot.

I yelled at him, telling him to stop and asking why he did that. He just thought it was the funniest thing and tried to do it again. My wife, who was sitting next to be, saw the whole thing – she was laughing too!

I confess that I sometimes do not understand my family, but then again, I'm absolutely sure they don't understand me.

Guess we're even . . . But licking the bottom of my feet?

Your son just has a fetish. The only weird thing about it is that he decided to act it out on his father.

I'm wearing socks from now on . . .

Malenkaya

So there is the spirit of a prankster with sick humor and a foot fetish of some sort, get over it . . . there could be worse things your 16-year old is doing.

misanthrope panda

Wow the normal one in a family of freaks, I can't relate personally but some of my friends could, run old man, as fast as you can.

That is just so gross! YEUCH!

Jelly

I'm scared for you

---

haha . . . that's funny . . . i'm sure he did it just to get a reaction out of you . . . kinda gross tho . . .

god_chic

Ha ha ha ha ha ha ha ha . . . that's too funny. I'd be laughing too right along next to your wife. Then again maybe I'd be freaked out too . . . ha ha ha ha ha ha

---

Your son needs to learn to control his impulses.

---

that's totally disgusting . . . . . . freaks

I agree with 1. your son must have a fetish. But I don't understand why his mother thought it was funny!

~CocaCola~

Har har har. Just be happy he's not smoking crack.

I don't think it's a foot fetish. I think he just enjoyed freaking you out and getting a reaction out of you. Not something I'd ever do myself, but I can understand why your wife was laughing.

It was the sixteen year old? Your wife laughed? Therapy quickly!

I think the weird part is that your sixteen year old son gives you foot rubs (the licking is weird too)

I would call that the "Bitter taste of defeet"

were it a foot fetish, i doubt ur son would be indulging in it with his dad, . . . like #13 said, i think he was probably just doing it to gross u out . . a tad overimpulsive yes, but well . . maybe its just his own brand of adolescent affection:P

He licked the bottom of your foot because he saw it on Spongebob, of course! lol, I'm not really sure . . . it does sound like a foot fetish, (' . . . likes to massage feet.') but who knows? I wouldn't worry about it too much. This confession cracked me up; I can just picture that happening to my husband!

Down Again

About six months ago I was on a job interview.

After the interview I went to the restroom just to stop shaking (very bad nerves). I looked in the mirror and saw that my zipper is completely down.

I died.

I went home and started looking for other jobs, for they must have noticed the white jockeys under the black slacks.

As it turns out, I guess they didn't notice. I got called back for a second interview. It went really well and I was offered the job. As I was leaving, the interviewer (same guy who I saw the first time) thanked me for checking my zipper this time.

I died again.

BWAH HAH HAH HAH!!! That is GREAT!!!!! :o)

Ha ha ha thanks for making my evening! I guess its true you need to leave an impression, thank goodness they have a sense of humor.

Awww! That is so sad and strangely funny at the same time. I'm sorry! But hey, at least you go the job, right? But the least they could have done was told you at the time, that way you wouldn't walk arounf like that being completely obliviouse!

~Sarah~

---

lol . . . that's classic! Well, at least they didn't judge you solely on your visual presentation.

---

lol that must be one cool guy! You are lucky to be working for them.

LMFAO!!! thats funny!

~*bijin*~

XI. THE KITCHEN SINK

Hah! Interviewers with a sense of humor! Hah!

I have to say, that is the funniest confession of the day!!!
LMFAO!!!!!!!!!!!!!!!!!!!!!!!!!!!!

Sounds like a cool work enviroment.

Hey, maybe you got the job BECAUSE your zipper was down.

Esquire

LOL. Don't be so melodramatic! You're a guy, grow some cajones!

OMG THAT IS THE FUNNIEST THING I'VE EVER HEARD OF!!!!!! Thanx 4
making my day!!!!!!!

GrL

---

lol omg u unwittingly just helped my nerves about my interview 2morow -
thankyou sooo much im glad it went so well 4 u!

~*leanne*~

LoL- it happens to the best of us, hon.

---

i got a job that i interviewed for with a popped button right across my
breasts. i didn't notice it until after the interview but when i got hired i
wasn't worried b/c the interviewer turned out to be gay!

~Gambitgirl~

Hahahahahahahahahaaaaa . . . . rotflmao . . . thanks for the good laugh,
I needed that. :)

Blue

Movie Magic

I was working craft services on a set of a movie in North Carolina.

The cast and crew were very cool! One of the scenes was of massive death and mayhem. Shot up, bloodied bodies everywhere.

I had a disposable camera with me in case any of the big stars were shooting that day (they weren't). So, when they wrapped the scene, the weapons wrangler gave an AK47 to pose with.

I stood over six of the shot up "victims" displaying them as my trophies. The next day I dropped the film off to be developed.

I confess that this was a big mistake. I was "detained" (not arrested) when I stopped back an hour later to pick up my pictures. I was questioned by a Deputy and released (thank God!).

The photos look fantastic!

LMAO . . . A picture of you, standing over dead bodies with a big grin on your face . . . DAY-UM, you can't make up this kind of comedy . . . LOL!!!
~~LilBaddy~~

You just made my day! I suddenly thought of the perfect gag for photo people. You know I hate the fact that these photo people actually look at people's pictures and sometimes comment about the pictures. It's annoying, I feel it's a violation of privacy. So right now, I have a nasty prank in mind.

I'm not sure what the law says, but that sounds like a total invasion of privacy to me, on the part of the photo shop.

HAHAHAHAHAAA*snort*HAHAHAHAAA!! That's AWESOME!!

That's kinda funny! We need confessions like this every once in a while amongst all of the cheaters, sicko, and crazies!

---

hey dude thats funny least u werent arrested

LOL- oh man, that has GOT to suck! At any rate, the people developing the pics should have figured that a mass murderer wouldn't take pictures of the dead bodies of their victims. I mean, unless they were an idiot. Oh well . . . {~Poppler~}

I wish I could've seen two things: The look on the face of the person developing your photos, and the look on YOUR face when you found out you were being detained for those photos. Hahahahaha

---

You should have taken a photo of you being detained

LMAO I actually LOL on that one. I usually don't. That's great! ~Sarah~

OMG, that is SO funny. Don't worry, you'll laugh about it too sooner or later.

That's . . killer! hah . . . . those photo guys . . I can just picture them fretting and panting with excitement as they called the constables. Morons. It wasn't a mistake . . . you rule.

JM

Umm i work as a photo lab technician (photo guy) at a CVS here in RI and it's our JOB to look at pictures, especially teenager picturs since certain things are illegal to sell to people. Nudity is allowed, but nude people touching or any naked person being touched in a sexual manner gets throw out sinc eits pornographic, underage drinking pics can't be printed, although it is tough to tell age, but we use best judgement since a 16 year old and a 21 year old can be very different. ALso not allowed are other illagel acts, I once had a pic of 2 kids doing graffiti AND smoking a joint, like 14 yr old kids, needless to say they didn't get those pics. But thats the law, love it or leave it, if you wanna take pics of porn, or violence, get a polarioid or a digital camera, then anything goes but with advantix or 35mm film, we are obliged to look at ALL pics as part of our job to ensure you dont get crappily developed pics, and to ensure yo dont get illegal stuff,a nd i HAVE seen MANY sexual pics and I'm surprised people don't realize its my job to look at them.

Two words- Digital Camera

SWEET! the betting hasseld by the cops makes this sotry even better! bet you were in Wilmington right? they have a movie studio down there ~Gambitgirl~

Actully, those people have to look at them by law. So if you dont want them get a digital cam or whatever.

Due To Technical Difficulties...

32, Male, Married. I have been having sex since I was 17. Tonight, for the first time ever, the little guy didn't "rise to the occasion".

My wife told me it was O.K., it happens some times (as if she knows first hand . . .). Then she rolled over and went to sleep.

I can't sleep.

It's 4:00am, I have to get up in two hours to go to work - and I can't stop thinking about this.

I confess that I know there is a myriad of things that can contribute to temporary erectile dysfunction. I'm just in denial right now, as in, "this doesn't happen to me!"

Best thing to do is just not worry about it. Your wife is right, it does happen to lots of guys, but obsessing over it only reinforces the problem. It happened to me a while back, and it drove me crazy for a few days, until I just resigned myself to not having sex for a while (there are, after all, other ways to have fun with a woman), and next thing you know . . . I was cured! If it bothers you enough, though, see a doctor.

The more stressed you get about it the worse it will be.

bless ya, dont worry too much, mite happen agen if u do worry. Could be due to stress, tiredness, illness and a million other reasons. Put it down as a one off and forget about it. The more you think about it, the more likely it is to happen again.

bibi, luv moi xxx

The more you stress about it, the worse it will get. So relax, don't worry about it, there are a million reasons that happens, maybe you were too tired, too hot, too cold, tired from a long at work, whatever . . . . just don't make a big deal out of it, or that will only compound the problem. It's really not the end of the world.

Well, don't stress over it. I mean, what's once in the course of a lifetime? And, I apologize, but for some reason this one had me laughing . . .

Sure, this doesn't happen to you . . . until now. The more freaked out you get, the worse it's going to get.

It happens - Don't worry about it. I suppose you could have just pleasured your wife by other means, so you could have at least gotten some sleep. As a woman, I'm telling you it's no big deal.

Whoah that happened to my boyfriend once but that was due to what was going on in his house and stuff (His mom's house is a really bad place for that) so you know maybe sh*t was just going on in your life. I'm sure your wife doesn't feel any differently at all abou tyou now, I doubt she even had any second thoughts about it. Don't worry!!! This is coming from a girl. I know.

It's about time that thing stopped working!!! My legs are sore!!

Look, if you stress over it, this may happen again . . . and again . . . and again. Do you really want that?

Happened to me not too long ago. Either the lighting wasn't right, or I was too stressed, or whatever. A couple of hours later, all was right with the world again. It happens.

These things happen, but if it continues to happen make sure not to neglect your wife. She shouldn't have to go without just because you're not "up to it".

Try ginsin :o)

Statistics show that it will happen to 1 in 7 men every year, for a period of about 2 weeks. Which means EVERY man will experience some form of impotence in his lifetime. So just relax, and take the advice of the other posts (webbie, please publish this as this little bit of info will relax him and other guys who read it).

This happend to my husband about three months back, and we are newlyweds so imagine my shock . . . but it wasn't that big of a deal, however what was a big deal was the fact he kept stressing over it which only made it worse. So my advice is to take a deep breath and don't worry about it, if this is the first time it probably won't be the last . . . and thats okay!

if you;ve been having sex for 15 years & this is the first time EVER you've had this problem you're doing pretty well. i've known 20 year old guy who weren't able to get it up for whatever reason: too tired, stressed out, too drunk or on drugs. chill out, if you fixate on this & freak that anxiety could inhibit you getting a boner nexdt time too. it DOES happen to most guys sooner or later

~Gambitgirl~

Adapt And Overcome

My wife is out of town on a business trip. I am pretty self sufficient in all areas save one.
Laundry.

XI. THE KITCHEN SINK

Today, since I was out of underwear, I tried on a pair of my wife's panties. A little (lot!) snug, but not too terribly binding. For the hell of it I wore them to work.

I just got home and still have them on. I feel as if I have conquered some major milestone in my 34 years on this earth.

Then again, all I did was wear a pair of very tight fitting French cut panties.

I am easily amused.

No, I will never tell my wife.

Why not tell your wife? What's the big deal? I know that I am a rather conservative person in most respects, but I would love it if my husband were to do something so different, and then have the guts to tell me about it! And if that's not enough, then you should tell her just so she knows why her underwear is stretched :)

Haha, that's priceless!

You're not the only one who has dome it! Welcome to the club!

Um..well whatever floats your boat right? I am glad you are easily amused b/c to most men, I think, that would be a bigger embarassment than washing them. Which btw you can do in the sink if you can't use complicated machinery)ie the washing machine). And people call me dumb. Sorry, but I am feeling really intelligent now. You made my day!! *Debbi*

---

thats funny!!
~iylya~

Tell her it will be funny

Ummm, you're making a big mistake here. Its not like she won't see them in the laundry and know she didn't wear them. Then you'll have some explaining to do.
MollyMayhem

Don't put it down until you try it ;)

Oohhh-kayyy. Whatever.

French cut panties? You're turning me on!
`Gramps`

You rock, dude.

aaaw lol what a cute confession but hmm she MAY find out . . especially
if theyre streched out with piss stains on em =D
-babypink-

Hey, I'm sure your wife wouldn't care. She might actually find it sexy! Ya
never know . . . whatever tickles your pickle.
ZeLdA

My Husband . . . Goodbye

That morning we woke up from greatest night we ever had (you
know what I mean), it was just incredible.

We had married two weeks earlier. We were set for our new life
together, he had a great job in Tower 1 and I painted. Brent was 27,
I was 25.

We actually met on a subway, I was going to college at Columbia
and Brent was going to NYU. Our wedding was in Napa Valley, CA.
My family loved him and he loved them.

Everything was perfect.

He wanted to stay home with me that morning and go to work late,
but I knew it would affect the raise he was trying to get. He made
me some coffee, kissed me, okay a little more, and then left.

I fell back asleep until I got this horrible feeling. I woke up and
turned on the TV. There it was. The 2nd plane hit. The phone rang,
it was my sister. I couldn't talk, I was just numb.

> I knew he was gone.
>
> I didn't talk for days. I couldn't get out of bed. I felt as if I was as dead as he was. Two months later I realized I was pregnant.
>
> Brent your baby is beautiful.

Oh my God . . . I'm almost crying here, and it takes a lot to get me to cry. I'm so sorry about your husband . . . That's so horrible . . . I just wish you well. You and your son. Good luck in the future . . . I wish I could say more . . . .

I am so sorry. You are a strong woman, and lucky to have his child. No one should ever have to suffer through something so awful.

Oh my God . . . . that's so sad!! I have chills all over right now. He left you a part of himself . . . a part that will always be there. What a great gift! God bless you both.

"Blueper"

---

omg im balling my eyes out . . I wish you the best of luck in your future

gwennie

Aww! that is soooo sad! i'm sorry that had to happen. Congratulations on the baby! i hope you have a good life with your new son/daughter.

*^*Boe*^*

Oh My God I really hope u have enough strength to get through this, i am soo incredibly sorry. this is by far the saddest confession i have ever heard, it just kinda goes to ur soul. may God bless you and give you and your children the will and strength to move on.Peace

~Sarah

I am so sorry. I guess I could never say I understand, because that must have been hell to go thru. My deepest sympathies and I bet that your husband is watching you both from Heaven.

:*(God will protect and provide for you and your baby.

~Crazee C~

Wow . . . I don't even know what to say. I'm sorry . . . .

Blitzed

I feel completely terrible for you, and this confession makes me think about how Ive shrugged off 9/11. My heart goes out to you and everyone that has lost a loved one.

God Bless you and your baby. You know your husband will watch over you forever.

Thank-you for making that confession. When my best friend died I thought I lost everything, I felt like I was the only perosn in the world going throuh it. But now I know different. All I want to say is that don't worry. Don't speak of his name in sadness but in happinesss. Knowing everything was "perfect" when he left. Think of all the memories that you had. I'm only 13 and I shouldn't even be saying anything but I want you to know you don't have to go through this alone.

Oh honey . . . Brent knows his baby is beautiful, he'll watch over him and you from heaven.

The Rogue

I am so sorry. His spirit is probably watching over you and the baby.

Sorry to hear that, but . . . these things happen. It's sad when people suffer because of what their governments do, but time will heal your wounds. Aaah, no worries, you'll get over it.

that was beautiful. i'm always happier when i hear the death of some one so young and so not ready to go and that a little piece of them is left . . . . be sure to tell your daughter about her Daddy and how wonderful he was. God Bless.

~Lael~

Started As An Experiment . . .

This is wrong, and I feel so very bad about it. I am a 26-year-old father of a beautiful, intelligent, 4-year-old boy.

For some unknown reason, I taught him that the color red was called "green" and the color green was called "red". It was just for fun, and my wife went along. This has been going on for about a year now. He calls the grass "red" and we laugh . . .

I was just hit with how bad, wrong, stupid this "joke" has been. Tomorrow, I will sit him down and explain that things are different now. I never ever meant any harm. It's just that he got into a fight, he shoved a neighbor's 6 year old how corrected him when he told her she had "green" hair (she is a red-head).

I am truly sorry son.

---

you may be a good father,but im sorry to say you have shit for brains if you didnt realise what affect that would have,just dont try any more of you stupid games,or your kid will look a twat at school,for his sake teach him correct terms,

---

Both you and your wife have a warped sense of humor.

That is extremely cruel - If he finds out how you lied to him about even something just as simple as colours, how hard do you think it will be for him to trust you again? Trust is something you may be able to establish easy, but it's extremely hard to regain once it's been disproven.

Hmm..I always wondered, in a "what if" kind of way, what would happen if you did that. I guess it was one guy's explanation of existentalism wayyy back when that got me thinking about it. Anyways, people are going to tell you that you're cruel and mean and the worst parent ever, and it WAS stupid. But parents tell kids some messed up stuff when they start out. It'll be a humorous anecdote for him when he gets to high school. Don't sweat it.

Stef

I actually wanted to 'experiment' like you did but to a much greater level. I wanted to raise a kid in a closed area and teach him everything in a different manner . . . water would actually be ice. If he was burnt it'd really mean he was frozen. Pizza, hamburgers, candybars and any food that most Americans perceive as 'good' would actually be bad to him. Brussel sprouts, raw onions and cabbage would be his foods of choice. Sick I guess.

At least you learned what you were doing before teaching a big lie. Phatboy.

well, i'm sure your sone won't turn into a serial killer or anything if the worst thing you ever did was teach him the wrong names for colors. what you might have to worry most about is if your son is going to start doubting everything you tell him from now on b/c he'll wonder if you're joking . . . this could get especially tricky when he asks where babies come from LOL

~Gambitgirl~

More importantly I think you should work on his anger control. Pushing people because he got corrected

((echo))

Tht is so mean - Tht doesnt sound like a joke 2 me. Ur both bad rents

Oh my God, you are cruel. Poor kid.

OMG !!!!!! YOu are such an idiot !!!!!! Do you know how much trouble he'll have when he gets to preschool ??????????

LOL I know it isnt funny to some but I am a parent. I have done some similar things out of kidding, I told my son once if he barked at trees that it helps the bark on the trees to grow, wich seemed harmless at the time but he still barks each time he passes a tree

How could you play with your child that way? Do you want to hurt him? ANYONE who hurts a child in such a way should be ashamed of themselves.

You should definitely rectify this situation A.S.A.P. There are enough psychological problems that we as humans have to face, without having the two people that we depend upon to teach us everything that we need to function in society not being honest. Breaking that trust before age five could have a detrimental effect on your future relationship with your son. A joke like that is not amusing or cute, it is cruel, and you have already seen the effects of your little "game", with the neighbor girl. My parents didn't tell me my first name {they used my middle name], and I had to learn from my first grade teacher, in front of the whole class, that my name wasn't what I thought it was. All of my life, I have had to explain to people my two names, and it is extremely tiring. Most normal children provide lots of amusement with their antics, so just try to enjoy your son for who he is, and teach him correctly from now on. good luck!

Laurel

That is twisted, to mess with your kid's head like that.

dareva

How awful! You sound sincerely sorry, though. I understand we often do little "cute" things and they end up back firing. Good luck. I'm sure you feel bad enough already.

I confess that when I started this Web site, I never thought it would reach so many people and touch as many lives as it has. As I read the new confessions that come in every day, I find some to be very similar to many we have received in the past. There are times when I even start to think that after reading over a quarter million confessions, I have just about heard it all. Then all I have to do is read a few more and there it is—something new that knocks me over! This may be the last confession of this book, but rest assured, every day, someone, somewhere will do something that he or she will be compelled to confess. And we will be right here, waiting for them.